The Reference Shelf®

The Business of Food

The Reference Shelf
Volume 85 • Number 2
H. W. Wilson
A Division of EBSCO Publishing, Inc.
Ipswich, Massachusetts
2013

The Reference Shelf

The books in this series contain reprints of articles, excerpts from books, addresses on current issues, and studies of social trends in the United States and other countries. There are six separately bound numbers in each volume, all of which are usually published in the same calendar year. Numbers one through five are each devoted to a single subject, providing background information and discussion from various points of view and concluding with an index and comprehensive bibliography that lists books, pamphlets, and articles on the subject. The final number of each volume is a collection of recent speeches. Books in the series may be purchased individually or on subscription.

Library of Congress Cataloging-in-Publication Data

The business of food.
    pages cm. -- (The reference shelf ; volume 85, number 2)
    Includes bibliographical references and index..
    ISBN 978-0-8242-1213-1 (issue 2) -- ISBN 978-0-8242-1211-7 (series) 1. Food--Social aspects. 2. Food habits. 3. Food consumption. 4. Food--Economic aspects. I. H.W. Wilson Company
    GN407.B87 2013
    394.1'2--dc23

                                                                            2013002196

Cover: © Radius Images/Corbis

Printed in the United States of America

Contents

1

The New Farm Movement

2

Media and How-To Cooking

3

Big Food Business

4

The Art of Food Writing

5

Open for Business

Preface

Food Movement Politics

Diet for a Small Planet (1971) was one of several books published during the 1970s that introduced a new notion of the relationship among food, cooking, and the planet. Frances Moore Lappé's book was overtly political, offering a conception of diet that held far greater implications for community than previously considered. The title was suggestive enough of the complex relationships Lappé wished to highlight as part and parcel of one's relationship to food. To act in one community is to effect change in other communities. While not the first to consider the question of food as a form of activism, Lappé's book may serve as an early articulation of the contemporary activism surrounding food movements. Lappé addressed a long-held disconnect among Americans in their understanding of the relationship between the consumption and the production of food.

Were Lappé to publish her work today, she would be just one of many blogger-activists publishing on subjects as far ranging as environmentalism and travelogues related to the food movement. The literature on food movements—local/slow food, vegetarianism/veganism, raw food, sustainable farming, true naturals, farmers markets, and so on—has proliferated in books, magazines, and blogs. In line with Lappé's ideals in the 1970s, these groups are defined by a sense of localism, a central belief in farm-to-table as a way of being in a sustainable world. "Buy local" becomes as much an economic necessity as a philosophical imperative. To varying degrees, food movement politics has informed parts of everyday American life. The most direct engagement, perhaps, for many occurs at the coffee shop, where the designation "free trade" beans ensures coffee drinkers are on the "right side" of food politics. But the growing concerns over environmentalism, sustainable agricultural practices, animal rights, and diet and health serve as a coalition of sorts that has emerged as a form of alternative, and in some forms, radicalized politics.

A collection of community magazines, publishing under the name Edible Communities, advances a common goal to "celebrate local foods, season by season." As many as seventy-five independent magazines have published under the Edible name, from cities small and large across the United States. *Edible Boston* offers stories from across the region, local businesses all contributing, the editors note, to the richness of Boston's food community. While readers will find the typical recipe and restaurant stories, the magazine is distinguished by its insight into the small business owners who collectively make up the many food movements. A story on Q's Nuts, for example, considers why its owner is "obsessed with flavor" in the creation of his sweet-roasted nuts. Readers learn of the creation of artisan cheese, produced on a 110-acre dairy farm in Framingham; about a new distillery in Ipswich creating boutique rums; and the culinary possibilities presented by a superbly photographed heirloom tomato. The magazine is well produced with fine photography. The stories suggest the epicurean tastes of people we have come to identify as "foodies"—those who take pleasure in the finer qualities of food. Foodies prefer healthy and organic foods. They may buy local, but they are tuned in to the international, too, in ways that are, for the most part, good for the planet and local producers. Besides highlighting specific foodie-related issues, the stories create a broader picture of a way of being in the world, of having a personal stake in one's community and one's food and food production. This idea is central to the emerging food movement politics.

The stories in the Edible magazines, available on the company's website, establish a collective imagination that is highly suggestive of an emerging consciousness about food and politics that has appeared in only a few moments in American history. One would need to revisit, as one example, the transcendentalists of Brook Farm in the 1840s in West Roxbury, Massachusetts. The group conducted an experiment in communal living, one based on the balance between labor and the farm in an increasingly industrialized world. Lappé's 1971 publication captures another moment. Michael Pollan, author of the highly influential *Omnivore's Dilemma* (2006), a study of the different ways food is produced, notes in his 2010 article "The Food Movement, Rising" for the *New York Review of Books* that "food in America has been more or less invisible, politically speaking, until recently." While food and farms have long been hotly debated subjects in the political domain, what Pollan points to is the emergence of a more pronounced activism underlying how one views food. The efficacy of this activism, Pollan notes, remains to be seen, particularly given the complexity of the problems Americans must confront about the food industry.

One of the major challenges the food movement must confront is the question of economics. To be a foodie who buys local, for example, is a decision that is informed by money. More often than not, buying local comes at a steeper price than if one were to buy from a major grocery-store chain. If food movements ask consumers to become wary of the mass food industry, one of the challenges for Americans is how to negotiate the costs. Pollan admits that the local food movement may well present an elitist lifestyle choice, as not all can afford to participate in the economics of the local farmers markets. The food movements suggest, however, that what is at stake is far more than the economics of farm-to-table dining. This may be where the politics emerge for the movements.

Going back to the 1970s, food movements have directly and indirectly provided food consumption and production alternatives to the dominant industries of mass food production. The battle with "big food," Pollan notes, comes down to both economics and politics, as many Americans have benefited from new perspectives and changes in the industry regarding what is a sound, sustainable food economy. If change has come slowly to the food industry, the influence of local movements has nonetheless changed the conversation for millions of consumers. This challenge to big food is evident in a wide range of issues, from Americans' battle with obesity to how the snack food industry targets children in advertising. More locally, Pollan views the participants in the local farmers markets as a new breed of communitarians, formative of new perspectives on personal responsibility and the production of food—giving rise to the local farmers and businesses such as the ones featured in the Edible magazines. A visit to a local farmers market appears suggestive of Pollan's vision of a community, where a conversation can be held with a farmer on the idiosyncrasies of the growing season and the produce available in the current week. This is local food politics and business, he notes, that by its very presence can effect change.

Nonetheless, the local food movement continues to work out the equation between consumer politics and food economics. One example of this complexity is the 2013 Farm Bill, which may be an important harbinger of the challenges ahead for the local food industry. In the bill, funding for the National Organic Certification Cost Share Program, as well as funding for organic farming research, was cut by $22 million, to the dismay of farmers across the country. Cost-share reimburses organic farmers up to $750 annually for organic certification costs. The question of what constitutes "organic" is a complicated issue for farmers, consumers, and the food industry. The widespread introduction of organic food and farming is one of the major areas of the dominant food industry directly influenced by the food movements. Organics has become big business, and the food industry has signed on to the extent that consumers may now purchase microwavable dinners labeled "organic." Organic farms, however, are mostly small operations, holding close to the ideals of the food movement. For these farmers, what is at stake is far more than the cost for certification; the broader challenge is to the viability of an alternative food chain, one that is closely aligned with consumer activism. What the 2013 Farm Bill highlights is the efficacy of the food movements, in this case, the organic farm industry, in a vital political and economic stage.

Consumers need not go long without a reminder of what is at stake in the food movements. In March 2012, "pink slime" hamburger caught the imagination of the United States with a cocktail of tasteless images, clever branding, and a story gone viral. Called by the meat industry "lean finely textured beef" (LFTB), this ground beef is composed of low-grade beef trimmings that undergo processing that includes something akin to an ammonia bath to kill E. coli, salmonella, and other bacteria. The images of "pink slime" in news stories were the makings of many a foodie's worst nightmare. For much of the public, the revelation of just how common LFTB is in beef products was a stark reminder of the journey concocted by the food industry for many of their favorite foods. Not everyone was caught unawares. Stakeholders in the beef industry viewed the story differently. The beef industry—along with governors from Texas, Kansas, and Iowa—blamed the media for sensationalizing the story of, as Mark Bittman of the *New York Times* put it, the "pink menace."

The emergence of the food movements can be closely aligned with the very existence of a food product like LFTB. To begin, the story illustrates the disjunctions the mass food industry has created in the food chain, a division between clear-eyed awareness of the food consumed and the complex processes for the production and delivery of that food. The geographic divisions that are now so commonplace in the food industry, the way produce travels across international borders, for example, is the everyday consciousness that localism confronts. The story pointed to the industrial production of livestock, which, because of its practices, heightened the development of disease as a part of the production process, requiring methods to combat E. coli and other bacteria. The remarkable part of the already remarkable story is that LFTB was a necessary and effective remedy to the problem of bacteria inherent in the mass production of beef.

As the "pink slime" story illustrates, the beef industry has long departed from the cultural practices of animal husbandry represented in nineteenth-century farming. The defensive postures of the governors of Texas, Kansas, and Iowa highlight the ways economics and politics frame the subject of animal food production. On the occasion of a new E. coli controversy, the underlying question of the ethical treatment of farm animals remains one of the most challenging issues. One of the central tenets of the various food movements is to question not only the effects of the mass food production but one's actions in the world of food. Lappé's *Diet for a Small Planet* outlines, for example, the challenges presented in the debate over the animal industry: "Anyone who questioned the American diet's reliance on beef—since cattle are the most wasteful converters of grain to meat—was perceived as challenging the American way of life."

Lappé advocated a vegetarian lifestyle. Add to this conversation veganism—a diet and lifestyle free of all animal products, including dairy—and the conversation on food becomes far more radicalized. Most of the food movements, however, are not strictly defined by vegetarianism. They do not hold to a monolithic agenda or single set of principles. If they share one character, one central to vegetarianism/veganism, it is tacit refusal. To campaign for animal rights, one does not need to refuse to consume chicken, beef, and fish. Rather, a common principle is the refusal to support an unsustainable way of life. Writing more than half a century ago, M. F. K. Fisher observed in *The Art of Eating* (1954) that "eating is not simply consuming calories but an act that defines who we are and how we see the world and its inhabitants." What may once have appeared to readers as a philosophical issue, far outside the conventions of the 1950s American diet, may now appear to be of its time, a formative movement that responds to the everyday realities of an increasingly small planet.

1

The New Farm Movement

(Photo by Robert Nickelsberg/Getty Images)

Moon in the Pond farm owner Dominic Palumbo, center left, sells organically grown eggplants at the weekly farmers market in Millerton, New York. The Moon in the Pond farm focuses on raising heritage breed livestock for meat and organic heirloom vegetables sold locally and at farmers markets.

America's New Farmer: A Slow and Local Practice

Global food culture is in the midst of a major transformation, driven by changing consumer preferences and an overall shift away from mass-produced food. In the United States, this transformation has come in the form of several interrelated shifts in consumer purchasing, cooking, and dining preferences, namely, the "slow food," "local food," and "alternative agriculture" movements. Taken as a whole, these movements represent a desire to avoid the ecological, ethical, and nutritional detriments of processed food and the large-scale agricultural industry, while simultaneously enhancing the quality and ethics of local food communities.

These growing food movements have taken hold primarily among affluent communities in and around urban areas, where consumers earn sufficient income to afford expensive alternatives to traditional, mass-produced products. Popular criticism of the ecological, social, and ethical detriments of the big-food industry is becoming more widespread; however, persons living in low-income communities are far less likely to be aware of shopping and dining alternatives. Further, low-income consumers are often faced with more immediate concerns with regard to meeting their daily needs, and many do not attend to the largely intellectual outrage over the perceived evils of the big-food industry.

Local Food Movement

The local food movement is an international consumer movement that seeks to encourage and facilitate consumers purchasing foods that are locally grown, produced, procured, and prepared. In part, the movement is one of economics, aimed at stimulating local economies by creating increased demand for locally produced products. Proponents of the movement sometimes call themselves "locavores," a name inspired by a popular San Francisco–based website promoting local food options.

The local food movement has taken hold in a number of American cities, as well as in parts of the United Kingdom and several other countries. The movement takes a variety of forms, including the establishment of farmers markets and food co-ops that specialize in locally produced products. Markets of these types have become increasingly popular in American cities and have come to form one of the cornerstones of the local food movement, as well as the related slow food and alternative agriculture movements.

The local food movement's focus on economics has earned support from those approaching local food as a way to build community cohesion. Co-op and local farmers markets promote cooperation among members of the immediate community, while also providing access to foods that have not been processed or stored for long voyages overseas. In many cases, consumers support local food because products produced locally tend to be superior in freshness and flavor to vegetables and meats procured through big-market retailers.

Defining the local food idea starts with defining the concept of "local" in terms of production and distribution. Some choose to define "local" in terms of the number of miles that food must travel to reach its final retail destination, while others define it in terms of states or regions. This aspect of local food becomes more important to those looking to reduce the greenhouse emissions caused by the global transport of food products.

Slow Food

Italian activist and writer Carlo Petrini was the founder of the "slow food" movement, and established the principles that have remained at the core of the movement as it has spread internationally. Similarly to the local food movement, the slow food movement encourages consumers to favor locally produced and procured foods in an effort to promote the consumption of more nutritious, better-tasting products while simultaneously stimulating local demand. Unlike the local food movement, Petrini and other slow food purists also promote the idea that consumers should limit their diets to foods that occur naturally in their geographic area or ecological zone. Consumers in the northeastern United States would simply not eat avocados or bananas if adhering to a strict slow food regimen.

The slow food movement also promotes the idea that consumers should limit their diet choices to products that are "fair trade," meaning purchased at a price that is equitable to farmers and/or ranchers. While the concept of fair trade has become a buzzword in dining and shopping, consumers and food-service professionals are currently attempting to create systems for determining guidelines for fairly obtained goods.

In addition, the slow food movement eschews the use of chemicals, hormones, and genetically altered crops that have become common in the industrial agricultural industry. Avoiding these products is believed to provide healthier dining options and access to foods that are superior in flavor, as it is widely accepted among adherents of these new food movements that processed and altered crops tend to be deficient in both nutritional value and the more aesthetic qualities of taste.

Like the local food movement, the slow food movement asks consumers to follow a number of shopping guidelines and to become educated by learning about the origin and other characteristics of various products. Therefore, local food fans support the farmers markets and local food co-op movements that have emerged in cities around the world, providing affordable access to products often sold directly by farmers and ranchers.

Alternative Agriculture

The increased demand for locally produced products, in conjunction with spreading dissatisfaction with the ecological and ethical hazards of industrial food production, has led to a new trend in the United States and other countries: alternative farming.

Hundreds of new small farms and alternative food-production businesses have been established, often in rural areas near major cities or in urban areas traditionally seen as unsuitable for farming.

In many cases, the farmers and ranchers operating these alternative agricultural enterprises are not the type of individuals traditionally associated with agriculture. Many are young people who began farming as a way to provide themselves with healthier and more flavorful food, but who have then turned this newfound interest into a career. To cite one example, Duke University student Emily Sloss, formerly a member of the university's Urban Planning Department, started a campus farm as an experiment in urban farming. Sloss utilized the educational resources of the school coupled with her own research to learn about the farming process, and she concentrated on vegetables known to grow well in the North Carolina climate. Over the course of her first two seasons, Sloss provided more than two tons of produce to the school cafeteria and was inspired to pursue farming as a career after graduation.

Like Sloss, many individuals not traditionally trained in agriculture have decided to try their hand at farming, with varying degrees of success. Some food writers and industry analysts have characterized this phenomenon as little more than a passing fad, but some believe that the movement may continue to gain steam and may eventually constitute a cornerstone of the American food market.

It is likely that many of those entering the alternative agriculture business are motivated by the fact that traditional farming, like curled mustaches and vintage fashion, is in vogue, especially among a subset of young adults in upper- and middle-class white communities. Undoubtedly, some who approach agriculture because it is trendy will find themselves motivated to remain in the field. In addition, the broader social movement away from industrial food products is enhanced by youth trends but based on more lasting environmental and social concerns, and this creates an economic incentive for the creation of businesses that provide alternatives to big-market retailers.

Challenges to the New Food Movement

Building the new food and farming industries beyond their current state is a difficult task, partially because the industrial food industry continues to strategically protect its share of the market. Increasingly, major food brands like Nestlé, Pepsi-Cola, and Kellogg are creating subordinate brands aimed at marketing products that appeal to ecologically minded and health-conscious consumers.

In some cases, these new products are superior in terms of nutritional value and the ethics of production methods, but purchasing any product from a mass-food retailer also supports the questionable manufacturing procedures of the company on a larger scale. In addition, the big-food industry spends millions in marketing each year to dilute concepts like "organic," "fair trade," and "farm fresh," producing products that are not nutritionally or ethically superior, but differ largely in marketing terminology.

In addition, though farmers are often underpaid and exploited by the dominant food production companies, a major shift toward local products could have devastating effects on the farmers and farming communities dependent on international sales. Concern for the welfare of these agricultural communities has led to the formation of a variety of companies aimed at supporting the ethical import of international products. A variety of companies in the United States and around the world now attempt to procure coffee and other types of produce in ways that support agricultural communities and provide farmers with a living wage. Some food analysts have suggested that ethical import of some crops must accompany a shift toward local or slow food in an effort to protect the small-farm industry worldwide.

For those hoping to ensure the integrity of the earth's ecological balance, purchasing local foods and supporting local farms will do little to address the overall effect of human culture on natural environments. More than 90 percent of the greenhouse gasses produced by the food industry come in the form of agricultural production, rather than the national or international transport of products. Buying locally therefore does little to affect this environmental consequence of food production. Shifting to a vegetarian diet and purchasing only products that can be produced with limited ecological impact are far more effective measures toward limiting the environmental impact of the food industry.

In addition, the cost of local, environmentally friendly, and ethically procured produce and other products remains too high for many consumers operating within a budget. This cost can be greatly reduced by utilizing food co-ops and farmers markets, but these resources tend to be seasonal and cannot, for most consumers, replace the need to purchase products from retail markets. If the new food movement is going to replace the big-food market in a substantial way, efforts to curtail the costs of alternative products will need to become a more widespread goal of the movement.

The Transition from Movement to Mainstream

The slow food movement has been ongoing since the 1980s and has continued to enjoy strong international popularity. The local food movement and alternative farming movements are both comparatively recent developments, but have gained increasing momentum as the proliferation of shopping and dining options combine to create a more powerful international shift in consumer trends and preferences.

Social, economic, and consumer patterns are constantly in a state of flux, hence the term *movement*, which is often used to describe a net shift in tastes or purchasing patterns. The full potential of the alternative food and farming trends will be recognized when these phenomena have evolved beyond the movement stage and have become an established part of mainstream food culture. For this to occur, consumers would need to permanently alter their views of shopping, cooking, and dining.

For an average restaurant owner or chef, local produce may be a desirable option when it can be obtained at a reasonable price. Locavores and slow food aficionados often flock to restaurants that offer specials such as local heirloom tomatoes or local berries and cream, but they may refuse to patronize the same restaurant during the off season when local products are unavailable or too expensive to purchase. This type of short-sighted consumer behavior does not serve the longevity of the move-ment because it penalizes a restaurant for being unable to afford the ideal products on all occasions.

Consumers must therefore make informed decisions to support restaurants that show the tendency to favor local food, and to increase their support whenever the restaurant can obtain and serve the idealized local cuisine. As the restaurant thrives and the owner and chef respond to customer support for their local offerings, these may become a more regular part of their menu, causing them to increase purchases from local farms and keeping the local farms alive in the process. In general, the new food and farming movements do not benefit from absolutism in consumers as much as they benefit from consumers who favor local and alternative options when they are available.

In addition, attracting the affluent consumer can help to build a steady subset of the food industry but will not cause major changes to the food industry as a whole. For this to occur, local and alternative products must be made available at vast-ly reduced prices to consumers in low-income communities. This type of change requires both a combination of grassroots involvement to set up new co-ops and farmers markets in low-income areas and dedicated support from companies and individuals with the resources to finance efforts to change dining, shopping, and eating habits within these communities. Until alternative products become a viable option for people at every income level, the new food phenomenon will remain a luxury movement and will never constitute a true challenge to industrial giants that currently dominate the food industry.

Slow Food Movement

Food Industry Watch, 2010

The name is intentional: Consider Slow Food the opposite of fast food. While the latter relies on cheap, processed ingredients that do not vary by location, the Slow Food movement urges people to eat fresh, local foods and regional specialties. Slow Food also calls for a rediscovery of traditional food production methods, and for a return to pleasurable meals enjoyed with friends, family and conversation. Established in 1989, Slow Food—a global organization called Slow Food International (SFI), with regional chapters called convivia in over 150 countries—offers a new way of thinking about food.

While few disagree that unprocessed, fresh foods are healthful and that supporting local producers benefits regional economies, critics argue that adherence to Slow Food principles is simply not realistic in today's world. Furthermore, many Americans live in urban or suburban areas that are far from the nearest farm. It is also difficult for modern Americans to spend hours each day shopping for, preparing and eating meals with others.

Still, Slow Food continues to gain support as people find ways to adapt the movement's principles to the reality of their schedules. Each regional chapter has the freedom to develop initiatives, like tastings or programs to market local foods, that are tailored to their area's needs. In the United States, Slow Food supporters have begun trying to make change by influencing food policy. Although the Obama administration has not officially endorsed the Slow Food movement, it has called for better nutrition in schools, increased school lunch funding, an emphasis on unprocessed food (especially during childhood) and programs like school gardens that help connect kids to food sources.

What Is the Slow Food Movement?

In 1986 McDonald's opened a franchise in Rome, Italy, not far from the famous Spanish Steps. This caught the attention of Carlo Petrini, a food writer and activist from a northern Italian town called Bra. The idea of a global fast food giant sitting so close to an Italian landmark in a country revered for its unique, fresh foods irritated Petrini. He came up with the idea of "slow food" as a half-joking, half-serious response to companies like McDonald's that have shifted world food consumption from regional cuisines to processed foods that are the same everywhere.

Slow Food became an official movement in December 1989, as Petrini formed Slow Food International, an organization dedicated to preserving local foods and food customs, and to reviving the idea of meals as communal affairs to be savored, not rushed. Because the Slow Food movement is concerned with how we eat, not just what we eat, in some ways it resembles the fair trade movement—another global effort focused on environmental, social and food issues.

Today SFI is a non-profit with over 100,000 members in 150 countries (Creighton, 2009). The movement—or at least some of its general concepts—are in sync with current food trends. Thanks to celebrity chefs, cooking shows, magazines and web sites the preparation and production of food has become a hot topic. At the same time, concerns about food contamination, environmental damage and health have led consumers to ask where their food comes from, and to shorten the distance between farm and fork. While critics of Slow Food deride the movement as elitist or impractical, most agree that the global food system needs a fix. According to the United Nations Food and Agriculture Organization (FAO), hunger is on the rise. Fifty million more people went hungry in 2007 than in 2006 (Walsh, 2008); at the same time, an overabundance of cheap processed food is driving up obesity rates in America. As highly processed convenience foods spread to markets around the world, they can raise health risks—and threaten the existence of regional cuisines and food traditions.

Tenets of the Slow Food Movement

SFI has articulated three major goals: education of taste; defending the right to material pleasure and conviviality; and preserving the survival of endangered foods and customs. These goals are in line with Slow Food's motto that food should be "good, clean and fair."

Changing Tastes

Many people eat fast food or processed food simply because it is familiar. Why spend money on a strange vegetable if you have no idea what it will taste like, or if your family will eat it? Slow Food believes that people can "educate" their palates and learn to distinguish differences in flavor—and appreciate the unique, delicious tastes of whole foods and regional specialties. The first step in this process is simple: Expand the menu. As people increase the diversity of foods that they eat, over time they will start noticing differences in taste. Slow Food encourages people to start by tasting foods that are unique to their area, and by attending events that offer a chance to taste new or unusual food products.

The Shared Table

Unlike a dietician, Slow Food is as concerned with how people eat as it is concerned with what people eat. Most commercial restaurants do not encourage lingering: Faster turnover means more tables seated per meal. Busy lifestyles and the availability of fast, packaged food lets people eat on the go, without utensils and while performing other chores. According to the Slow Food movement, quick, solitary eating compromises the pleasure of meal time, and runs counter to the traditional idea of meal time as a foundation for family and community. Slow Food encourages people to eat with others, in leisurely settings, savoring tastes and allowing the meal to become an enjoyable shared experience.

Protecting "Endangered Foods"

Thanks to the global food industry, it is now possible to eat the same meal in New York, Paris, Beijing, Mexico City and rural Nebraska. According to Slow Food, one of the downsides of food globalization is the loss of regional specialties and agricultural products that used to form the cornerstone of local meals. A Slow Food program called the Ark of Taste aims to preserve these endangered foods by supporting their producers and by strengthening markets for local food; in the United States the Slow Food Ark of Taste is working to protect foods like the American chestnut and the black turkey. Besides the foods themselves, Slow Food wants to protect traditional methods of food production that are in danger of being lost or forgotten.

Support and Criticism of the Slow Food Movement

Slow Food has gained significant momentum in recent years, thanks in part to increased worries about food safety and quality. However, the movement has also earned its share of criticism.

Supporters of the Slow Food Movement Say:

In a world where obesity rates and health care costs are rising, the Slow Food movement and its initiatives promote minimally-processed, nutrient-dense foods that have been linked to good health.

Although Slow Food activities are aimed at specialty foods like heirloom tomatoes and unique French cheeses, the movement is also working to preserve staple foods like rice crops in Asia. Many of these foods—and the traditions that make them—are in danger of being lost, as small producers and regional food cultures are replaced by the global food industry.

Efforts to preserve and promote regional or traditional foods have the added benefit of supporting the livelihoods of small-scale farmers, producers and manufacturers, including those who have no viable economic alternatives to agricultural production.

Slow Food encourages environmentally-friendly, sustainable food production, but does not encourage strict rules like "never buy non-organic foods."

Slow Food tries to take a positive approach by emphasizing the benefits of healthful, traditional eating instead of highlighting the dangers of eating processed or fast food.

Community supported agriculture (CSA) programs and farmers' markets help link urban residents to their food producers. People who participate in CSAs can buy shares of a farm's seasonal output directly from the farmers.

In addition to the nutritional and environmental benefits of slow food, the movement urges people to re-connect food with fellowship by taking the time to share meals with family and friends.

Critics of the Slow Food Movement Say:

Industrial, large-scale farming is the only efficient way to feed the world's growing population.

Genetically-modified organisms (GMOs) and other industrial innovations produce crops that provide greater returns with less cost. Advocates of industrial farming add that in order to yield as much food as the world's growing population requires, traditional food production methods are no longer adequate.

Slow Food programs are aimed at "fancy" foods that most consumers will never buy on a regular basis.

For many people, fast food and pre-packaged meals are the most affordable and convenient source of calories.

It is not realistic to expect everyone—especially residents of urban and suburban areas—to purchase the majority of their foods from local farms or producers.

While consumers may agree that food producers deserve fair pay, those who do not earn enough themselves often save money by buying cheap food. Because food is a necessity, not a luxury, it cannot be removed from the budget entirely—so people with insufficient income are more likely to cut corners. Those who must work long hours to cover their bills also have less time to shop and cook.

> *Some health and food advocates have begun to connect the dots between US food policy and the amount of highly processed foods in our food supply.*

Slow Food Initiatives and Organization

Slow Food International is the global slow food organization, which operates at the local level as chapters called convivia. Regional convivia appeared in the United States in the early 1990s, organizing first in Portland, Oregon, and San Francisco. In 2000, the headquarters of Slow Food USA opened in New York, and today there are Slow Food convivia in every state.

Convivia are purposefully given freedom to develop their own programs and approaches; this way they are able to integrate organically with the communities in which they operate. Forming a convivium is simple: Slow Food advocates join together, discuss their aims and interests, and request support from headquarters. Activities undertaken by the convivia vary, but most groups host events and tastings, partner with local food producers and help bring other Slow Food initiatives to life in their communities.

At the international level, Slow Food operates a number of programs. It also runs a culinary school, the University of Gastronomic Sciences, which teaches courses on cooking as well as food science and social issues related to food. Ongoing major initiatives include Terra Madre, which brings small-scale food producers together to exchange ideas about food production; the Ark of Taste, which preserves endangered local foods and food production traditions; and the Presidium program, which provides marketing assistance to traditional food producers who have difficulty bringing their goods to market. In the United States, Slow Food programs include RAFT (Renewing America's Food Traditions), which links food producers with chefs and consumers to understand traditional foods and production methods; the US Youth Food Movement, the national chapter of a global alliance dedicated to food sustainability and justice; and Slow Food in Schools, which tackles issues related to school lunch programs and has helped to popularize school gardens.

Perhaps the most famous Slow Food International event is the Salon of Taste, a five-day food festival that takes place every two years. San Francisco hosted the first US version of the Salon, dubbed Slow Food Nation, in 2008.

Slow Food Principles and US Food Policy

Although the Slow Food movement does not proscribe diets composed exclusively of organic foods, Slow Food is vehemently opposed to genetically modified organisms and GMO crops. Monsanto, the world's largest producer of genetically modified crop seeds, is headquartered in Missouri. As much as 60 percent of the food Americans eat contain some genetically modified ingredients (Gustin, 2009). GMOs are cost-effective, especially for the industrial farms that have come to dominate the US food production landscape, because they produce more resilient and abundant crops. In fact, some GMO supporters claim that GMO crops should be embraced by environmentalists—after all, they allow greater yields with less water, fertilizer and pesticide.

Some health and food advocates have begun to connect the dots between US food policy and the amount of highly processed foods in our food supply. Americans are also becoming more aware of the environmental impacts of large-scale industrial farming, a production system that also jeopardizes the small, local producers championed by Slow Food. Most US food policy is linked to the Farm Bill, a sizeable piece of agricultural legislation that establishes farm subsidies, incentives and other guidelines for food production. Updated every four or five years, the Farm Bill has become a battleground for local food proponents who want to see fewer incentives for mass-produced processed foods. A common example of how the Farm Bill contradicts Slow Food principles is the issue of corn. Lobbyists and legislators from corn states have helped keep corn subsidies and price supports in place, making corn a very cheap commodity crop, capable of being processed into cheap inputs for manufactured food. The rise of corn syrup and high fructose corn syrup (HFCS) in processed food is linked in part to these conditions, as corn-based sweeteners are very cheap. A processed ingredient like HFCS would have no place on a Slow Food menu.

The issue of school lunch has become another highly charged issue for food and health advocates, and Slow Food USA is actively trying to shape policy in this debate. Every five years Congress writes a new Child Nutrition Act that sets guidelines and funding for school meal programs which are administered by the US Department of Agriculture (USDA). One of the chief criticisms of school lunches is that they are built on processed, salty and fatty foods. This has to do with supply: A list of 180 USDA commodity foods—especially beef and cheese—make up approximately 20 percent of food used to prepare school meals. These commodities are often processed—not served fresh (Lubrano, 2010). The remainder of school lunch ingredients is purchased by schools and reimbursed by the government, but reimbursement limitations encourage the use of cheap, processed foods.

The Obama administration has pledged to improve childhood health and nutrition; Michelle Obama's signature initiative is a campaign to reduce childhood obesity. As Congress prepares to authorize a new Child Nutrition Act, President Obama has called for gradual increases in school lunch funding over the next decade, and Secretary of Agriculture Tom Vilsack backs recommendations by the Institute of Medicine (IOM) to put more produce and whole grains in school lunches. If approved, these recommendations would take effect in 2011. Vilsack has also called for increased reimbursement budgets so schools could afford better ingredients.

Slow Food USA has called for the Child Nutrition Act to revise National School Lunch Program rules to invest $50 million in "Farm to School" programs that link local farms with local schools; to establish stronger nutrition standards for school food, including foods sold in vending machines on school grounds; and to increase school lunch funding by $1 billion per year so schools have more purchasing choices ("Time for lunch," 2010).

A reauthorization of the Child Nutrition Act reached Congress in spring 2010. This version offers some funding increases and improved nutrition standards, but not as much funding as Slow Food USA or the Obama administration have requested. Additional changes are possible before a final vote, which is expected by the end of 2010.

Slow Cities

The Slow Food movement has begun to influence policy and planning at the municipal level via the Cittaslow network. Cittaslow ("slow city") began in Italy in 1999, then spread to other cities in Europe. Today there are over 100 Slow Cities around the world, most of them in Europe, although the concept has spread as far as South Korea and Australia.

Slow Cities agree to follow a set of zoning, planning and environmental principles aimed at promoting eco-friendly development, community, local character and regional foods; they also agree to reduce air, noise and light pollution with measures like banning car alarms and neon signs in public squares, and removing advertising billboards from their centers. Adherence to these standards is largely self-monitored but evaluated by Cittaslow International headquarters in Italy. Each Slow City must submit periodic reports about their progress toward Cittaslow goals. In order to become a Slow City, a city must meet a population standard of 50,000 people or fewer. It must also form a committee and work with Cittaslow International to receive guidance and approval.

The first—and only—Slow City in the United States is Sonoma Valley, California. Located in the state's wine country about 40 miles north of San Francisco, Sonoma Valley received its Slow City designation in 2009. Like other members of the Cittaslow network, Sonoma can now leverage its Slow City status in marketing materials, hoping to draw visitors who are interested in environmental or gastronomic tourism.

Bringing Local Food to the Lunch Line

By Susan McCrory
Edible Boston, September 7, 2012

Even if the first day of school is no longer a consideration for you at this time of year, it's hard to ignore the fact that our society still operates on an academic-year kind of mentality. September equals "school" in the macro sense: it marks the re-start of formal obligations and the end of a more relaxed, summer-induced attitude. Not so for the Food Service Director (FSD) in your town. Of the handful you'll hear from below—those in Framingham, Arlington, Boston, Lynn and Concord—nary a one said s/he slows down in the summer. Instead, each gave a wry chuckle at the prospect.

Ironically, it's fair to say that, not even a generation ago, few of us were aware of who filled the role of Food Service Director and what went into feeding our school kids lunch each day. That cultural landscape has changed dramatically. Obesity rates are rising, municipalities are strapped for cash, a growing number of families rely on school meals to nourish their children and, as a nation, we've become increasingly concerned with where, literally, our food comes from.

These societal factors, alone, place Food Service Directors in a particularly "hot seat." Yet they don't even begin to touch on the financial challenges of operating within the most heavily regulated food-related industry in the country. Here's how the National School Lunch Program works. The NSLP is a federally-assisted meal program administered on the state level. Decisions about what foods to serve, and how to prepare them are made by local school food authorities—in other words, Food Service Directors.

Schools that participate in the NSLP receive cash subsidies and donated foods from the USDA for each meal they serve. In return, they must serve lunches that meet Federal nutrition requirements, plus offer free or reduced-price lunches to eligible children. For the 2011–12 school year, the reimbursement rate for paid lunch in the forty-eight contiguous states was $0.26. Free lunches were reimbursed at $2.77 per meal, and reduced-price lunches at $2.37 per meal, according to the School Nutrition Association. As these numbers reveal, if an FSD wants to take advantage of cash reimbursements and "entitlement" (i.e., donated) foods from the USDA, the incumbent nutritional guidelines must be met for under $3.00 per student meal, all costs included. Sound tricky? And now, the guidelines are changing. The Federal government's new My Plate requirements mean that schools will now need to double the quantity of fruits and vegetables served each day. Yet the adjusted rate of reimbursement per student will be a mere $.06.

Amidst these rules, regulations and opportunities, some within the school foods industry have reached out to local farmers as a means of procuring fresh, nutritious produce to help them meet Federal nutritional requirements and operate in the black. One of the primary ways of doing so is through the Massachusetts Farm to School program, a grassroots project based out of Amherst, MA, which has helped connect farmers with schools since 2004. The benefits of creating sustainable local food purchasing relationships are obvious, and manifold. Farmers gain the security of consistent, reliable demand. Schools districts participate in strengthening the local economy and reinforce the need to eat healthfully. School kids benefit from more frequent access to healthy, locally-grown produce and foods cooked from scratch, which in turn means less consumption of the substandard processed foods that traditionally appear in lunch lines.

To date, there are approximately ninety-five Farm to School programs in place in the Commonwealth, involving more than two-hundred school districts preferentially serving local foods. According to director Kelly Erwin, Massachusetts' inherent strength rests with the fact that growers are geographically close to consumers, literally one with the community. This makes them an obvious resource when it comes to procuring food. The concept of marrying local farms with local schools, which ultimately invigorates local economies while nourishing students, is so powerful, in fact, that the USDA now offers Farm to School grants, available both to eligible school districts and individual schools. (Like the NSLP, such grants are administered on the state level through the Massachusetts Department of Elementary and Secondary School of Education, or MDESE).

On the face of it, the Farm to School model makes abundant sense on many levels—public health, local economies, the environment. No one in his/her right mind would be against it. But that doesn't mean it's easy to implement. I set out to speak with a few of the Food Service Directors in the Boston area about the challenges they are encountering in making locally-procured foods part of school lunch.

The Seasons

One of the first, obvious challenges for Food Service Directors in bringing state produce into their schools is New England's short growing season. Last frost dates can range from late April to early June, first frost dates from early September to the end of October, sometimes later. Those approximately 120–180 days do not handily overlap with the school "serving season"—the mandated 180 days of the academic year running roughly from September to June.

This disconnect eliminates quite a few local-grown products. For example, zucchini and broccoli "whither out," according to Brendan Ryan, the straight-talking Food Service Director in Framingham, MA. Ryan receives butternut and spaghetti squash through his Farm to School connections, in addition to zucchini, sweet potatoes, apples and Brussels sprouts. Ryan says his staff will fast-freeze the Brussels sprouts, for example, if the quantity received is too great to prepare and serve before spoiling. They can effectively store the produce in "Cook-Chill" bags (thick-gauge plastic bags that close at the top with a metal staple) and "quick menu" the food into the lunch line with relative ease. There is no added cost to Ryan's budget for the prep work involved.

In Concord, where Alden Cadwell has been shaking up the system in his first year as Food Service Director, Clearview Farm in Sterling, MA, supplies "second" tomatoes and zucchini in late August, which Cadwell's staff then stews, blitzes and/or shreds before freezing. As the school year progresses, the stored, local vegetable appears at lunch as pizza, pasta, tomato soup, zucchini browns or in stir-fry. Keeping up with the late summer harvest therefore means there's a lot of in-house processing of food that occurs before school begins. (You'll recall the wry laugh, above.) Cadwell has yet to figure out the labor costs involved, saying they depend on the amount of produce he actually receives and the efficiency of the systems he and staff develop over time. But "tons" of fresh produce is slated to arrive for Concord school kids early this fall, including lettuce, snap peas, summer squash, cucumbers, apples and peaches.

In Arlington, Food Services Director Denise Boucher takes advantage of locally-grown apples, squashes and tomatoes harvested from Massachusetts farms in the fall. But she has found that the minimum quantities required by some of the farmers participating in Farm to School presents a challenge she has yet to overcome. Even with support waiting in the wings from Farm to School staffers, Boucher feels strapped for time to research potential new relationships with local farmers. Therefore, even while eager to grow Arlington's local foods procurement, she's poised for a second consecutive year of facility-rebuilding in Arlington that has placed logistical challenges on her lunchroom staff at multiple schools.

Indeed, Brendan Ryan of Framingham noted that remaining "fluid" is a necessity for any Food Service Director because of the varying quantities of food stuffs that come in, which may be more or less than what's needed—as true for the locally-grown produce received through Farm to School relationships as for government-supplied commodities such as cheese, milk, dry goods, etc. Cadwell concurred about time constraints. The two farms he currently does business with—the previously mentioned Clearview, plus Verrill Farm, just up the road in Concord—are plenty from an administrative standpoint once government contracts figure in. He does all the paperwork.

In the final analysis, it takes time to explore and develop financially viable business relationships with farmers, especially when the growing season is short.

The Taste Test: Or Getting Kids to Eat

As any parent knows, the labor and care that go into preparing meals does not mean a child will "dig in." At home, this can be maddening. At school, it's expensive and counterproductive to the goal of changing mindsets and eating habits.

At Boston Public Schools (BPS), the largest of the public school districts in New England, participating in the Farm to School Program has been made possible through grants and collaborations amongst many state organizations and agencies. BPS Farm to School Coordinator Kim Szeto has been on the job for approximately four years, and now works with Michael Peck, Boston's new, progressively-minded

Director of the Department of Food and Nutrition Services. Szeto has seen the original pilot program of six participating schools grow to forty-four Boston public schools with full kitchen cafeterias where Massachusetts-grown produce is regularly on the menu (BPS does not currently have the onsite storage space to stockpile local produce in kitchen freezers, nor has it located an off-site facility to do the same). But while the supply-side of the equation may not pose a challenge when you're serving over 34,000 meals per day (K–12), and can commit to purchasing over 58,000 locally-grown apples and pears in a four-month period as Boston did last fall, the demand side of things—the kid side—can be tricky.

In order to expose students to fresh produce they may never have seen before, let alone tried, Szeto instituted "Local Lunch Thursdays." During the 2011–12 academic year, accompanied by a small Farm to School "team" consisting of parents, teachers and a USDA-funded Fresh Fruit and Vegetable Coordinator, Szeto visited approximately two dozen public schools with a whole vegetable or fruit in hand. Students were able to experience how, say, a carrot or cabbage looks, weighs and feels before it becomes the coleslaw on their plates. Locally-grown collard greens, green beans, broccoli, butternut squash and pears represent some of the other foods introduced to BPS students during these Thursday meetings. Strategically, the food discussed in the morning anticipated that day's lunch menu, so that students could put their knowledge, and taste buds, to immediate use. They also received nutrition information cards and a take-home recipe to further their learning and make it stick. All said, over 6,000 pounds of locally-grown produce was served in BPS from September through December alone of last year.

The education piece is similarly important in the city of Lynn, where over 9,000 school lunches are served daily (K–12). Kevin Richardson, six years on the job as Lynn's FSD and employed by Chartwells School Dining Services, which collaborates with the Farm to School program, chooses a fruit or vegetable each week that is highlighted on the lunch menu and posted as such in the serving line. At the 5–12 grade levels, Richardson commented that the kids appear to be "very responsive" to the featured items, be they whole peaches, apples or pears. Still, locally grown produce is not picture perfect, of the "warehouse-stored" variety, he observed, and some kids balk. Continually educating students, he says, is important if the Farm to School initiative is to grow.

In Framingham, taste tests are done for entree items to ensure some modicum of success in the serving line. Ryan told me that cod and roasted pork have been very well-received by students. Ignoring popular wisdom, he stands by what he's seen: kids will eat fish. "You have to present and cook it right," he says. This means a 3.5 ounce portion of cod or haddock, baked in the oven. For the mythically dreaded Brussels sprout, Ryan roasts them with extra virgin olive oil in a balsamic reduction whose caramelized sweetness fights the characteristic bitterness of the sprout. Down the proverbial hatch they go. Alden Cadwell in Concord also conducts taste tests, particularly for students at the elementary and middle-school level since they tend to be pickier. Even with initial test runs, however, some recipes just flop, he admits. Those locally-grown sweet potatoes will have to be coaxed into a final form

> *In order to expose students to fresh produce they may never have seen before, let alone tried, Szeto instituted "Local Lunch Thursdays."*

other than sweet-potato and garbanzo bean "tater tots."

Both Ryan of Framingham and Boston's Szeto spoke realistically about how connected kids are to the local angle. Put differently, taste and peer opinion matter. In Ryan's view, only a small number of kids grasp the importance of eating local. "You don't [participate in Farm to School] for the monetary gain, or for an 'atta boy!' pat on the back. It's for helping the local economy," he says. To support learning in a hands-on way, Ryan has overseen the planting of organic Saxonville Gardens, an impressive vegetable and herb garden on the grounds of Framingham High School in which secondary-school students help out (a farm in school, as Ryan likes to think of it). This past year the garden yielded eight-hundred gallons of tomato sauce, thirty gallons of basil pesto, two-hundred cantaloupes and 120 lbs of carrots—plus small amounts of peppers, eggplant and various herbs used in meals served.

Similarly, Szeto feels that the "fresh and local" tag doesn't always move the school-age kids she works with in Boston. Plain and simple, the food has to taste good. Mangoes and red peppers may be easy sells, "but their friends need to like it!" Szeto insists.

The Cost

With a short growing season and kids' finicky taste buds collectively agreed upon as obvious obstacles, a third formidable challenge in bringing local foods into schools is budgetary concerns. Yes, money—the proverbial elephant in the room. For at least two of the Food Service Directors interviewed for this article, the per meal food cost, excluding overhead, utensils, etc., runs approximately $1.50. Since dining services is a fee-for-service industry, a Food Service Director should be overseeing an operation that at least breaks even. Profits from meals purchased (regardless of the degree of federal reimbursement) might be spent on new equipment, new staff, new foods.

Settling on a price point is therefore arguably the greatest challenge for Food Service Directors. Yet price point obviously matters to the farmer as well, especially when it can be more profitable to sell wholesale to grocery stores or retail directly to customers via farmers markets, farms stands and CSAs. Still, the business model for local foods procurement is working, thanks in part to the networking efforts of Farm to School staff and a growing number of Food Service Directors in Massachusetts willing to think out of the box. "The classic [FSD] is focused on the per-meal cost, and will think 'not possible,'" says Cadwell. Yet he will tell you it is.

Cadwell looked at operating costs and the sourcing of food across the board in Concord and has begun piecemealing together an enviably healthy, fiscally sound school food program. Instead of one or two big volume sellers (traditionally, chicken patties, chicken nuggets and pizza), Cadwell has introduced several "good" sellers instead, including a pulled-pork sandwich and honey chicken. He makes up the money elsewhere, he says, with vegetarian offerings such as mac 'n' cheese, grilled cheeses and a baked potato bar, all of which are popular with students. The number of school lunches served grew in Concord this year, helping Cadwell to a 5 percent profit margin. In Framingham, participation in the lunch program has been rising on a regular basis, according to Ryan, but he felt it hard to discern whether the growth was due to the poor economy and more children relying on reduced-fare meals or because of the increasing appeal of his food.

Richardson of Lynn spoke candidly of the pending Federal requirements for serving more fresh fruits, vegetables and whole grains to students each day. The $.06 reimbursement rate represents "a big concern" for Food Service Directors in general, certainly those wanting to look first to local farmers to meet the forthcoming increase in demand. Likewise, Szeto of Boston was frank. Her current budget for fresh fruit and vegetables is less than $.20 per serving. Doubling the quantity of produce with only an additional $.06 from the Federal government presents a serious challenge. She has "no new answer" for it, allowing that it will require some pretty innovative planning on the part of Peck, herself, the menu planner and the nutritionist on staff. Yet it is not Boston's problem alone. Beyond budgetary constraints, what also concerns Szeto is the false dichotomy that arises as a result between procuring greater quantities of locally-grown, fresh food and the increased costs of training staff (or a third party) to prepare it.

The Time

Finally, perhaps the thorniest point of contention to consider in the "good food in schools" debate: the issue of how much time kids get to spend in the lunchroom eating the strictly regulated, often deliberately procured and carefully presented foods that grown-ups want so badly for kids to eat. Many students move in and out of their cafeteria in twenty minutes. Union contracts are involved, as are state and federal benchmarks for standardized testing.

Arlington's Boucher laments the lack of time conducive to socializing (yes!) and savoring food as more than jet fuel. How can the positive peer influence of seeing a friend consume butternut squash actually come into play when you barely have time to connect with that friend? Szeto also regrets the daily reality of a twenty-minute lunch, implying that it undermines the change in attitude and eating culture she feels the BPS Farm to School program can help foment in the city's school-age children. Rather than integral, the cafeteria—broadly speaking, learning about nutrition and healthy eating habits—is viewed as tangential to a child's formal education.

This brings us to the takeaway. There is more than one challenge in implementing the Farm to School model for Massachusetts Food Service Directors. But the overarching need is to bring together good-food education with demand and supply in a way that is sustainably profitable for all parties, allowing them to move in the same, progressive direction at the same time. In order to evaluate success appropriate expectations must be set. We must be realistic; America is never going to return to being a fully agrarian society. Instead, you just keep innovating and making things work since, in the optimistic words of Alden Cadwell, "anything is possible."

Sue McCrory is the former Editor & Host of WBUR's Public Radio Kitchen. *She lives in Arlington with her husband and children.*

Sandhills Farm to Table Co-op Goal: Meeting Local Food Needs with Local Food

By James Matson and Jeremiah Thayer
Rural Cooperatives, January 2012

Editor's note: The authors are both business consultants with Matson Consulting, a co-op business development firm based in Aiken, S.C. Matson is a former co-op development specialist with USDA Rural Development.

Since its inception two years ago, Sandhills Farm to Table Cooperative (Sandhills)— a multi-stakeholder enterprise—has made a huge impact in the rural community surrounding Moore County, N.C. Sandhills is providing fresh local food to more than 1,600 co-op members, while donating more than $30,000 to local schools and nonprofit organizations. In addition, it has had a tremendous impact on thirty-five producer-members, paying them more than 70 percent of the retail food dollars their co-op collects. Their multi-stakeholder model is providing inspiration for several other rural cooperatives being developed in North Carolina that are seeking locally based solutions to local food needs.

Expanding the Co-op Model

From its inception, Sandhills Farm to Table Cooperative has redefined the traditional cooperative model. Typically, a co-op is focused on benefiting one class of stakeholder, be it a producer-owned, worker-owned or consumer-owned cooperative. However, many cooperatives are unable to operate successfully within the traditional "single stakeholder" business model. But when there are multiple types of members represented by one co-op, addressing more diverse concerns is a challenge—which Sandhills has been designed to accomplish.

By including three different stakeholder groups (producer-farmers, consumer-customers and employees) in the decision-making structure of its operations, Sandhills has been able to expand the scope of benefits. It is one of the first local food cooperatives in the country in which the farmers, consumers and staff are all equal owners.

"People are less concerned about price, and the farmers are working to provide the best possible produce to their neighbors," says Jan Leitschuh, director of marketing and farmer relations for the co-op. "We're trying to be a cooperative in the truest sense of the word." While co-op leaders determined that the multi-stakeholder business structure was the best way to address the concerns of each party involved, the process is still evolving. They say the flexibility of the cooperative structure is the key to sustaining growth.

Ultimately, Sandhills would tweak the multi-stakeholder format through the use of the "one member, one vote" concept, partnered with a board of seven directors. Two board members are elected directly by each of the three stakeholder classes. These six directors then appoint one additional, unaffiliated board member to provide balance and objectivity.

Reaching Consensus

The decision-making process posed an interesting challenge. The ideal of a "consensus" was never really considered. A simple majority vote of board members would allow any two interest groups to override the interest of the third, which is inconsistent with Sandhills' guiding principle: "We're all in this together."

A creative alternative emerged. Decisions are made by a simple majority vote, with the provision that at least one representative of each interest group must agree. The format of the cooperative serves as a watershed, expanding the benefit base beyond the stakeholders and into the community in which the cooperative resides.

Linking Producers with Consumers

Sandhills Farm to Table Cooperative is an outgrowth of a wave of Community Supported Agriculture (CSA) co-ops that began springing up across the nation in the 1990s. At its core, Sandhills is a multi-farm CSA cooperative. This multi-farm format allows the co-op to expand on the benefits of traditional CSAs. In a typical CSA, consumer-members financially support local producers and, in turn, they are supplied with regular "shares" in the form of produce distributed throughout the season.

In Sandhills' case, once customers become members, they are able to sign up for a subscription to receive "produce boxes," which are distributed on a regular schedule at various "gathering sites" located throughout the area. The multi-farm CSA format employed by Sandhills ensures that the co-op can offer a greater variety of produce as well as provide joint marketing and sales logistics. Similarly, the consumer-members receive the benefit of receiving their produce at gathering sites on a regular basis, instead of just when certain crops are in season.

While serving as a conduit for local food demand (which influences producers' planting decisions), Sandhills also serves to bring producers and consumers closer together. "The co-op has been very successful in building a positive relationship between the farmers and community," says John Blue, a Sandhills farmer-member. "It has stimulated interest in using local products that we, as farmers, could have never accomplished as individuals."

This "consumer connection" is especially important for "transitioning farmers," those who are too large to make a living by selling at farmers markets, but not big enough to access large-scale producer markets. Or these farmers may be transitioning from producing one crop type to another. By participating in the cooperative, many of these producers have been able to succeed.

"A full-time farmer transitioning from commodity crops, like tobacco, into direct-to-consumer sales finds it difficult to adjust his production and marketing practices to meet the demand for locally grown, fresh fruits and vegetables," says Taylor Williams, an agent with North Carolina Cooperative Extension. "Sandhills Farm to Table helps the farmer expand and diversify production and marketing practices to meet the demand for locally grown, fresh fruits and vegetables. It is no exaggeration to say that two dozen farmers in our county have been able to survive and succeed because of their participation in this cooperative."

Sandhills returns local dollars to the community, primarily through payment to farmers for their produce. In 2011 alone, 35 farmer producers were paid at least 70 percent of the retail food dollars from the co-op's produce sales.

Community Impacts

While Sandhills includes the functions of a traditional CSA, it has become much more than that to the local community. The co-op's goals have always included community building. An example of this can be seen in the use of "gathering sites," rather than simple "pick-up locations." Jan Leitschuh says that the idea was to make the gathering sites a place where people could get to know their neighbors, swap recipes and generally have a more pleasant experience than is experienced at a typical "get your box and go"-type pick-up site. She sees the gathering sites as one of the key benefits of Sandhills Farm to Table, compared to other cooperative models.

While community building is accomplished through the strengthening of producer-consumer ties, it is also accomplished by fostering volunteerism. People begin to understand that "we're all in this together." In 2010, Sandhills was the recipient of more than 2,500 hours of volunteer services from members and others. Most of this donated time was used to operate the weekly gathering sites at churches and elementary schools.

Working together to meet the personal needs of the cooperative members also helps meet the needs of people and organizations outside the cooperative. Through donations to gathering site hosts in 2011, more than $30,000 was given to three public elementary schools, three churches and several other local, nonprofit organizations. That amount is up from about $10,000 in 2010.

In addition to its role as a CSA, the co-op is also on the cutting edge of the emerging "food hub" trend, in which the Internet becomes a marketing vehicle for local producers and a shopping platform for consumers. Through the use of Sandhills' website, the co-op offers services much like a "pre-order" farmers market. Orders are placed via the website, then a "market day" is scheduled on which food and nonfood items are picked up and a final bill is determined.

The use of market days allows producers to include food items that probably would not "survive" in the produce boxes, as well as to include more highly processed items, such as cured meats, jams, jellies and baked goods. Because they provide a source of guaranteed sales, market days have also allowed producers to include more difficult-to-store items, such as grass-fed beef, pork, and lamb; sausages; breads; and jams.

While the website format allows producers to find a sure market, it also opens the door for new business ventures in the community.

A recent survey identified several areas where there was a potential market, but uncertainty existed about local producers to meet the demand. One result of this is the Olde Time Bakery. Business owner Leslie Covington says she was willing to start the bakery due largely to Sandhills Farm to Table Cooperative. "I broke even my first month, primarily selling directly to Sandhills members on a limited basis," Covington says. "I can't wait to be able to offer subscriptions."

Working with Low-Income Households

Sandhills' service region includes several USDA-designated "food deserts," which are defined as "a low-income census tract where a substantial number of residents have limited access to a supermarket or large grocery store." Even in many areas not designated as a food desert, a significant percentage of the population may lack access to healthy foods.

Sandhills takes its commitment to address food insecurity in the community seriously. In 2010, the co-op donated more than three tons of produce—which farmers were paid for—to needy residents of Moore County. The food donations were made through a local food bank and food pantries, a friend-to-friend program, and directly to families in need.

To ensure that community members have access to fresh healthy, locally produced foods, Sandhills has partnered with West Southern Pines Citizens for Change (WSP) to enact the "Affordable, Healthy Local Food Access Initiative." This grassroots, self-empowerment initiative in a low-income, minority neighborhood aims to increase access to healthy local food. WSP's 1,600 low-income residents currently have no access to healthy—much less, local—food. Many of them also lack transportation to get to better food sources. Both children and adults there are experiencing severe diet-related health issues.

"The West Southern Pines initiative will add the crucial piece of making healthy food more accessible in an economically depressed area while supporting local farmers, the local economy and our at-risk school children," says Kathy Byron, director of the Communities In Schools (CIS) FirstSchool Garden Program, a project partner.

Community Enrichment

A CSA's activities tend to slump in winter, when most of the farmer-members are not growing crops. Sandhills has seized this opportunity to start the "SF2T University" ("SF2T" is often used as an acronym for the co-op). The informal "teach what you know" format allows people to teach community-based classes based on experience or expertise.

While serving as a conduit for local food demand (which influences producers' planting decisions), Sandhills also serves to bring producers and consumers closer together. "The co-op has been very successful in building a positive relationship between the farmers and community," says John Blue, a Sandhills farmer-member.

Part of the resurgence of demand for local foods corresponds to an increased interest in cooking at home. However, many of Sandhills' subscribers did not know how to properly prepare the produce they were getting from the co-op. Recognizing this need, Sandhills not only began offering regular cooking classes that work with foods included in that week's produce box from the CSA, but it also began offering canning and food preservation classes to capitalize on the abundance of some foods during harvest.

Sandhills' weekly newsletter, produced by Leitschuh, features recipes that use food from the co-op's CSA produce boxes in ways that help broaden consumers' palates while encouraging the "exploration" of new foods. A recent member survey found that 73 percent of respondents were increasing their frequency of cooking meals "from scratch" at home after becoming a co-op member. Cooking, canning and recipe use are all areas Sandhills is focusing on in an attempt to teach "lost skills" to a new generation.

Looking to the Future

Sandhills has big plans for the future. After being awarded a Farmers Market Promotion Grant in November 2011 from USDA, the cooperative's goals include expanding current offerings to include a number of value-added foods like meats, breads and locally prepared soups. The grant will enable the co-op to expand its influence even farther in the community.

By purchasing new transportation equipment and electronic payment system point-of-sale devices, Sandhills will be able to offer foods to community members it has not reached to date, especially those in low-income communities where access to supermarkets is limited. The co-op intends to continue the formation of community-learning classes, as well as adding new members and subscriptions in the coming year.

Influence Spreads

Sandhills is inspiring communities beyond its own. Because of the co-op's pioneering work in the multi-stakeholder arena, its business model is being adopted by others and its influence is spreading. Sandhills' members believe that sharing knowledge and know-how in order to promote community on a larger scale is a foundation of cooperative philosophy.

"I am indebted to this group for their willingness and proactive efforts to expand their own project to become a regional initiative, and for their unselfish sharing of not only their success but their knowledge and experience," says Mark Tucker, North Carolina Cooperative Extension director for Forsyth County. "This dissemination of information has allowed for others to replicate similar efforts in additional areas of our state."

The success of Sandhills Farm to Table is attributable both to its unique, multi-stakeholder structure and to Sandhills' actions to benefit many community groups beyond its own members. Multi-stakeholder cooperatives are proving that the best way to solve community issues is often with a community solution. While still evolving, these co-ops can help offer local solutions to local issues, following the spirit of the cooperative through information sharing and propagation, mutually benefiting every level of stakeholder. These co-ops exemplify the best aspects of cooperatives by helping to identify an issue, take initiative and form a community of interest to solve it.

"Sandhills Farm to Table Cooperative's intent and actions are a reflection of a new-values system of commerce," says its founder, Fenton Wilkinson. "It is not a business, but a community endeavor with the mission of meeting local food needs with local food," he continues, saying this reflects the co-op's belief that: We're all in this together.

"When asked: 'Is SF2T for-profit?' I have to say yes, but not in the usual sense," Wilkinson adds. "With all parties to the transaction being equal owners, we all profit from our relationship to our community and with each other."

A New Prescription for the Local Food Movement

By Kendra Klein
The Nation, October 12, 2012

At dawn, at the loading dock behind the kitchen at St. Joseph Mercy Hospital of Ann Arbor, Michigan, small lift loaders and handcarts trundle boxes from food trucks to storage rooms. The perishables go straight to immense walk-in refrigerators packed with processed produce—buckets of cubed melons, bags of pre-washed lettuce, packages of onions diced by the quarter-, half-, and three-quarter inch.

That St. Joe's executive chef can peel open a three-pound bag of diced onions and dump it into the steel cauldron he calls a soup pot is an efficiency triumph of no small consequence. Preparing the soup du jour from whole ingredients—all sixty-five gallons of it—would take hours of chopping.

When you're making soup for 600, changing your grocery list can quickly get complicated. Hospitals like St. Joe's are emerging as the next frontier of the local food movement, but they are struggling to navigate the tensions between their new food goals and their reliance on standardized, low-cost products delivered dependably day in and day out. The question is, Can the local food movement scale up to meet institutional demand without losing sight of its original values?

Last fall, as part of the hospital's sustainable food efforts, St. Joe's loading dock had a new visitor. Farmer Richard Andres arrived from just down the road with 200 pounds of his green beans—local, organic, and grown by a family farmer. They were a point of pride for the hospital's good food advocates, including CEO Rob Casalou and chief clinical dietitian Lisa McDowell. Like Farm to School initiatives, which are flourishing with support from Michelle Obama's anti-obesity campaign, St. Joe's sees enthusiasm for fresh local produce as a way to encourage healthier eating while supporting local farm economies.

In the kitchen, however, Andres's superbly fresh beans meant eight hours of washing, snipping and slicing. Even St. Joe's food purchasing coordinator sidled out from behind her computer to help get the job done. "Nobody understands how long it takes to prepare certain things," says Executive Chef Ryan Kendall. "If it's from a major food distributor, it comes in ready to rock and roll."

Farmers' markets have long been the darlings of the local food movement, but the bags of goods exchanging hands at some 7,000 locations nationwide represent less than 1 percent of total US agricultural production. Meanwhile, vast quantities of food crisscross the nation in the industrial food supply stream, quietly showing up, day after day, at the loading docks of the largest food buyers.

"Farmers' markets are an important part of building local food systems," says James Barham, an agricultural economist at the US Department of Agriculture, "but more fundamental change will come from connecting small and mid-sized local farmers with institutional purchasers that are expressing ever more demand for sustainable food." Even small shifts in institutions' purchasing can have major consequences. An average hospital food budget can run upwards of $4 million, while the healthcare sector as a whole commands $12 billion worth of food and beverage purchases annually.

Buying food at that scale means relying on certain industrial-style standards. To tap the institutional market, local food advocates would do well to learn about the workings of the mysterious middle ground of wholesalers, processors and distributors that move the majority of food from farm to fork. Efficiency and convenience reign in this realm. The online ordering form for St. Joe's main distributor, Gordon Food Service, is the ultimate in one-stop-shopping (hence the common industry term "broadline" distributor). Chicken noodle soup, hamburger patties, paper plates, orange juice—just click and you shall receive. Most orders show up at St. Joe's loading dock within twenty four hours by way of a Gordon truck.

The company's guaranteed supply (which evades the vagaries of weather and season thanks to its global reach) is crucial for menu planning. It takes a team of dieticians to develop targeted diets for St. Joe's patients. Patients with kidney disease can't have black beans, and heart patients can't exceed two grams of sodium per day. Changes can take weeks of planning and paperwork.

The widget-like standardization of food sourced through the conventional supply stream also helps hospitals meet exacting federal dietary guidelines. Broadline distributors sourcing from poultry giants like Tyson and Perdue can deliver entire pallets of chicken breasts that are each within a fraction of the targeted four-ounce weight. In contrast, locally sourced chicken breasts might come in a four- to eight-ounce range, requiring staff to mete out perfect portions.

Gordon Food Service is part of the hospital's contract with Entegra, one of a handful of powerful national Group Purchasing Organizations (GPOs) that act as a gateway between hospitals and the companies they buy from. Hospitals commit to purchasing 80 to 90 percent of their food budget through their GPO. In turn, the GPO pools hundreds of hospitals' buying power to negotiate lower prices and secure rebates, often with the most recognizable names in the food business. GPOs source through broadline distributors like Gordon, SYSCO and US Foods, whose shipping and stocking requirements can be significant barriers to small and mid-sized farmers and local food companies seeking to plug in to the supply chain.

Although scores of hospitals across the country are achieving new food goals through creativity and commitment, it often requires swimming upstream against entrenched contracts, efficiency constraints, and cost restrictions. "You have to remember," Kendall says, "it's a business."

But the business of hospitals is also to protect people's health. Within the healthcare sector, there has been an explosion of interest in enacting that mission through foodservice departments. St. Joe's is one of 400 hospitals nationwide that have signed the Healthy Food in Health Care Pledge that articulates this approach. Generated by the nonprofit coalition Health Care Without Harm, the pledge states that healthy food is not just about the back-of-the-package nutrition facts but must come from a food system that is environmentally sound, economically viable and socially just.

Like the first hospitals to ban smoking on their grounds, St. Joe's is putting its moral weight behind societal change through its new food initiatives. "It's not just about the food we serve," says CEO Rob Casalou, "it's about the message, the symbolism of it." The hospital has revamped menus to incorporate seasonal produce, switched to rBGH-free dairy products and lunch meats produced without antibiotics or added hormones and reduced meat servings as a way to model healthier choices and reduce greenhouse gas emissions. The most dramatic evidence of their commitment is the twenty acres of St. Joe's sprawling property that have been plowed under to create an educational farm. The crops are incorporated into patient meals and cafeteria offerings, and patrons can pick up a bag of fresh fare from a farm stand in the hospital lobby each Monday.

Hospital-grown food is as local as it gets, but St. Joe's has more expansive plans. Along with over 100 hospitals in the state, they are aiming for twenty percent of their food purchases to be Michigan grown by 2020 in alignment with the Michigan Good Food Charter. How that food gets to the hospital may determine whether it upholds the values often assumed to be inherent to buying local—creating a diverse food system with decision-making power closer to the ground and with money in a greater share of hands. "Local" has been imagined as an inoculation against the co-optation of big agribusiness because it's about changing the *structure* of the food system rather than substituting sustainable for conventional products. But can the values implied by the farmer-to-customer handshake of a farmers' market transaction be maintained when the supply chain lengthens, when price becomes less negotiable, or when product standardization comes into play?

Advocates for so-called food hubs hope that they can; they aim to combine the social and environmental values of alternative food movements with industrial values of efficiency and convenience. According to the US Department of Agriculture's Know Your Farmer, Know Your Food initiative, a food hub is a business or organization that manages the aggregation, distribution, and marketing of source-identified food from local and regional producers to help them meet wholesale, retail and institutional demand. The middlemen and infrastructure that could have satisfied this role have largely been lost in recent decades because of corporate concentration, leaving an increasingly bifurcated system that favors small-scale direct markets and large-scale commodity markets.

While over 170 food hubs have emerged across the country, broadline distributors are also responding to increased demand for local products. With a solid hold on the healthcare market, these companies offer hospitals a way to achieve their goals with the utmost convenience—just look for the "local" symbol in the online ordering catalog. While many hospitals applaud these new options, some point to

How that food gets to the hospital may determine whether it upholds the values often assumed to be inherent to buying local—creating a diverse food system with decision-making power closer to the ground and with money in a greater share of hands.

concerns about the looseness of the term *local*. Distributors like US Foods have marked products like Doritos and Pepsi-Cola as local because they come from nearby processing plants. A fascination with food miles is the thinnest reading of the term, glossing over production methods and ownership structures for a rote counting of distance on a map. St. Joe's interest in Richard Andres's green beans is not simply that they come from twenty-nine miles away but that they are grown by an independent family farmer who practices environmentally responsible agricultural methods.

Food hubs, because of their supply chain transparency and values-based missions, can ensure that institutional purchasers are getting the sort of local food they're aiming for. That's why St. Joe's is doing anything they can to help the nascent Washtenaw Food Hub in their region get off the ground.

However, guaranteeing that the green beans come in the door ready to rock and roll remains a challenge for many food hubs, both because processing equipment and distribution infrastructure are costly, and because their leadership can be long on vision and short on business savvy. Michigan advocates would do well to talk to their neighbors across the Great Lakes. The failure of the Producers & Buyers Cooperative in Wisconsin serves as a cautionary tale. The food hub attempted to ride on enthusiasm and trust between its members but soon ran up against stark business realities including lack of sufficient capital and management expertise and the need for a broader set of buyers secured with binding contracts. Two hours south along Highway 53, the Fifth Season Cooperative is successfully serving hospital and college clients by partnering with broadline distributor Reinhart FoodService. The alliance captures the best of both worlds, ensuring transparency related to social and environmental values on one hand and providing infrastructure, efficiency and expertise on the other.

Creating a new food hub may not always be the answer. Much like family farmers, small independent distributors are disappearing from the food system. Hospitals keen on supporting their local economy should beware they don't favor new hubs at the expense of these companies. With a mixture of prodding and support, some hospitals are finding that local distributors can act as food hubs themselves by strengthening ties with family farmers and increasing the transparency in their supply chain from farm to hospital.

If efforts like St. Joe's thrive, hospitals and their fellow institutional purchasers will play a major role in moving the local food movement beyond farmers' markets to engage more farmers, acres and eaters. But the leap in scale from an individual's buying three onions at a farmers' market to a hospital's buying 300 cases of local onions is not simply one of numbers; it presents a different game entirely. "Middle-men" is still a dirty word in some local-food circles, but if the movement hopes to expand beyond boutique status, it will need to embrace it. The real innovation will be developing that missing middle ground in a way that honors a comprehensive range of social, environmental and economic values.

Pastoral Romance

By Brent Cunningham
Lapham's Quarterly, December 12, 2012

Betty Jo Patton spent her childhood on a 240-acre farm in Mason County, West Virginia, in the 1930s. Her family raised what it ate, from tomatoes to turkeys, pears to pigs. They picked, plucked, slaughtered, butchered, cured, canned, preserved, and rendered. They drew water from a well, cooked on a wood stove, and the bathroom was an outhouse.

Phoebe Patton Randolph, Betty Jo's thirty-two-year-old granddaughter, has a dream of returning to the farm, which has been in the family since 1863 and is an hour's drive from her home in the suburbs of Huntington, a city of nearly fifty thousand people along the Ohio River. Phoebe is an architect and a mother of one (soon to be two) boys, who is deeply involved in efforts to revitalize Huntington, a moribund Rust Belt community unsure of what can replace the defunct factories that drove its economy for a hundred years. She grew up with stories of life on the farm as she watched the empty farmhouse sag into disrepair.

Recently, over lunch in Betty Jo's cozy house in a quiet Huntington neighborhood, I listened to them talk about the farm, and I eventually asked Betty Jo what she thought of her granddaughter's notion of returning to the land. Betty Jo smiled, but was blunt: "Leave it. There's nothing romantic about it."

Leave it? But isn't Green Acres the place to be? Listening to the conversation about food reform that has unspooled in this country over the last decade, it's hard to avoid the idea that in terms of food production and consumption, we once had it right—before industrialization and then globalization sullied our Eden. Nostalgia glistens on that conversation like dew on an heirloom tomato: the belief that in a not-so-distant past, families routinely sat down to happy meals whipped up from scratch by mom or grandma. That in the 1950s, housewives had to be tricked by Madison Avenue marketers into abandoning beloved family recipes in favor of new Betty Crocker cake mixes. That the family farm was at the center of an ennobling way of life.

Evidence of the nostalgia abounds. There is an endless series of books by urban food revolutionaries who flee the professional world for the simple pleasures of rural life, if only for a year or so: *Growing A Farmer: How I Learned to Live Off the Land; Coop: A Family, a Farm, and the Pursuit of One Good Egg; The Bucolic Plague: How Two Manhattanites Became Gentlemen Farmers: An Unconventional Memoir.* A new crop sprouts each year. There's Michael Pollan's admonition, in his bestselling book

Food Rules, to not "eat anything your great-grandmother wouldn't recognize as food." And then there are countless articles about the young and educated putting off grad school to become organic farmers. A March 5 [2012], piece in the *New York Times* is typical. Under the headline, "In New Food Culture, a Young Generation of Farmers Emerges," it delivers a predictable blend: twenty-somethings who quit engineering jobs to farm in Corvallis, Oregon—microbrews, Subaru, multiple piercings, indie rock, yoga. This back-to-the-landism is of a piece with the nineteenth-century, do-it-yourself fever that has swept certain neighborhoods of Brooklyn, complete with handlebar mustaches, jodhpur boots, classic cocktails, soda shops, and restaurants with wagon wheels on the walls.

The surest sign that this nostalgia has reached a critical mass, though, is that food companies have begun to board the retro bus. PepsiCo now has throwback cans for Pepsi (the red-white-and-blue one Cindy Crawford famously guzzled in the 1990s) and Mountain Dew (featuring a cartoon hillbilly from the 1960s) in which they've replaced "bad" high-fructose corn syrup with "good" cane sugar. Frito-Lay is resurrecting a Doritos chip from the 1980s (taco-flavored, a sombrero on the package). When nostalgia is co-opted by corporate America and sold back to us, as it invariably is, the backlash can't be far behind. Consider this the opening salvo.

It's unlikely that most serious food reformers think America can or should dismantle our industrial food system and return to an agrarian way of life. But the idea that "Food used to be better" so pervades the rhetoric about what ails our modern food system that it is hard not to conclude that rolling back the clock would provide at least some of the answers. The trouble is, it wouldn't. And even if it would, the prospect of a return to Green Acres just isn't very appealing to a lot of people who know what life there is really like.

I came to Huntington last November with my wife, the food writer Jane Black, to research a book about the effort to build a healthier food culture there. This is where celebrity chef Jamie Oliver last year debuted his reality television show, *Jamie Oliver's Food Revolution*, after the Huntington metro area was labeled the nation's most unhealthy community by a 2008 Centers for Disease Control study. It is a place that has suffered the familiar litany of postindustrial woes: a decimated manufacturing base, a shrinking population, a drug problem. It is also precisely the kind of place where the food-reform movement must take hold if it is to deliver on its promise of large-scale and enduring change.

How would the messages and assumptions that have powered the movement in the elite enclaves where it took root over the last decade—like Brooklyn, where we live, Berkeley, Washington, DC, etc.—play in communities like Huntington? Places where most people don't consider Applebee's and Wal-Mart to be the enemy. Where the familiar and the consistent are valued over the new and the exotic, especially when it comes to what's for dinner. Where a significant portion of the population lives in poverty or perilously close to it.

Jane and I suspected that the environmental, social justice, it-just-tastes-better case for eating seasonally and sustainably that our foodie friends consider self-evident would be met with skepticism—or shrugs—by people who have more pressing concerns than the plight of tomato pickers in Florida or the fact that cows are meant to eat grass, not corn. Nostalgia, though, did not immediately register with us as part of the movement's message problem. Perhaps because we live in the same world as the people who write those My-Year-Doing-X books, foodie nostalgia only seemed an innocuous, if annoying, bit of yuppie indulgence.

But in Huntington we kept meeting people like Betty Jo. Alma Keeney, for instance, who also grew up on a farm, is baffled by her daughter-in-law Shelly's decision to launch a goat-cheese business. Shelly runs the fledgling Yellow Goat Farm with her friend, Dominique Wong, and together they tend their Nubian and Alpine dairy goats on a small plot in Proctorville, Ohio, just across the river from Huntington. The eighty-seven-year-old Alma, Shelley told us, prefers individually wrapped American slices of cheese, not "farm food," which brings back memories of hard times. Jane and I started thinking about the uncritical, even simplistic way that our agricultural past—and our kitchen-table past—are referenced in American society generally, and in the conversation about food reform specifically.

The farmer is among the most enduring figures in the American pantheon. "Those who labor in the earth are the chosen people of God," wrote Thomas Jefferson in *Notes on the State of Virginia*, his classic work on the promise of the American experiment. The agrarian ideal—a belief that the family farm is the soul of the nation, a pure embodiment of our democracy—is a recurring theme in the national narrative. In 1782, J. Hector St. John de Crèvecoeur, in his *Letters from an American Farmer*, celebrated the notion of independence and self-sufficiency that is central to the story: "Where is that station which can confer a more substantial system of felicity than that of an American farmer, possessing freedom of action, freedom of thoughts, ruled by a mode of government which requires but little from us?"

The exalted status of the farmer has influenced political strategy and policy decisions throughout our history: in New Deal legislation that sought to place the family farm, which struggled mightily during the Depression, on par with other industries primarily through price supports; in an amendment to the Selective Service Act of 1940, which granted deferments to young men who were "necessary to and regularly engaged in an agricultural occupation"; in the creation of the US food-assistance program in 1954, which pitted the stalwart American farmer against the menace of Soviet collectivized agriculture. And it surely informs the nostalgia that shrouds today's food-reform movement. One can essentially trace a through line from Thomas Jefferson's romantic image of the farmer to a recent defense of rural America in the *Washington Post* by Tom Vilsack, the US Secretary of Agriculture: "There's a value system there. Service is important for rural folks. Country is important, patriotism is important."

Today most of us are so removed from the agricultural life, and so ignorant about its realities, that this wholesome and nostalgic lens is the only one we know. Research by the FrameWorks Institute, a think tank employed by nonprofits to strategically reframe public conversation about social issues, found that for Americans, "Rural Utopia" is the dominant image of life beyond the cities and suburbs: a countryside "filled with poor but noble, tough and hard-working people living healthier and fundamentally better lives than the rest of us." This despite the fact that the reality in rural America today is one of decline: unemployment, rising divorce rates, a scramble to get out. According to the Bureau of Labor Statistics, farming is the nation's fourth-most-dangerous job.

Still, nostalgia has been a useful tool for the food-reform movement. It has provided a blueprint for how to think about and act on the daunting environmental, moral, and health problems associated with our industrial food-system for people who have the resources—financial, social, and educational—that allow them to participate in the movement if they so choose, and that predispose them to be sympathetic to the cause in the first place. Whether they started raising chickens in their backyards or simply became better informed about how their food is produced, this idea that we've lost our way has helped make food *important*, and in ways that go beyond simple sustenance.

Most of these food revolutionaries won't become actual farmers, and most of those who do—including those microbrew-swilling kids in Corvallis—won't make a career of it. But the movement has, I suspect, permanently changed their attitudes toward food, and this alone is already forcing modest systemic change. Since 1994 the number of farmers' markets in the US has risen from 1,700 to more than 6,000. And between 2000 and 2009, organic-food sales grew from $6 billion to nearly $25 billion—still less than 4 percent of total US food sales, but it's a start. Twenty years from now, most of these young "farmers" will have rejoined the professional ranks. Like their middle-class forefathers who tuned in, turned on, and dropped out in the 1960s, the appeal of financial security and a climate-controlled office will, in most cases, win out. That said, they probably won't be regulars at McDonald's, and they'll instill these values in their own kids.

Nevertheless, a "bourgeois nostalgia" pervades the food-reform movement, as Amy Trubek, an anthropologist at the University of Vermont who studies food and culture, points out. This is a perception of our food history that is the luxury of people who have little or no experience with farming, or more generally with manual labor. A perception that appeals to those who have never had to cook from scratch, let alone milk cows, kill chickens, and bake bread, just to get food on the table every day. A perception of people for whom it makes perfect sense to redefine their *leisure* time to include things like making *guanciale* or Meyer-lemon marmalade. As such, it may not resonate with great swaths of the public who don't fit this demographic profile, and it is a perception that ignores some crucial truths about our food history.

The reality of America's food past is far more complicated, and troubling, than is suggested by the romantic image at the heart of our foodie nostalgia. In *Revolution at the Table* and its sequel, *Paradox of Plenty*, the historian Harvey Levenstein provides a more sober, and ultimately more useful, accounting of that past. Levenstein shows how, starting in the late nineteenth century and continuing through the twentieth, food preparation steadily migrated outside the home. The reason is simple: if you have no choice but to plan and prepare multiple meals every day, cooking not only isn't cool, it's tedious and damned hard work.

Jane and I experienced this firsthand in West Virginia. We both are skilled and enthusiastic cooks, and as part of the reporting for the book, we wanted to see how well, and local, we could eat, and for how much money, preparing three meals a day. But we also understood that we were the kind of people for whom cooking is a hobby. Outside our door in Brooklyn, there is a cornucopia of options for the nights when we are busy or not in the mood to cook. In Huntington, though, most of those options are missing. Three months in we began

> *Most of these food revolutionaries won't become actual farmers, and most of those who do—including those microbrew-swilling kids in Corvallis—won't make a career of it. But the movement has, I suspect, permanently changed their attitudes toward food, and this alone is already forcing modest systemic change.*

to notice, with dismay, that as soon as one meal was finished, we had to start thinking about the next. Four months in, the joy of cooking was replaced by a growing irritation, a longing to amble down the block for *banh mi* or a bowl of ramen. By mid-March, Jane wrote in her journal, "Officially sick of cooking."

Between 1880 and 1930, the fruits of industrialization—canning, bottling, the growth of food manufacturers and restaurants—enabled the outsourcing of food preparation that Levenstein describes. Improved transportation—first the railroad and then the automobile—and food-preservation processes—refrigerated rail cars, for instance—brought an end to seasonal and regional restrictions on what we ate. Soon, people in Kentucky had the same food choices as those in New York or California.

The standardization of the American diet, so bemoaned by people like me, is what many—maybe even most—people want at mealtime. It is reassuring to have what everyone else has. The desire to have the same Big Mac in Syracuse as in San Diego is a big part of why fast-food outlets became America's default dining-out option, and why suggesting that as a nation we return to a more seasonal and regional way of eating will be a tough sell.

The family farm itself was not immune to these developments. By the 1920s and '30s, the gap between city and farm diets had begun to collapse, as processed foods became high-status items in rural areas. Poor Appalachian farmers began to prefer canned hams to country hams; farm women who could afford store-bought canned vegetables and other processed food embraced this new convenience without a second thought that they were abandoning a purer, nobler way of life.

There's a reason that less than two percent of people in this country are engaged in farming today, and it isn't simply that they've been driven off the land by Cargill and ADM. Just like Betty Jo Patton, many of them wanted things to be easier. This revolution at the table—the one that produced the food culture that today's revolutionaries are trying to counter—was considered a tremendous leap forward. It was modern. It gave people time for things other than keeping the family fed.

There is an even more fundamental concern about our nostalgia: America's food system has always depended on the exploitation of someone, whether it was indentured servants, slaves, tenant farmers, braceros and other guest workers, or, now, immigrants. In his ode to the American farmer, Crèvecoeur made it clear that he had a little help on his farm. "My Negroes are tolerably faithful and healthy," he wrote. This is an aspect of our agricultural heritage that rarely gets mentioned in the mainstream conversation about food-system reform, and it raises thorny questions about who actually grows, harvests, processes, and prepares the food in a capitalist society. We have no history of a food system that does not depend on oppression of some sort, and it seems unlikely that we will be able to create a future system that avoids this fate. The leaders of the food revolution have, in recent years, begun to speak out on the matter of farm-worker rights. But few acknowledge—at least in the public debate—that if a central goal of the movement is a more equitable food system, then the notion that we once had it right is deeply problematic.

Exploitation is as true in the kitchen as in the field. Women have always borne the burden of transforming the raw to the cooked in the American home. Interestingly, it was a confluence of these two inconvenient truths about our food past—its reliance on women and exploited labor—that helped set the stage for our national embrace of fast food.

During the Gilded Age following the end of the Civil War, and continuing into the early twentieth century, America's rapidly expanding ranks of wealthy industrialists used extravagant dinner parties, featuring French haute cuisine, as a way to showcase their status. Hosts and hostesses sought to outdo one another: chefs were imported from France; eight courses were standard, as were menu cards, elaborate centerpieces, and a labor-intensive style of service known as *À la Russe*, which involved a butler carving and arranging the food on plates at a sideboard, which were then delivered to guests by servants. (The traditional style had been to fill the table with platters and bowls and let the guests serve themselves.)

The fetish for French cuisine, and all the attendant showmanship, quickly trickled down, and the nation's middle-class, which also was expanding, sought pecuniary emulation of this conspicuous consumption. Competitive dinner parties became a fixture of middle-class social life. And it wasn't just at dinner; there were also multicourse luncheons and high teas to pull together. The problem, though, was that middle-class households couldn't afford the number and quality of servants necessary for this kind of entertaining. This "servant problem," as Levenstein calls it, became something of an obsession for American housewives, who saw it as the main obstacle to fulfilling society's expectations of them.

Their plight led to various time-saving experiments, including cooperative kitchens—in which meals for multiple families were prepared for pickup in a central location—and the first home-meal delivery services. The former failed because they were regarded as a violation of the "ideal of American family life," a critique that had more than a whiff of antisocialist sentiment. The latter, it turns out, was simply an idea ahead of its time. These delivery services conformed to what was then considered the standard for a "proper meal": three courses and a menu that changed daily. As such, they were too expensive to be sustainable. The inability to solve the middle-class servant problem led, eventually, to a new conception in American society of what constituted a proper meal: simpler, cheaper, and of course, faster. We know how that story turned out.

By misrepresenting—or misunderstanding—our food history, we make a realistic conversation about what to change and how to change it more difficult than it already is. America will not revert to a nation of family farms. Convenience will always be important. Seasonal and regional limitations on what we eat can only go so far. If Americans want to cook like their grandmothers, fine, but the fact is our grandmothers, by and large, made only a handful of meals, they made them over and over again, and they used plenty of shortcuts, courtesy of the industrial age. My grandmother's cornbread, which still remains the gold standard for cornbread in my family twenty years after her death, began with a Martha White mix.

Nostalgia is part of a larger message problem that food revolutionaries face as they attempt to broaden the appeal of their cause. For example, when Wal-Mart announced earlier this year that it would, over the next five years, reduce the amount of sodium by 25 percent and added sugars by 10 percent in its house brands, and pressure other food manufacturers whose products it carries to follow suit, the overwhelming response from within the food-reform community was, "That's not good enough."

In Huntington, and in communities across the country, Wal-Mart is where a lot of people get their food. They like the way the food there tastes. If that food has less sugar and salt—incrementally less so that they will still like the way it tastes—that is an important, and realistic, step toward a healthier food culture. Wal-Mart has many bad policies, but it's shortsighted to write off every initiative just because it comes from Wal-Mart. New ideas about food need to conform to people's social and economic aspirations, and those aspirations are going to be different in 2011 than they were in 1900, and they will be different, too, in Huntington, West Virginia, than in Brooklyn, New York. Achieving fundamental and lasting change in our food system will require the efforts of those yuppie farmers in Oregon who can afford to step outside the mainstream food culture and, as they say, vote with their forks. It will also require the more hard-won, incremental reforms at the big food processors and sellers, like Wal-Mart, that feed the great mass of people who either can't or won't vote with their forks.

Somewhere in the middle of these two efforts, hopefully, we can eventually arrive at a food system that makes sense for the twenty-first century. But the process of figuring out what that will look like needs to begin with a full and honest accounting of where we've been, and what's possible given where we are.

The Local-Global Food Connection

By Amy Mayer
Harvest Public Media, November 21, 2012

The United States is the world's leading corn producer and exporter. But sending corn and other food abroad is just part of the equation when it comes to figuring out how we'll feed the global population, projected to reach nine billion by 2050.

Corn from the United States is used as livestock feed to support the increasing demand for meat in China, India and other countries with growing middle classes. The US also has a history of food aid to poor nations. But World Food Prize Laureate and former international aid worker Catherine Bertini applauded bi-partisan efforts to re-focus American food policy on farming when she spoke recently at the University of Nebraska, Lincoln.

"The administration, now for the first time in a long time, decided yes, it's a good idea to put more effort into agriculture development," she said.

That means helping farmers succeed, not just distributing food to the hungry. Governments, non-profits and private businesses all have a place in the effort. Seed companies, for example, are developing technologies specific to regions all over the globe.

"Generally the most productive genetics are the ones that are developed within the area where the plant breeding has been done," said Mike Vander Logt, the chief operating officer of WinField, a Land-o-Lakes subsidiary. He said advances in seed technology can have global impact, but the biggest players know to innovate locally—wherever that is. If your target market is China, set up a lab there. Eventually, the technology will help Chinese farmers increase yield.

Bertini said the US government's Feed the Future program—a commitment to help ensure the world has enough to eat—emphasizes local food production. In places where people are hungry, the program supports small farming efforts because those have a ripple effect.

"The World Bank says that agricultural productivity is two to four times more effective than any other productivity in alleviating poverty," she said.

Today, the world's growing population relies on a combination of international trade, food aid from the rich countries to the poor as needed, and increased local production, even here in the United States.

"We need to produce as much to feed the world as we can, but also people like to eat locally grown foods, too, so there's a case for both sides of agriculture," said Greg Rinehart, a farmer in Boone County, Iowa.

> *Today, the world's growing population relies on a combination of international trade, food aid from the rich countries to the poor as needed, and increased local production, even here in the United States.*

That's reflected on his farm. He and his family grow fruit and vegetables on 100 acres and sell at farmers' markets. But on 700 acres, they grow traditional corn and soybeans.

"We don't actually know exactly where it's going," Rinehart said of the row crops, "But we know it's not being wasted, it's being used somewhere in the food chain, whether in the United States or being exported to many countries in the world."

Given the rich soil and well-developed infrastructure here, Midwestern farmers are likely to continue playing an important role on the world food scene. But Iowa State University economist Bruce Babcock said the goal of domestic production around the world isn't as far-off as many people seem to think.

"The overwhelming supply of calories and food that is consumed in most countries comes from the country that is the consuming country," he said.

So the persistent challenge is distribution. And even the rich countries haven't yet figured out how to get food to everyone who needs it.

Top Ten Barriers to Local Food Access for Low-Income Individuals

localFoodconnection.org

Local Food Connection is a non-profit organization that purchases produce, meat and other products from small family farmers and donates this food to low-income families. As part of our main program, we enroll families in Community Supported Agriculture (CSA) groups, through which they receive a box of fresh, organic produce every week for approximately twenty weeks. Running concurrently with the CSA program, we offer our clients opportunities to learn about nutrition and healthy meal preparation. They earn points for each educational activity completed and can use these points to purchase kitchen equipment. We have begun our tenth year of work in the Iowa City, Iowa, region. We also serve Fairfield, Des Moines and Cedar Rapids, Iowa.

The "Top Ten Barriers" list was compiled by Local Foods Connection staff and volunteers, as well as social service agency personnel who serve the same populations we do. LFC serves single mothers, people with exceptional medical needs, immigrants, refugees and racial minorities in cities ranging in size from 9,000 to 200,000 people. We realize that people living in bigger cities or smaller towns, in Iowa or elsewhere in the country, might experience additional obstacles unique to their environment and consequently might not be well-represented on this list. Furthermore, we understand that some of the challenges on this list are confronted not only by low-income families, but by people of all income levels wishing to purchase more local foods and to add fresh food to their diet.

Local Foods Connection is excited to start a conversation about the "Top Ten Barriers to Local Food Access for Low-Income Individuals" with other communities around the country. We want to share our thoughts, to expand upon the list and to work together towards new solutions to these problems.

> *Parents skip meals to make sure there is enough food for their children. For parents, it is more important to ensure that their children have enough food and "are full" than it is to provide children with a healthy diet.*

1. Financial Restrictions

We believe that cost is the greatest obstacle low-income individuals face in accessing fresh, and especially organic and locally-produced, food.

- The cost of vegetables and fruit rose 120 percent between 1985 and 2000, while the price of junk like sodas and sweets went up less than 50 percent on average. (source 3)

- Fresh food often doesn't provide as many calories per dollar as processed food.

- Fresh food doesn't stay fresh as long as processed food.

- Fresh food requires more labor to make into appealing, satisfying meals than processed food.

- Eating a variety of colorful fresh fruits and vegetables, as recommended by the USDA, is expensive. Even though some fruits and vegetables can be bought at Farmers Markets for a good price, purchasing products of different nutritional contents on a regular basis throughout the year is costly.

- Eating out-of-season fresh fruits and vegetables is even more expensive.

We believe that healthy food is often one of the first things cut from a family's budget when they are experiencing financial difficulties. Faced with limited resources,

- One out of six Americans turns to government food assistance programs.

- People skip meals.

- People substitute less expensive, less nutritious alternatives.

- People go to soup kitchens or food pantries.

- Parents skip meals to make sure there is enough food for their children. For parents, it is more important to ensure that their children have enough food and "are full" than it is to provide children with a healthy diet.

- People cannot afford a balanced meal.

- People choose to pay bills (e.g., rent, utilities, and prescription drugs) instead of buying food. (source 2)

We believe that individuals depending upon supplemental food assistance from the government can be restricted in the types of food they are allowed to purchase.

- The government places restrictions on where food assistance coupons can be used. For example, WIC coupons cannot be used at the New Pioneer Co-op, the natural food stores in the Iowa City/Coralville area.

- Organic foods are not always eligible for purchase with WIC coupons. Individual states make the decision. (source 9)

2. Preparation and Storage of Food

We believe that low-income families lack, and cannot afford, much of the equipment and companion ingredients needed to prepare fresh food into a variety of interesting, fulfilling meals throughout the year.

Individuals might lack such basic ingredients as: cooking oil, garlic/onion, butter, milk, flour, spices, etc. Purchasing basic kitchen equipment can be an obstacle as well, such as blenders and adequate pots/pans for recipes that aren't "one-pot" meals. Major appliances might be absent from their lives or might be inadequate for storage and food preparation. Lots of low-income folks live doubled up (with friends or family members) or in rooming houses where they may be lucky to have one shelf in the fridge for cold storage. Appliances can be unreliable—a cooktop with one working burner, for instance.

3. Distribution of Food

We believe that individuals and families have trouble knowing where to buy fresh local food, in addition to having difficulties getting to these locations. The challenges individuals face can be specific to the area in which they live, be it an urban, suburban or rural environment. Low-income individuals might live in areas with restricted access to affordable, healthy/fresh foods.

- Cars
  - One-stop grocery shopping is easier for low-income individuals because it saves time and gas money.
  - Going to the farmer's market or a grocery store featuring local foods would require making an additional trip.
- Public transportation
  - It is not always adequate or easy to use.
  - Carrying groceries on a bus or subway is difficult, especially with children.
  - It is often inadequate in rural areas.
- Big cities often have food deserts, where only convenience stores are available for food shopping in low-income areas.
- Food delivery services can be expensive, if available at all.

4. Lack of Knowledge and Education—Low-Income Individuals

We believe that low-income individuals might lack knowledge on how to prepare fresh food for a variety of reasons, including lack of quality education, inexperience of family members, and popular cultural influences. Individuals often lack:

- An understanding of the meanings and benefits of fresh, organic, and local food.
- Awareness of the health benefits of eating fresh food.

- Confidence in preparing fresh food.
- Skills in preparing fresh food in fast, easy ways.
- Knowledge of ways to make produce attractive to children.

5. Cultural Values and Lifestyles

We believe that low-income individuals might lack experience eating meals highlighting fresh food.

- Eating habits developed during childhood, memories from holidays and other celebratory occasions, and positive, community-centered experiences might have centered on comfort foods made with lard, fat, sugar, as well as processed foods.
- An individual's life might be lacking in pleasurable and affirmative food-related experiences. Children attending crowded public schools, for example, are forced to eat lunch hurriedly, in shifts as short as 20 minutes, so that maximum use can be made of cafeteria space.
- Individuals living in urban and suburban settings might be completely disconnected from the agricultural origins of the food they eat. Never having seen a vegetable, a grain, or a fruit growing on a plant, they might be unaware of the simple form food has in its original state, and the changes it undergoes during processing.
- We believe that low-income families are accustomed to eating fast food because a great deal of fast food advertising targets low-income families and these restaurants are clustered in low-income communities.
- Families seeking emergency food assistance often receive boxed, canned, and processed food, which has a longer shelf life and can be more easily transported than fresh food. Families who depend on food pantries to survive long-term financial crises can become accustomed to convenience foods.

6. Disabilities

We believe that individuals with disabilities who take care of themselves, and those who depend upon others to care for them, face even more obstacles to local food access than those faced by the low-income population in general. There is a very high correlation between having a disability and having a low income.

- To remain eligible to receive services through Medicaid, individuals are forced to remain at a very low-income level, hindering their ability to purchase fresh food. (source 5)
- Undiagnosed individuals with mental retardation usually don't know how to use the stove or even the oven. They often rely on microwave and take-out.
- Diagnosed individuals with mental retardation might receive funding for services and have access to Support Community Living (SCL). SCL is a

one-on-one service that teaches, assists and creates skills for individuals with disabilities. The goal of SCL is to work toward specific goals and increase client's independent living skills and community development. SCL clients can have goals that help them learn about nutrition and how to cook and shop wisely.

- However, SCL workers might not be educated in the areas of fresh food, nutrition and cooking.

- Recipes need to be easy and only a few steps long.

- Similar challenges are faced by individuals with physical and mental illness and brain injury. These individuals might be eligible for Consumer Directed Attendant Care (CDAC). CDAC workers can grocery shop and prepare meals for clients.

- However, CDAC workers might not be educated in nutrition and cooking.

7. Preparation and Storage of Food—Social Service Agencies

We believe that the variety of social service agencies which are in a position to assist their low-income clients increase their consumption of local and fresh foods often lack the time, funding, experience and education to do so. Examples of the types of agencies and organizations that we believe could help their clients learn more about local and fresh food include: food pantries, neighborhood centers, Lion's Clubs, churches, homeless and domestic violence shelters, medical clinics, family resource centers, and environmental action groups.

- Few staff members at social service agencies have the extra time to add the component of local foods to their work.

- These agencies might not have adequate space, kitchen equipment and utensils with which to prepare fresh food.

- These agencies might lack the major appliances for the storage, refrigeration and freezing of fresh food.

- These agencies might lack the extra volunteers to process and store fresh ingredients safely.

8. Fulfillment of Government Nutrition Standards—Agencies and Institutions

We believe that state and federal restrictions on food purchasing can negatively affect the decision to acquire local foods by agencies and institutions that serve food to their clients, such as senior centers and school districts. If government money is used to purchase foods at an institution, it might be required to meet government nutrition standards. Reconfiguring a menu to incorporate local foods and continue to meet these standards can be a burden.

9. Lack of Education—Social Service Agencies

We believe that the knowledge and understanding of local and fresh foods can be limited at all levels with a social service agency's workforce.

- Workers at these agencies might lack the same knowledge of nutrition and lack fresh food preparation skills as the clients do.

- Agency administration might not have considered the potential positive relationship between improving their clients' health through their diet, and improving other aspects of their clients' lives. In order for agency staff to integrate nutrition and food into their interactions with clients, there must be interest in and commitment from the agencies' supervisors or board of directors.

10. Lack of Education—General Population

We believe that if the general public understood the obstacles to local food that low-income families face they would support programs and organizations that increase this population's access to good, fresh food. We believe that the general public lacks knowledge of:

- The extent of poverty in Iowa.

- The causes of poverty.

- How poverty affects food shopping habits.

Feedback

Local Foods Connection is excited about starting a conversation about this list! Please join the discussion at Sustainable Table's forum and share your experiences with everyone!

- Would you change the order of any item on the list? (1 = greatest obstacle; 10 = least obstacle)

- Would you add any item to this list?

- Can you share an experience you have had with any of these obstacles?

- Do you disagree with anything we have said?

- What solutions do you have to offer?

With special thanks to: Tiffany Boyle, the Lead Family Services Coordinator for the ARC of Southeast Iowa, which assists developmentally disabled individuals in our community to realize their full potential in how they live, learn, work and play.

Katherine Nydam-Olivier, a social worker who works primarily with people who are homeless in Iowa City.

This document was prepared as a community service by volunteers. The initiative for the creation of this document came from the Iowa Valley Resource Conservation and Development Office's I Food Initiative, a project to help strengthen the local food network in Southeast Iowa.

Our first version of the "Top Ten" list was presented at a workshop at the Iowa Network for Community Agriculture.

Bibliography

1. *2007 Hunger in Iowa Report* by Susan Roberts and Erin Feld (and the 2003 report)
2. The Hartford Food System: A Guide to Developing Community Food Programs, Replication Manual put out by World Hunger Year
3. *Don't Eat This Book: Fast Food and the Supersizing of America* by Morgan Spurlock
4. *Iowans Fit for Life, Active and Eating Smart: Nutrition and Physical Activity* by the Iowa Department of Public Health,1, Nutrition and Physical Activity.
5. Eligibility requirements for individuals with disabilities: www.socialsecurity.gov and http://www.cms.hhs.gov/home/medicaid.asp
6. The ARC of East Central Iowa
7. Living Well Iowa (run in this area by Keith Ruff through the Evert Conner Center)
8. *Retail and Consumer Aspects of the Organic Milk Market* by Carolyn Dimitri and Kathryn M. Venezia for the US Dept. of Agriculture, May 2007
9. Frequently asked questions of the WIC program
10. *Are Lower Income Households Willing and Able to Budget for Fruits and Vegetables?* by Hayden Stewart and Noel Blisard for the USDA: Economic Research Service, January 2008
11. *Dynamics of Poverty and Food Sufficiency* by David Ribar and Karen Hamrick for the USDA: Economic Research Service, September 2003
12. *Household Food Security in the United States, 2006* by Mark Nord, Margaret Andrews and Steven Carlson for the USDA: Economic Research Service, November 2007

2
Media and How-To Cooking

Bobby Flay at the Whole Foods Grand Tasting Village at the 2012 South Beach Wine and Food Festival on February 26, 2012, in Miami Beach, Florida.

Celebrity Chefs and Foodie Culture

Good cooking can be a powerful phenomenon because of both the sensual pleasures of eating an excellent meal and the social influence of food within society. For these and many other reasons, a great chef holds an honored place in many societies. Any food writer or historian who attempts to compile a list of history's great chefs can do little more than add a footnote to a centuries-old debate. Judging cooking, like judging any other subjective art form, is a matter of personal taste, and the criteria that make a chef "great" as opposed to just "good" are open to interpretation.

A great chef may be defined, for instance, by his or her skill in the craft of cooking, including the chef's ability to create dishes that are visibly tantalizing and aesthetically organized to enhance the sensory experience of the meal, even before the first bite. Other chefs may be lauded for their innovation and imagination, reaching beyond the capabilities of their peers to imagine new directions of flavor and technique. In addition, the importance of a chef's work can be determined by their influence, in terms of both how their work influences the cuisine of peers and their lasting inspiration to subsequent generations of eaters and cooks. It is in the category of influence that we see the emergence of "celebrity chefs," those whose combinations of skills have gained them a level of fame beyond the kitchen or the insular world of fine cuisine.

The concept of the celebrity chef is not new, as several prominent European chefs achieved international fame in the 1700s, before even the printed news could carry their name across national boundaries. These early celebrities were popular enough that word of mouth was sufficient to create fame. The "television chef" emerged as a subset of the celebrity chef phenomenon in the 1960s, with innovators such as Julia Child, whose televised cooking show made her a household name around the world. While some of the popular television chefs may have been considered great chefs even before the television era, many have achieved fame based on their personalities and ability to teach, rather than just on the innovative quality of their cuisine. In this way, the rise of the television celebrity has substantively altered the celebrity-chef phenomenon to the point that modern celebrity chefs are far less likely to have a lasting impact on global cuisine.

In the same way that television cooking shows created a new category of celebrity chef, the invention of reality shows and reality-based cooking series led to an unprecedented proliferation of chefs who have achieved national or international fame as television stars. Cable and television networks now compete to promote the next "hot" celebrity chef in an effort to garner high ratings. Several networks have even produced series, such as *Iron Chef* and *Top Chef*, in which up-and-coming chefs compete in cooking competitions. The winners of these competitions will not be rewarded with peer recognition as a leading chef but will gain a certain level of popular recognition—and this element, far more than critical or peer acknowledgement, can lead to fortune.

The Rise of the Celebrity Chef

Before the era of television, a chef could only achieve fame on the strength of his or her cuisine, though personality and skill with teaching have always been important secondary characteristics for those seeking to make a name for themselves in the profession. Many of the earliest chefs to achieve international recognition were from France, and French cuisine has had an enormous international impact, especially in countries where European colonization played a role in the foundation of modern populations.

Many food writers and historians have pointed to Marie Antoine Carême as one of the first true celebrity chefs. Carême is credited with, among other things, the invention of the most widely recognized chef's hat, in addition to being the first major proponent of the *grande* style of French cooking. Carême rose to fame in the first decades of the 1800s and often plied his trade to cook extravagant meals for French and other European royalty. Also from France was Auguste Escoffier, whose French cuisine rose to international prominence through the Hotel Savoy in London. Escoffier's take on traditional French cooking set a standard that would transcend the more transitory cooking fads that came and went in the twentieth century, and it remains foundational to the cuisine, inspiring hundreds of chefs who have followed his example.

The phenomenon of the celebrity chef changed significantly with the debut of the first cooking shows on television. The individuals chosen to star in these shows were not recognized as "master chefs" in the same way as Escoffier or the greats of the past, but were chosen because they had personality traits that made them excellent teachers and ambassadors for the art of cooking. Fanny Cradock, whose cooking program ran from the 1950s to the 1970s in the United Kingdom, and Child, whose cooking program debuted in 1963 on American television, were the first in what would become a lasting facet of food culture, the "how-to" cooking program.

As Child and Cradock became household names, they helped to introduce a higher caliber of cuisine to home cooks around the world, concentrating on presenting basic dishes and techniques in a way that was accessible to a broad audience. Child and Cradock were joined by chefs such as Graham Kerr of *The Galloping Gourmet* and American chef James Beard, whose television programs and related books were highly influential to a generation of aspiring cooks. The television cooking programs not only helped to popularize home cooking but also increased demand and interest in the work of professional chefs, whose training and expertise represented a level of cuisine that stood apart from the basic yet satisfying dishes presented in television programs or cookbooks such as *The Joy of Cooking* (1931).

One of the first restaurant chefs to achieve major celebrity without hosting a television cooking show was Paul Prudhomme, chef at K-Paul's Louisiana Kitchen in New Orleans. Prudhomme became a major international symbol on the strength of American cuisine, and Prudhomme is largely credited with popularizing Cajun cuisine worldwide. Other American chefs who made a major splash include Alice Waters, whose Berkeley, California, Chez Panisse restaurant opened in 1971. By the 1980s, as chefs who trained in Waters's style began making a name for themselves around the United States, Waters became a major figure in the industry.

Other notable chefs who followed in the United States include Wolfgang Puck, whose Hollywood restaurant Spago became world renowned. Puck, who later became a television and cookbook celebrity as well, introduced global audiences to what has since been dubbed "California cuisine," a distinctly American blend of recipes, but presented in a manner that paid homage to the formal French and British chefs. Charlie Trotter, who opened his restaurant in 1987 in Chicago, is another American chef who developed a significant amount of fame, largely built on the fame of his eponymous restaurant.

Another chef who had a major impact on the evolution of the celebrity-chef phenomenon was Paul Bocuse, a French chef based in Lyon who has been credited with inspiring a major evolution in traditional French cuisine. Bocuse was a major originator of "nouvelle cuisine" but was also one of the first in a new generation of media-savvy chefs who knew how to use the press to build their own reputation. Puck, whose Hollywood restaurant catapulted him into the spotlight, was, like Bocuse, a shrewd manipulator of the media, transforming his growing fame as a chef into a personal brand, packaged to maximize mass-media appeal.

Cooking for the Television

The celebrity chefs of the 1980s paved the way for a new generation of celebrity chefs that rose to prominence in the 1990s. The cable channel Food Network aired its first programs in 1993, and it was the first television network entirely dedicated to the culinary world. The network's initial lineup featured up-and-coming celebrity chef Emeril Lagasse and renowned French chef Jacques Pépin.

Lagasse rose to prominence in the cooking world by working as the executive chef of Commander's Palace, a famous New Orleans restaurant that had formerly been run by Prudhomme. Lagasse was seen by many in the cooking world as the successor to Prudhomme's legacy, and his stint at Commander's Palace began with the restaurant being acknowledged as one of the best in the country in the early 1990s. While his cooking skill was widely acknowledged, Lagasse's rise to superstardom as a television celebrity was based largely on the chef's personality and ability to create a television persona that was memorable to audiences.

One of Lagasse's signature techniques used on his cooking shows is to "kick it up a notch," with salt or spices often added to the dish, with Lagasse shouting "Bam!," which became his signature expression and is now a branded trademark of his product-related culinary empire. Lagasse also marketed a line of spices, under the name "Emeril's Essences," that viewers could use to "kick things up a notch," and the creation of his signature techniques and catchphrases served as a powerful tool for marketing these peripheral products.

As legions of fans echoed Lagasse's "Bam!" and tossed Emeril's Essences into their dishes, they were ironically mimicking a technique that would never be taught in a professional cooking program because the addition of raw spice mix is at best a mediocre cooking technique. Herbs and spices are best when fresh, and many flavorings are first toasted to bring out the flavors and oils in the spice. It is unlikely that Lagasse does much "bamming" while working in a restaurant like Emperor's Palace; nonetheless, this signature move became both a shrewd marketing gimmick and an important part of the chef's brand-recognition strategy, even as it represented the worst of the techniques Lagasse helped to introduce to television audiences.

The Food Network and cable cooking shows blended into the many reality-television series of the 2000s, which saw a new army of chef celebrities come to the fore. The reality-television genre provided the culinary world with a new avenue of expression, beyond the how-to cooking series of chefs like Pépin, Lagasse, and Bocuse. The reality genre promised to take viewers behind the veil of the kitchen door to see the various culinary and interpersonal dramas that occurred in working kitchens and the lives of professional chefs.

In addition, the Japanese series *Iron Chef* popularized the televised "cooking contest" genre, in which chefs competed to win favor from celebrity judges. This type of series became enormously popular and spawned dozens of new shows in the same category, including *Top Chef* and *Iron Chef America*, featuring widely popular American celebrity chef Bobby Flay. The cooking-contest genre offers audience members a window into the kitchen while simultaneously providing viewers with the momentary vicarious thrill of being a restaurant critic, as they pass armchair judgments on the cuisine and behavior of the various chefs, putting aside the slight complication that the viewers cannot taste or smell the cuisine in question.

The Effect of Media on Culinary Culture

The reality and cooking-contest genres have changed the cooking industry, providing chefs with a new avenue to achieve success in the industry while simultaneously raising public awareness about the cooking and dining industry across the board. Cooking shows have significantly increased public interest in culinary education and in the various facets of dining and cooking that were once reserved for professional critics, chefs, and advanced gourmands.

In addition, a relatively new subgenre of cooking shows has emerged investigating the ins and outs of the cooking and dining industries and presenting to the public the many challenges faced by restaurant owners and chefs trying to succeed in the business. There are even shows where professional chefs visit failing or floundering restaurants in an effort to rescue the business by providing the owners and chefs with a "recipe" for success.

Reality television is not, in fact, "real," but is instead a genre of fiction that seeks to present the illusion of reality to viewers while still being able to provide the behind-the-scenes insight into the lives of the characters that is only possible in a scripted and staged situation. The characters featured on culinary reality series are, in some cases at least, actual cooks, chefs, and restaurateurs, and the situations presented in each episode are based on real events or at least on events that could feasibly occur in a real kitchen. However, the rise of the television chef has also been accompanied by the rise of kitchen fiction as television producers seek to craft an image of culinary culture that is more gripping than the realities of day-to-day life in the industry.

Just as Lagasse "kicks things up" at the expense of dispensing a higher caliber of cooking instruction, television obscures reality in order to maximize marketing potential. Some of the restaurants owned by celebrity chefs or featured in restaurant reality series have received abhorrent reviews from qualified critics but continue to enjoy high levels of business, partly from customers hoping to appear on television and partly from those who take their dining advice from the celebrity personalities they have come to feel they can trust. So for all the benefits enjoyed by chefs and restaurants as a result of so much television attention, the media era of cooking and dining has also diluted the art and craft of cooking and has led to a situation where fame can, and often does, beat out talent.

Kitchen Gods

By Lisa Abend
Time, June 21, 2010

They start behind the counter and end up in the spotlight. How the phenomenon of the celebrity chef has transformed the restaurant industry and even changed the way we eat

David Chang was asleep in his aisle seat on a recent flight to Melbourne when searing pain jolted him awake: a flight attendant had accidentally spilled boiling water on his arm. That the worst scalding of the Manhattan megachef's life occurred in business class rather than in a busy kitchen was perhaps surprising. But that was nothing compared with what awaited him on the ground. Soon after he landed, news of the accident made the Australian papers and then, thanks to the global hum of diligent foodies at their keyboards, quickly appeared on websites around the world. The shocking headline: "Chef Burned."

It's been a few decades since we started turning cooks into stars, and still the phenomenon continues to grow. These days, the Emerils, Marios and Gordons of the world scarcely need the qualifier chef—they are celebrities, plain and simple. But between the television shows, the food festivals, the Vegas outposts, the spaghetti-sauce labels bearing their names and the fans rabidly tracking everything from new dishes to failed love affairs and, yes, accidental airline injuries, it's easy to overlook the impact that fame has had on the once disparaged profession of cooking. In the Food Network era, the phenomenon of the celebrity chef has utterly transformed the restaurant industry and, in the process, changed the very nature of how we eat.

There's a reason restaurant food sales in the US have jumped from $42.8 billion in 1970 to a projected $520 billion in 2010, and it's not just that more women have entered the workforce. As best-selling food author Michael Pollan recently noted, the age of the TV chef has coincided with a dramatic decline in home cooking. Pollan, who was named by *Time* as one of this year's 100 most influential people in the world—as was Chang—argued that by making food a spectacle, shows like *Iron Chef* and *The F Word* have reinforced the message that cooking is best left to the professionals. By turning chefs into entertainers—whether performing onscreen or via the impeccable platings in their restaurants—we have widened the breach between ourselves and the once ordinary task of cooking.

And yet our alienation from food and its preparation is matched only by our obsession with it. Huge parts of the population now seek out artisanal cheeses at their local farmers' markets, and run-of-the-mill restaurants attempt to cater to their newly refined tastes, serving salads made of fancy lettuce. Lots of ordinary folk now aspire to have their own $1,100 Thermomix food processor and blog about every course of every restaurant meal they eat. (The camera-happy movement has gotten so bad that Grant Achatz, the famously avant-garde chef of Chicago's Alinea, recently chastised diners who take photos—and video—of the food he serves.) These trends are fed by chefs' newfound prominence but also prod them to attain ever greater influence. In a world in which what and how we eat have become fetishized, celebrity chefs are finding new ways to harness their star power—and not just to make money.

The Start of the Rock-Star Chef

The term *foodie* was coined in the early 1980s, at about the same time Wolfgang Puck began serving gourmet pizzas at his buzzy Spago restaurant in Los Angeles. But it took another decade before Puck really kicked off the celebrity phenomenon by turning his attention to the culinary desert that was Las Vegas. At the time, everyone thought he was crazy. Crazy, too, the cable channel (today's Food Network) that launched a few months later in 1993, in the remarkable belief that audiences would watch round-the-clock food programming. The same adjective would also apply across the ocean, to Britain's enfant terrible Marco Pierre White, who by 1995 had not only become the youngest chef to earn three Michelin stars but also had a reputation for ejecting customers who were critical of his food. "Those stories you heard about him, about how he would be shagging someone's wife upstairs while her husband was eating in the dining room downstairs," says Jay Rayner, restaurant critic for the British newspaper the *Observer*, "that was the start of the rock-star chef."

It's not that there weren't famous cooks before then. As far back as the 19th century, Europe's aristocracy was agog about Marie Antoine Carême's elaborate dishes. And within more recent memory, Julia Child used television to help turn America's housewives on to the glories of the French table and to turn herself into a star. But none of that comes close to the renown of today's celebrity chefs, which can be attributed not only to the multiple restaurants and bad-boy personas but also to *Food Network*. Today the channel averages a million viewers a day and is so popular that in late May it launched a culinary spin-off called *Cooking Channel*, whose programming will include new shows with Bobby Flay and Emeril Lagasse. Culinary programs are also populating major networks like Fox, which this month began airing its seventh season of *Hell's Kitchen*. In that show, Gordon Ramsay, the five-continent chef whose offscreen empire includes restaurants in Dubai and Cape Town, berates low-skill contestants into becoming better cooks. Ramsay and Bravo's popular *Top Chef* series have prompted NBC and CBS to prep their own reality-kitchen shows.

The Internet has also played an important role: on websites like Grub Street (1 million page views per day) and Eater (2 million), chef groupies can breathlessly track every charity event and opening—sometimes before the chef has gone public with the news. A whole subindustry of agents and publicists has sprung up to manage everything from a chef's media appearances to his hairstyle. And, yes, the chefs are mostly he's: although women are entering the profession in ever greater numbers, the vast majority of celebrity chefs are male.

*The term **Foodie** was coined in the early 1980s, at about the same time Wolfgang Puck began serving gourmet pizzas at his buzzy Spago restaurant in Los Angeles. But it took another decade before Puck really kicked off the celebrity phenomenon by turning his attention to the culinary desert that was Las Vegas.*

All the fawning has propelled a profession once considered little better than servitude to the ranks of the glamorous and profitable. "I hate the word, but it's all about establishing a brand," says Mario Batali, whose endeavors include fifteen restaurants, countless awards, a television show that had him tooling around Spain with Gwyneth Paltrow and a full line of cookware products. "Because once you have that, all these other opportunities open up, and you have this giant soapbox."

Food Revolutions

Perhaps no one knows that better than Jamie Oliver. In 1999 the lowly line cook began taping *The Naked Chef* (he wasn't dressed down—his recipes were), which turned the twenty-four-year-old into a national star in Britain. "I would make focaccia with semolina on the show, and semolina would sell out across the country," he says. "You quickly learn that you have a responsibility."

In between making gobs of money—doing endorsements for a supermarket chain, launching a dating website for food lovers, etc.—Oliver has worked hard to improve people's eating habits. He collected more than 270,000 signatures in favor of improving school meals and delivered the petition to 10 Downing Street; eventually the British government pledged £650 million ($940 million) to the task. This spring he launched the TV show *Food Revolution*, which tracks his dietary-reform efforts in Huntington, W.Va., one of the most overweight cities in the US. He has also set up educational kitchens in Huntington as well as in Britain and Australia, to give families cooking lessons on how to prepare simple, healthy meals.

In other words, Oliver has become a culinary activist. "At heart, I'm probably no more political than anyone else," he says. "But because of what I do, people listen to me. And right now there's a massive need for information."

Oliver is hardly alone in trying to educate consumers and shape public policy. In recent years, the pioneering Alice Waters has seen her Edible Schoolyard project, which uses gardening to teach children about where their food comes from, spread from Berkeley, Calif., to New Orleans; Greensboro, NC; and Brooklyn, NY. Dan Barber, a New York chef leading the effort to make agriculture more sustainable, has become so influential that he has spoken at Davos. This month, Michelle Obama got more than 500 chefs—including Rachael Ray—to join her initiative against childhood obesity. And everywhere, lesser-known cooks are teaching locals about the value of eating well-raised food. If there are green markets popping up all over the US and diners scanning menus for the name of the farm that grew the carrots they're about to eat, we have chefs to thank.

Celebrity has had salutary effects on the profession of cooking as well. "Thirty years ago, most people who worked in restaurant kitchens had either just gotten out of the Army or were on their way to jail," says Batali. "Now you get all these people who went to college, then found their passion in cooking. The level is suddenly much higher because the people cooking are a lot smarter."

Most major culinary schools are going through an unprecedented growth spurt. For example, applications to the Culinary Institute of America, the premier cooking school in the US, have jumped 50 percent in the past six years. That may have something to do with the economy. At the venerable Cordon Bleu in Paris, communications director Sandra Messier notes, "we've seen a lot of students using their severance packages from their old jobs to pay tuition."

Cheering As if He Were Mick Jagger

For every potential cook who puts herself through an expensive culinary program or grinding apprenticeship, there are many more who seek to bypass all the years of drudgery and enter the profession through a new channel: reality TV. This year thousands of people applied for seventeen slots on the seventh season of *Top Chef* (which premieres June 16). Some of the applicants are well-trained rising stars with James Beard awards under their toques. But most are nobodies rolling the dice.

Jodie Thompson, thirty, a British travel agent, managed to beat some 20,000 other applicants to become one of the lucky 500 who got to audition this spring for *MasterChef*, the British counterpart to *Top Chef*. In a London conference room, she unpacked a Tupperware container from her bag and carefully plated the rosemary-scented roasted duck breast she had prepared earlier. She waited nervously as, cameras rolling, a producer took a bite and asked why she had chosen this route to launch her culinary career. "My brother went to catering school for two years," Thompson replied. "I thought this would be more direct."

And she's right. These shows have a history of turning contestants into celebrity chefs. James Nathan is one of them. In 2008 he was working as a mechanic in Glastonbury, in the south of England, when, on a whim, he sent in an application to *MasterChef*. After wooing the producers at his audition with an onion-and-goat-cheese tart, he went on to win the competition. The attention was intoxicating. "Cabdrivers would lean out their windows and say, 'Well done, James,'" he recalls. Best of all, he got the job of his dreams. Despite the fact that he had no experience outside the show, his newfound fame helped him land a position as junior sous-chef for two-Michelin-starred Michael Caines.

"We've created a symbiotic relationship between the television chef and the serious restaurant chef, where each furthers the efforts of the other," says Ferran Adrià, perhaps the world's most famous chef. Each year more than one million people try to get reservations at El Bulli, a small, fifty-seat restaurant in northeastern Spain he started running in 1984. When the dean of molecular gastronomy speaks at chefs' conferences, people rise to their feet and cheer as if he were Mick Jagger. When Adrià announced in January that in 2012 he would be closing his restaurant for two years, every major media outlet in the world covered the news.

Adrià, forty-eight, has achieved all of this without ever starring in a television show or opening another restaurant. His reputation stems almost entirely from his wildly innovative cooking, which by playing with diners' expectations—serving, for example, a cocktail that manages to be simultaneously hot and cold—forces people to re-examine their ideas about food. But he knows his prominence owes at least a small debt to the audience for great food that Jamie and Mario and all the others have helped create.

He, in turn, is pushing the boundaries of the chef even further. In March, Adrià was named the new face of a major Spanish tourism campaign. In the fall, he will co-teach a course in science and gastronomy at Harvard. And in 2014 he will launch a culinary think tank to train new generations of cooks to approach food with maximum creativity.

Yet Adrià is still in his kitchen every night during the six months of the year that El Bulli is open. If both Batali and *Top Chef* judge Tom Colicchio have recently made news for getting back into the kitchen, it's because most celebrity chefs spend far more time these days doing media appearances and traveling from restaurant to restaurant than cooking. "You can't blame them," says Rayner, who has become a bit of a celebrity himself, thanks to his role as judge on *Top Chef Masters*. "Before, cheffing was a bloody hard job and poorly paid at that. They've found a way to make it work."

Cook It Raw

Still, there's a fine line between making it work and selling out. Not many chefs have crossed it—Rocco DiSpirito probably should have skipped *Dancing with the Stars*—but the threat is always there. "The one thing that will turn back the tide of celebrity is being seen as inauthentic at the thing that made you famous in the first place," says Joshua Gamson, a sociologist at the University of San Francisco. "So the question is, Can you be a celebrity chef and maintain your authenticity as a cook?"

It's a question that keeps Chang up at night. If chefs are today's rock stars, few of them more closely fit the model than the thirty-two-year-old behind the extraordinarily popular Momofuku restaurants in New York City. His style of intensely flavorful, technically proficient cooking, served in restaurants stripped of haute cuisine's pretenses, has coincided perfectly with the dining zeitgeist and catapulted him to fame. (His outsize temper, colorful language and penchant for late-night drinking may also have played a role.) In the six years since opening his first restaurant, Chang has been accosted by autograph seekers while working out at the gym, had his underwear preferences publicized in *Vanity Fair* and read reports (all untrue) of restaurants he is supposedly opening in Seoul, Tokyo and London.

But now, in the wake of his fifth opening in New York, as he fends off investment offers from around the world and grapples with the ever present question of whether to do his own television show, Chang says his health is suffering from the stress and that he hardly ever cooks anymore. He still cares about making delicious food, but these days he sees his primary responsibility as taking care of the people who work for him, including helping them set up their own restaurants so that, with any luck, they can become famous too.

In January, Chang stopped to catch his breath and joined twelve other acclaimed chefs at a gathering in Italy called Cook It Raw. The event—it hopes to become a movement—prompts participants to think about the future of gastronomy by encouraging them to explore the connection between environmental consciousness and creativity. The chefs fished from local lagoons, met with the region's winemakers and farmers and even attended a pig slaughter.

On the final night, they cooked a dinner together, one course per chef. In keeping with the environmental theme, the recipes were supposed to use as little energy as possible. As each dish came up, the chefs would gather round and marvel at their colleague's technique. "To see each guy's creativity, to watch his perfectionism, was amazing," says Chang, who contributed a kimchi made from local radicchio. "It was so great to be actually cooking with them. You forget that's what it's all about."

The fifty or so guests who dined that night in the candlelit cellar of an Italian castle were similarly dazzled. But even those who were not at the dinner can experience it. Like everything else in a world that has turned food into fetish and cooking into spectacle, the highlights are available on YouTube.

How *Food Network Star* Whipped a Hashtag into a Giada Bump

By Michael Humphrey
Forbes, July 9, 2012

Food Network Star has become *The Voice* of cooking shows, at least when it comes to Social Media engagement. By mixing #FNStar and #FNStarTrivia into the contest's content, Food Network is serving up some big social engagement increases.

For example, buzz around Season 8's premiere jumped 300 percent over Season 7. That's impressive, but the increase of Twitter followers really tells the story:

During the first half of the season, @FoodNetwork gained 67,000 new Twitter followers, an average of 1,825 per day. But it wasn't just the show that benefited—the efforts rocketed their stars' followings too.

Call it the Giada Bump, because it's worth noting that the mentor stars didn't all get the same return. Alton Brown has had the biggest percentage increase, but Giada is the big winner overall, with Bobby Flay also building on his half-million-plus followers.

Here were the increases after six episodes:

- Giada De Laurentiis (@GDeLaurentiis) gained 36,000 new followers.

- Bobby Flay (@bflay) gained 29,000 followers.

- Alton Brown (@altonbrown) gained 26,000 followers.

What matters to Food Network is the overall lift. And it doesn't stop at Twitter. A 250 percent increase in website traffic on Monday—where fans cast votes, read blogs and look at photos and videos—is another testament to success in engagement efforts.

In this email conversation with Angela Moore, vice president of Digital for Food Network, we discuss the rapid evolution in Social Media for all networks, what FN wants to do with that new engagement and how it helps its celebrities finesse their social presence.

We're starting to see more hashtags on screens now. I wonder, was this something you had to sell at Food Network or do you think everyone is on board with integrating social media now?

Both TV networks and their audiences have come a long way in the past couple of years in terms of familiarity with on-air social media integrations.

A recent Accenture study reported the following in terms of social media integrations on TV:

- Overall 64 percent of those surveyed said they could recall seeing symbols and images associated with social media, including the Facebook "Like" button, while watching TV.

- In terms of specific symbols, 42 percent said they remembered seeing—and understood how to interact with—the Facebook "Like" symbol, while 18 percent said the same for Twitter hashtags appearing on TV.

For Food Network, it was a collaborative process between the digital and marketing teams to test and hone in on the best social media executions for our audience. For example, we started with more generic call-to-actions ("Tweet with @FoodNetwork using #Chopped!"), then began to get more specific ("What would you make with this basket of #Chopped ingredients?"). Now, if we know that talent will be tweeting for a show, we'll call that out on-air too. It's an ongoing evolution to discover what strikes a chord with our audience.

The Reality of Reality TV: Jillian Hopke's Sweet Victory in the *Cupcake Wars*

By Lynnette Porter
Popmatters.com, October 9, 2012

Jillian Hopke has a good track record for making her most cherished dreams come true. When she was three years old, she watched the Walt Disney World Christmas Day Parade on television and knew that she someday wanted to be a Disney performer in that parade.

Orlando, Florida, is a long way from her hometown of Plymouth, Massachusetts, and although most three-year-olds are little stars to their family, the reality of becoming a performer tarnishes most children's dreams long before they grow up. Not so with little Jillian, who continued to work toward her dream. At university, she earned degrees in both dance and marketing, which would prove to be a winning combination in her future careers. By 2007 she had achieved what she now calls her "previous lifelong dream" as a Disney performer in the televised holiday parade. Recently she joked that "lucky for cupcake lovers everywhere, I've had a new dream since then."

Hopke's talent and perseverance, first at Disney and now as an entertainment specialist who develops and directs the characters and live entertainment at Legoland, guided her to success in her second career, as baker and creator of Orlando-based cupcake company Jillycakes. In fact, the skills gained as a performer and through her first television appearance helped her and colleague Daylyn Graff win the 34th America's Cup challenge on the Food Network's *Cupcake Wars*.

The Jillycakes duo's secret ingredient for success in the stress-inducing reality TV baking competition sounds simple: Improvise! That word became Hopke's mantra during the multi-month process of being selected for the show. She learned about the online casting call when a good friend suggested she audition. "At first I didn't take him very seriously but, knowing of our years of experience performing for local theme parks, he said 'we already know you make the best cupcakes, plus you would make great television.' So I took his advice and wrote [an essay] from the heart. I never dreamed they would actually choose us!" After Jillycakes made the first cut, "the video audition tape that was requested by our casting agent didn't come until many months later."

In their humorous audition video, which can still be seen on YouTube (see below), Hopke persuades the Food Network to bring Jillycakes into *Cupcake Wars* because, in addition to baking exquisite cupcakes, she and Graff are "good improvisers." Hopke knew that they "both have a natural comfort in front of an audience. We have had so much experience speaking and performing for large groups of people that we don't exhibit much of the nervous energy that many people do on camera. I just thrive on anything creative, so to be able combine my love for the stage and my passion for cupcakes was a natural fit for me."

Talent and performance experience, no matter how valuable, can only take contestants so far in their preparation for reality television. *Cupcake Wars* pits teams of two bakers against each other during several rounds of competition, with one team going home after each round. Cupcake warriors never know the ingredients or design themes that may be part of a round's baking requirements. Hopke emphasizes, "believe me when I tell you that *nothing* can prepare you for what might be on that inspiration table or for the chaos that ensues."

No one told her what to wear, either. What advice would have been most helpful prior to filming the episode? "I wish someone had told me to wear non-skid shoes," she laughs. While they waited to hear when they would be on the show, Hopke and Graff carefully developed a strategy to handle the twin challenges of a baking competition and on-camera performance. "We knew it was going to be a think-on-your-feet game," Hopke explains, "so we spent months perfecting just the right vanilla and chocolate cake recipes that we knew could be turned into anything if we were to finally get on the show. We wanted to be ready—or as ready as you can possibly be when someone tells you to put fish in a cupcake!"

When Jillycakes arrived on set, the episode's theme was the America's Cup race. The first of three rounds of competition required the bakers to select an ingredient from a table of oceanic delights—perfect for dinner but not typically for dessert. Hopke chose tilapia, which went over surprisingly well with the judges. In fact, Hopke and Graff sailed through the first round but had more difficulty in the second, which required them to use fillings and flavors more typically associated with cupcakes, such as champagne (for toasting a Cup victory) or strawberries (to go swimmingly with that champagne).

The bakers thought they had a winning, well-decorated cupcake assortment to present to the three judges, but one expressed a difference in taste. French pastry chef Florian Bellanger "was upset by how unnatural things tasted. With the exception of the champagne extract, everything else was made from actual fruit, just a little too much of it, I guess, [but] he had the insight to know we could do better. I thank him for that now. I think our cupcakes have been refined to a more balanced flavor now, so it was a critique that hurt [at the time] but helped in the long run."

Coming up with creative fillings or flavors is hardly new to Hopke, who learned to bake by helping her mother and grandmother in the kitchen. "Usually the best ideas come to me when I'm hungry. That's how we ended up with our crazy Thanksgiving dinner cupcake. I live for the holiday sandwich from Earl of Sandwich, [but] unfortunately my craving came up a week short of its availability, so I made a cupcake that was a turkey dinner to go, complete with mashed potato 'icing.' We like to make cupcakes that are a true flavor experience rather than a flavored cupcake. We want you to eat them and think 'I can't believe that was a cupcake.'"

"We knew it was going to be a think-on-your-feet game," Hopke explains, *"so we spent months perfecting just the right vanilla and chocolate cake recipes that we knew could be turned into anything if we were to finally get on the show. We wanted to be ready—or as ready as you can possibly be when someone tells you to put fish in a cupcake!"*

Improvising new flavor combinations and cupcake designs from one round to the next is only part of a *Cupcake Wars* battle. The top two bakers also have to design a display to hold a thousand cupcakes—and everything must be completed within two hours. The Jillycakes team sketched a sleek racing vessel to hold the tiers of cupcakes they concocted while carpenters built the stand to the bakers' specifications. "The third round was the most difficult, for both teams, I would say. We had just been beaten down by the judges pretty badly coming off of round two, and our spirits were rather low. It took a couple minutes to realize that we had actually made it through and that we were going to have to make some significant changes to step up the game for the final round."

The last round of fiercely intense competition takes place while camera operators circle the kitchen or zoom in for close-ups. A typical part of each episode is a baking crisis, such as a forgotten or incorrectly measured ingredient, stubborn cupcakes that refuse to rise on time, or the struggle to decorate every one of the thousand cupcakes vying for the judges' attention. Hopke quickly learned to ignore the camera while she worked. "You have such a limited amount of time to do things [that] you get into this tunnel vision zone, and the cameras fade into the distance. It's a lot like the scene in the *Matrix* where time slows down. If only the time clock would do the same," she laments. "I don't care how many assistants they give you. It will always be a mad dash to the finish!"

At the dramatic conclusion of Season 6, Episode 12, the camera lingered on Hopke and the other finalist as they waited to hear the winner's name. "Congratulations… Jillian! You're the winner of *Cupcake Wars!*" On television, a widely grinning Hopke and Graff briefly celebrate their victory before the show ends with film featuring Jillycakes' display at the America's Cup reception in San Francisco. In Orlando, the bakers' family and friends who gathered for a *Cupcake Wars* viewing party likely didn't see these final shots. Once they heard "Jillian," the cheers and applause drowned out everything else.

The reality of a show like *Cupcake Wars* is that it can boost a business overnight, but celebrity also has a price. Companies promoted on TV must meet or exceed customers' expectations for an award-winning product. Hopke and Graff embrace the opportunity to expand not only their business but their creativity in developing new flavors and cakes of all sizes. "We don't ever want to be limited in what we offer to people, and we will be adding all three of the 'normal' round two flavors to our current offerings. We continue to evolve every day, and we are always open to suggestions and custom flavor requests. We made cupcakes for the grand opening of a salon/spa, and we customized their flavors to be representative of the spa experience [by using] green tea, chai, honey, and spices. Just like in the competition, it's all about what clients need and what will best represent their theme."

In addition to expanding business "through more community outreach and eventually through a retail location," the company plans to offer more services, such as "a new type of in-home party for all ages with cupcake-baking demos and decorating tips." With such tasty ideas, Jillycakes is becoming far more than an online-order cupcake company. Requests for cupcakes not only arrive from across the US but now from other countries. "I certainly didn't expect any international business, and yet people flying in from Norway on vacation have placed an order for when they arrive."

Other types of response to the *Cupcake Wars* win surprised Hopke, who expected an increase in sales but had not thought about the extent to which the television episode might affect her personally. She jokes about "how much I look like Amy Poehler. I've been getting [that comparison] for years, but the side-by-side screenshots posted by random strangers on the Internet were certainly unexpected."

Since their *Cupcake Wars* episode was broadcast in September, the company's website has received so many congratulatory emails that Hopke posted a message thanking everyone but noting that it might take a while to read all messages. The business' celebrity also means more television in Hopke's and Graff's future. Jillycakes received hundreds of votes on the Food Network's Facebook page and will battle other fan favorites during a special *Cupcake Wars's* Season 8 episode. After making two of her lifetime dreams come true, Hopke now has to set a new goal for herself—maybe a second victory in the *Cupcake Wars*. She assures her fans that she is "certainly up to [another baking] challenge—just let me get a little rest in first!"

Chocolate-Dipped Candies, and Geo. Abowd & Son, Confectioners

By Maureen Abowd
Rose Water & Orange Blossoms.com, November 30, 2012

The last time my Uncle Tom saw his father before he died, he was at the stove. Grandpa (my *Jiddo* who did not want to be called *Jiddo*, but rather the all-American *Grandpa*) was in his mid-80's, and he had something important to tell his physician son, so he sent for him at the hospital where Tom was making his rounds. Tom rushed off the job, a little miffed at what could be so important.

When he arrived, Grandpa was working quietly at the stove melting chocolate. *I wanted to be sure you know how this is done*, he told Tom, and proceeded to demonstrate the proper technique for tempering chocolate for dipping.

I heard this and a treasure-trove of other stories not long ago, when my mother and her brothers and sisters got together back in Ohio. It was a little reunion, a moment to hug each other, and for them to feast on memories that only they can share. Uncle Tom is a historian of the highest order of his father's life, going deep into the psyche and story of a man he adored. Uncle held forth at the siblings' reunion, showing photos and documents of the life of his parents, tidbits that begged for more time to get every last detail.

The sisters, my mother the youngest of them, sat on the couch with their rose corsages made for the Abowd siblings by cousin Anne to honor the day. They passed to each other old photos, one after the other of the family, and even pieces of stationery, incredible to have been saved by a loving son all these years, letterhead from my grandfather's candy store.

My grandfather, Richard George Abowd, became a confectioner as a teenage boy. I imagine he wasn't much older than my nephew, his great-grandson and namesake. I use the old-school word "confectioner" whenever I can, and I take pride in telling people: *My grandfather was a confectioner*. Such a description lends a kind of stamp of approval to my own pursuits, and a heritage that speaks to authenticity.

Confections were not, however, my grandfather's idea of his destiny. He wanted to study, and he wanted to study law, at the University of Michigan. From the time he came to Michigan's Upper Peninsula in 1896, a five-year-old on the arm of his mother (Afifa, herself just a teen girl, but a strong one, a tough one), he started preparing. He learned to read, write, and speak English in an Arabic-only household. He worked jobs to save money so that he could make his way to Minnesota, where he would start his high school college-prep program at St. Thomas Academy. Things were looking bright until the day, not long after he arrived in Minnesota, when he was called to the headmaster's office. Young Richard's parents were there, and they would be leaving immediately with their son.

Their destination was Fostoria, Ohio, where a Lebanese friend was going to help my grandfather open a business to support the family, a candy store. Richard had the smarts and

I use the old-school word "confectioner" whenever I can, and I take pride in telling people: My grandfather was a confectioner. Such a description lends a kind of stamp of approval to my own pursuits, and a heritage that speaks to authenticity.

the language to make a better go of things than his parents had on the cold, harsh, rather untillable land they had tried to farm in the U.P.

The shop window was emblazoned not with my grandfather's name, but rather his own father's name. My great-grandfather George would sit in his chair by the cash register and give the candies away to the little children who came in, much to Richard's irritation after the work he put into making them, no doubt swiftly, for a profit.

A Hershey chocolate salesman taught Grandpa to temper the chocolate, and about the sorts of inclusions (nuts, marshmallows, dried fruit) that taste good chocolate-covered. When he married my grandmother Alice, Grandpa showed her how to temper chocolate, and my mom and uncle tell me she covered everything in sight with chocolate. It was a family affair. The children would help and carry the sheet pans of wet candies to the back stairs to cool and dry, just as I did as a child when my mother dipped chocolates every Christmas.

I personally remember my grandmother's pretzels, coated in white chocolate and resting on waxed paper to dry in the basement of their home on Maple Street. That was quite possibly my first taste of salty-sweet pleasure. I was five years old. My mom and Uncle Tom said they never saw their mother eat a bite of the candy, not one bite. She made it and made it and made some more, but the candy was boxed and given away or eaten by the family. The joy was in the doing.

Once his candy shop became nicely established, Grandpa was "strongly encouraged" to hand the business off to his brother, who proceeded to run it into the ground while Grandpa moved on to something else that would support his own family (a hotel, The New Ohio Hotel).

The University of Michigan became relegated to my grandfather's unrequited dreams, one of those lifelong unmet ambitions that can drive a man to bitterness, or at least to drink. Instead, Richard gave his own seven children the educations he had wanted so badly for himself. They went on to give their own children—many, many of them—extraordinary educations that their father would be proud of. Meanwhile my grandfather was a self-educated man, reading several newspapers every day sitting at his desk at the hotel, and engaging in discussions about all manner of subjects with everyone who would talk, especially his loyal weekly Rotarians.

Yet just before he died, Grandpa had something important on his mind. His thoughts no doubt ran to so many of his life events, and what could have, should have, would have happened, if only. . . . But his mind also went to what *did* happen, the perfected techniques of dipping chocolates, a confectioner's heritage worth passing on.

Chocolate-Dipped Candies

Choose high quality chocolate—Callebaut, Sharffenberger, Green & Black's, or even a big organic bar from Trader Joe's—and avoid regular chocolate chips; they don't melt well. Choose all sorts of inclusions for dipping; I usually pick three or four to do in one candy-making session, about a cup of each in their own small bowls. Be sure to have everything ready for dipping before tempering the chocolate, so that you can work swiftly once the chocolate is ready. Make as much or as little chocolate as you like, though the more you use, the easier it is to keep the chocolate tempered while you work. The quantity of candies in the end depends on the size of your drops and your inclusions, but a pound of chocolate yields about 3 dozen 1-inch candies.

1 pound semi-sweet chocolate (not chips for cookies), preferably about 60 percent cacao, finely chopped

> For dipping:
> - Nuts, roasted and salted (peanuts, almonds, pecans, you name it)
> - Rice Krispies
> - Marshmallows
> - Pretzels
> - Toasted coconut (sweetened or unsweetened; crush the toasted coconut flakes for uniformity)
> - Dried fruit (cherries, cranberries, raisins, apricots, blueberries, you name it)

Line two sheet pans with waxed paper. Place the nuts and other inclusions each in their own small bowl for dipping, each with their own teaspoon for dipping.

Temper the chocolate. Do this by melting the chocolate gently either in the microwave (15-second increments, stir between) or over a barely simmering double boiler, very slowly, to 110 degrees. Cool down by seeding the melted chocolate with more finely chopped chocolate and stirring frequently until it reaches 84 degrees (use less seeding as the chocolate gets into the 80's, or the seed won't melt well). Warm back up very gently to 89–91 degrees and keep the chocolate at that temperature for dipping.

To dip the chocolates:

Work swiftly to keep the chocolate tempered, at 88–91 degrees throughout this process. Pour about a cup of chocolate over the nuts or other inclusions in one of the small bowls set up earlier. Stir until coated. Using a teaspoon, drop a small quantity (4–5 almonds, for example) onto the waxed paper, arranging the nuts on top of one another to form the piece of candy. Repeat until all of the inclusion is dipped. Repeat this process for each bowl of inclusions, dipping one bowl of inclusions at a time before pouring chocolate into the next bowl.

The chocolate may cool too much and go out of temper (it thickens). Place it back on the double boiler or in the microwave at five-second intervals to bring it back to temperature (88–91 degrees) and continue working.

Place the sheet pans of candies in a cool, dry spot to set up and harden. Box for gifts, or place in little paper cups on a platter or tiered plate stand to serve, extra special.

Bobby Flay Would Like You to Know That He's Not the Screaming Type

By Anna Roth
SFWeekly, August 2, 2012

Last week we published an installment of Michael Leaverton's darkly funny Food on TV column criticizing Bobby Flay for not behaving badly enough in his new restaurant fix-it show, *3 Days to Open*:

> Also, Bobby Flay's mild and tempered personality forgets to scream and rage at the owner of the chicken wing place for needing Bobby Flay's help. It should have. The owner needed to be screamed at, with all his over-talking and over-thinking and not-listening-to-Bobby-Flay. Chef Ramsay would have observed the odd, hyperactive fellow, measured him up, realized that he was about to make some of the best television of his career, and then fileted him raw on the sidewalk, cutting him psychologically back to the womb and reducing him, as if he were a balsamic, into a sticky blob of tears and sweat.

We never expected to discuss the review with Bobby Flay himself. But this week the blogging gods must have been in a benevolent mood, because Bobby Flay wanted to discuss it with us.

It all started three days ago, when this e-mail arrived via the feedback form on our website:

Michael,

Sorry to hear you didn't like the show. I did it as a six-show limited series. The last thing I wanted to do was scream and yell like GR or Robert Irvine. It's not my teaching or mentoring style in my restaurants so I didn't want to represent myself in any other way than how I really am.

The list of shows, books, etc. was hysterical. Thanks for taking the time to watch and write.

BF

PERSONAL INFO:
Bobby Flay
NY Ny
[redacted]@gmail.com
212 807 7400

After our initial amazement and glee faded, Bobby Flay's note started to make us a little uncomfortable. Not about publishing the piece, because the belligerence and bullying of Ramsay and Irvine really does make better television (the episodes where they can't find enough to scream about always put us to sleep), but because his note made us admit how much we're entertained by the drama and heartbreak of the worst type of reality TV: the mean shows. We love seeing people shamed and bullied on television. We just prefer not to think about it, so we can continue watching them.

Plus, we've got nothing against Bobby Flay. What's not to like? He's one of the Food Network's old guard who worked his way up through restaurant kitchens, so he knows his stuff. By all accounts he's a nice guy, and we've enjoyed his gently self-mocking guest spots on *Portlandia* and *Entourage*.

Mostly we don't think about him much at all, since his approach to reality TV has always been so laid-back. Bobby Flay's the unofficial dad of the Food Network—encouraging but straight-shooting, administering authority through quiet anger and disappointment. From someone you respect, and we do respect Bobby Flay, disappointment is so much worse than yelling. If this e-mail was actually from him (and we had a hunch it was), we felt obliged to hear his side of things.

The phone number on the e-mail, as those of you who immediately called it already know, turned out to be the main line at Mesa Grill, Bobby Flay's flagship restaurant in New York. The hostess transferred us to management, who referred us to Bobby Flay's publicist, who did not seem pleased to hear that Bobby Flay was e-mailing media on his own initiative. But she promised to "feel him out" about the possibility of a follow-up interview, and lo and behold the next morning she called with news that, against all odds, Bobby Flay was eager to speak with us. So we left a message on Bobby Flay's voicemail, and a few hours later Bobby Flay himself called us back.

Talking to Bobby Flay on the phone is exactly like you'd imagine it. He was nice, articulate, kind of funny, and very intent on getting his message across, which seemed to be that television Bobby Flay is the same as real-life Bobby Flay, and neither is the screaming type.

"I didn't want to do a show with yelling and screaming and drama. Everyone mentors and teaches in their own way, and I've never found yelling and screaming to be effective in my business life. I always say, 'don't tell, show,' which is why my sleeves are always rolled up . . . You get a lot more out of it that way, and people respect you—which doesn't happen overnight and doesn't happen with fear. That's my style and I'm not changing it for television."

On if the Food Network Ever Pushes Him to Be More Dramatic:

"Listen, I've had a long relationship with the Food Network. [17 years!] I've grown up on the Food Network. I've always been the exact person I have been and they've come to accept that that's who I'm going to be. I'm not a pushover—the phrase "tough love" comes up a lot—I just try to get people to think about things in a common-sense way . . . On *Food Network Star*, I always found myself mentoring from the judging table, and they tell me they like that part of me where you can see the real-life experience going through my head."

On His Approach to Mentorship in the New Show, Which He Also Produced:

"On 3 *Days to Open* it's really simple. . . . [These are] people who have never opened a restaurant before, they've put up their money or their family's money or their friend's money and there's a lot on the line besides how good their chicken fingers will be. My feeling was, look, I've done this for a long time, and made plenty of mistakes in my career to get to the success I've had in the restaurant business, so why not help people get there before they make 400 mistakes in the wrong direction. It's really a tough and perplexing business. People have no idea what they're getting into.

"I only did six [episodes] and won't do any more because they're exhausting for me. When I open a restaurant I have a team of people to open it with me. In this case it's just me dealing with the front of house, back of house, health inspectors . . . 400 things to deal with, and I end up doing a lot of it myself or getting [the restaurant owners] to do it with me. It's very difficult."

On How He Found the Review, Why He Wrote in, and if He Often Sends E-mails Like This:

"Never. I think I was doing a search for 3 *Days to Open* to see what people were saying about the show—with a few exceptions it's gotten a lot of good buzz. Up to a few years ago I used to get upset about things like this, because it would feel personal to me. I'm just myself on these shows, and I'd feel like, wow, that guy really doesn't like me—and that hurts anyone's feelings. I don't get upset about it anymore.

"That part where [Leaverton] copied my Wikipedia page was hysterical, it took a lot of effort just to type it all. I don't take this review incredibly seriously . . . I just wanted to write to him because a) I think it's funny, and b) I just want him to know what I was thinking. Here's what I was thinking when I came up with the show, just so you know."

[Michael Leaverton responds: Thanks, Bobby! I don't take these reviews all that seriously, either. A few weeks ago I spent the entire time writing about how the judges on *Master Chef* use their utensils when they eat, for example.]

Of course, Bobby Flay is a public figure with an image to protect. What we found so odd and refreshing about the whole encounter was that Bobby Flay is doing the image-protecting himself.

> *Talking to Bobby Flay on the phone is exactly like you'd imagine it. He was nice, articulate, kind of funny, and very intent on getting his message across, which seemed to be that television Bobby Flay is the same as real-life Bobby Flay, and neither is the screaming type.*

Maybe because it's not an image? Maybe he's just a regular guy who's trying to be understood? We don't know Bobby Flay well enough to say. But we'll think on it. Right after we finish this episode of *Toddlers & Tiaras* on Netflix.

Food Rules

By Ali Lorraine, Babriel Beltrone, and D.M. Levine
Adweek, September 19, 2011

*Once the province of how-to cooking shows, food media, more popular than ever, has
extended its reach—but has it become too big?*

Next week, ABC's *All My Children* will be replaced after four decades on the air
by *The Chew*, a lifestyle show whose hosts include three chefs and which stars
the food in your refrigerator. Who could have predicted that network TV would
trade sex, scandal, and drama for dough hooks and mixing bowls? But consumers'
relationship with food now has less to do with lining stomachs and more to do with
entertainment and reaction to an economy that fosters domesticity.

It stands to reason that food media would be doing quite well—and it is. Food-
related TV programming has exploded; the mainstay stand-and-stir cooking shows
are expanding and splintering into myriad permutations, from reality shows and
competitions to, at last count, eleven shows just about cake and cupcakes. Culinary
apps on how to braise beef or make a graham cracker crust are proliferating almost
daily (Martha Stewart's Smoothies and Cookies hit No. 1 in paid iPad lifestyle apps
this summer), and a plethora of blogs leaves no food need or fetish untouched.

Even battered print media is doing fine when it comes to cuisine. "For the first
time since I started tracking magazines in the 1980s, food has become the No. 1
category for three years in a row," says Samir Husni, director of the Magazine Innovation Center at the University of Mississippi School of Journalism.

While it seems the interest in food is reaching a peak, it has gone beyond mere
fad and become, at its base, a lifestyle shift.

"I believe this new food moment is really just us catching up," says author, former *Gourmet* editor-in-chief, and *Gilt Taste* editorial adviser Ruth Reichl. "Other
countries have been thinking about food in an interesting way for most of their history. That *Gourmet* started in 1941 as the first epicurean magazine in this country is
absurd. In France, one of the great cookbook writers did recipe radio in the 1930s."

From a TV perspective, the shift is part of what journalist and food author Michael Pollan has called the transformation of cooking "from something you do to
something you watch." Behind us are not only Julia Child and the Frugal Gourmet—and the housewives they catered to—but also the Food Network's original
stand-and-stir recipe of prime-time shows. Yes, its daytime programs lean toward
how to cook—albeit quickly and effectively, cutting corners encouraged—but also

From *Adweek* 52.32 (19 September 2011): 32–36. Copyrighted 2013. Prometheus Global Media. 96846:213JM. Reprinted
with permission. All rights reserved.

how to wear the new fall clothes and how to improve your sex life. Its prime-time offerings? Shows such as *The Great Food Truck Race* and *Restaurant: Impossible*.

And, of course, given both the recession and the growing number of foodies who also want to cook, how-to shows have not lost their allure. Despite an increase in two-income households and the number of prepared and prepackaged foods in the aisles, an economy as flat as a kimchi pancake means more meals at home, and, in turn, the trying out of recipes and the need for food budget tips. According to a 2011 Food Marketing Institute US Grocery Shopper Trends study, for instance, 61 percent of households with kids are preparing more meals at home than they did last year.

Entertainment, however, rules. Ratings for many competition shows are going strong. *The Next Food Network Star's* seventh season finale drew 4.23 million viewers, according to Nielsen, approximately 1.91 million of which were 18–49, nearly doubling the June 5 season premiere's audience of 2.23 million viewers. That it includes viewers relatively young is no coincidence; the food space wouldn't have expanded and splintered without a corresponding change in audience. According to a 2010 Harris Poll, 50 percent of Americans watch TV shows about cooking and no, they weren't all women. Forty-six percent of men said they watch cooking shows very often or occasionally, 57 percent of boomers watch cooking shows very often or occasionally, and 43 percent of the 18–33 crowd do the same.

Laureen Ong, president of the Travel Channel, which offers such programs as the stunt-eating *Man v. Food Nation* and the gross-out *Bizarre Foods* with Andrew Zimmern (bull penis soup, anyone?), says, "I would give a nod to our sister network Food Network for raising the interest level to being more than just a utility. It found a contemporary and entertaining way to address the food space, and that's why so many people in the general entertainment space are playing in the food category."

Food is now "more than just a meal to feed your family—it's an experience," adds Dustin Smith, head of communications at TLC, whose shows include *Cake Boss* and *Next Great Baker*. "Docu series and competition formats emerged in response, treating food and chefs and the cooking process as high-energy entertainment. . . . Food ends up becoming another character in these series, rather than a theme or genre."

Viewers also find food personalities, many of whom are a mix of raw aggression and finesse, extraordinarily compelling. On Fox's *Hell's Kitchen*, Gordon Ramsay may bully a restaurant owner into fixing a failing business, but he's also a nurturer who steps behind the stove and whips up pretty, delicate dishes. (Out of all food shows, by the way, *Hell's Kitchen* has the highest ad revenue, averaging $125,000 for a 30-second spot.)

> **Targeting men, whether for magazines or TV, was inevitable, given the data. According to the U.S. Bureau of Labor Statistics, last year 41 percent of men did food preparation or cleanup, compared with 68 percent of women.**

And celebrity chefs are now purveyors of a nightlife that combines food, movie stars, and, increasingly, the world of fashion. Just last week, Marcus Samuelsson, who has competed in Bravo's *Top Chef Masters*, hosted a party at his New York restaurant, Red Rooster, for a line of clothes from Edun, started by Bono and his wife, Ali Hewson.

The changing makeup of the audience has meant dollars from advertisers outside the mainstay of food and other consumer packaged goods. There is a "much more diverse portfolio of advertising categories, including a lot of support from automotive as well as retail and even expanding into telecom and financial," says Mike Rosen, president of media buying agency Starcom.

A glance at the sponsors of Bravo's *Top Chef Masters* illustrates that shift clearly: The show receives support from home-appliance brand KitchenAid but also luxury-car manufacturer Lexus. During its third season, which aired in 2011, upscale credit card Chase Sapphire signed on for the first time.

Food magazines have mostly fared as well as TV. The glaring exception is *Gourmet,* a victim of Condé Nast's cost-cutting measures; its demise speaks to the democratization of food media and the sense that *Gourmet* was snobby and old.

Food Network Magazine, launched in 2009, has displayed one of the most impressive circulation trajectories regardless of genre: For the first half of 2011, according to the latest report from the Audit Bureau of Circulations, average total circulation was 1.5 million, with more than 338,000 single copies sold, a 5 percent increase over the prior reporting period. For the sixth time since its launch, it's raising its rate base, to 1.4 million, effective with the January/February 2012 issue, according to the company.

The brightly colored magazine—geared toward moms—is big on the network's celebrity chefs, easy dinner recipes, "fun" ideas like PB-and-J cake, and 50 recipes to make with bacon. "The magazine's been incredibly successful at bringing a sense of accessibility and fun to the epicurean magazine world, which not long ago was perceived as extremely 'precious,'" says Vicki Wellington, publisher and chief revenue officer at *Food Network Magazine*.

The publications themselves tend to fall into two mass-market categories: those that stick to recipes, like *Everyday Food, Cooking Light,* and *Taste of Home*; and those that add liberal doses of lifestyle content, which, in addition to *Food Network Magazine*, includes the more sophisticated *Saveur* and *Food & Wine. Bon Appétit* is headed in this latter direction under new editor-in-chief Adam Rapoport, who hopes to add men and younger food-blog readers to the magazine's mostly female, middle-age readership. He's also throwing in some glamour: Gwyneth Paltrow is on the cover of the June 2011 issue.

Targeting men, whether for magazines or TV, was inevitable, given the data. According to the US Bureau of Labor Statistics, last year 41 percent of men did food preparation or cleanup, compared with 68 percent of women. In 2003, the same study found 20 percent of men reported doing housework as opposed to 55 percent of women. Apps popular with men, such as How to Cook Everything and Weber's

On the Grill, were the third and fourth (respectively) most downloaded lifestyle apps for iPads and iPhones last year, according to Apple.

Advertisers spent more than $315 million in food-related print publications during the first half of 2011, according to an *Adweek* tally of data for ten titles from Publishers Information Bureau. While that represented a roughly 1.4 percent overall decrease for the same magazines for the same period in 2010, several large-circulation magazines showed increases: *Bon Appétit, Food & Wine, Saveur,* and *Food Network Magazine* all drew more revenue.

Bon Appétit publisher Pamela Drucker Mann attributes much of the change to packaged food advertisers like Kellogg's and Nestlé, which have had to scale back their buys in some food titles, as rising production costs and consumer flight to generics simultaneously squeeze their spending. From January through July of 2011, Kellogg's advertising, for example, was down 28 percent across the titles *Bon Appétit* defines as its competitive set: *Cooking Light, Everyday Food, Every Day with Rachael Ray, Food Network Magazine, Food & Wine,* and *Saveur.* But increased interest from other categories helped offset that drop. Business technology was up 45 percent, health and pharmaceutical up 35 percent, beauty up 14 percent, and auto up 10 percent in those same titles, according to Mann.

Niche media has grown as well. Even author Dave Eggers is getting in on the game: His publishing house, McSweeney's, recently launched the new food and lifestyle quarterly *Lucky Peach* with chef David Chang. The politics of food alone—having mostly to do with where it has been sourced and whether it's organic—has given birth to a deluge of popular blogs, such as *Sustainable Table* (sustainabletable.org), and magazines like *Gastronomica: The Journal of Food and Culture.* Readers, says Darra Goldstein, editor-in-chief of the quarterly, "range from hip 20-somethings to the kind of well-heeled readership that also likes *The New Yorker*." Andrew Knowlton, restaurant editor at *Bon Appétit* and a former *Iron Chef* America judge (a Food Network program), adds that "those celebrity chefs people love and some of the food community takes for granted . . . are educating the public on the politics of food. People might roll their eyes at spending so much on an heirloom tomato, but the fact [that] they have an opinion on an heirloom tomato can only be a good thing."

Indeed, the more we think about food, the more aware we are of what we're eating. It's no coincidence that the boom in food media comes when obesity in America is at an all-time high and Americans are realizing their bad eating habits are shortening life expectancies.

But the expansion also suggests that a bust is on its way. The sheer number of choices is overwhelming, which may be why there's been some slippage in the TV landscape: Food Network's Nielsen rating slipped 4 percent year-over-year, *Top Chef's* most recent season premiere drew 1.66 million viewers, down more than 1 million from the series' highwater mark of season five, and *Every Day with Rachel Ray* magazine lost 14 percent in ad revenue from last year, according to the MPA, Association of Magazine Media. And critics say the glut of reality-show competitions associated with cuisine has cheapened the culinary landscape. The field is becoming so crowded, goes the argument, that food media is being pushed to absurd extremes.

More likely, however, these slips are not indicative of the larger picture. Not only has consumer interest in food translated into increasing gourmand tastes, food is also a leveler of class, as Pollan has noted: "If Julia [Child] took the fear out of cooking, these shows take the fear—the social anxiety—out of ordering in restaurants. . . . Then, at the judges' table [in shows like *Top Chef*], we learn how to taste and how to talk about food."

"Being a chef or tasting good food doesn't mean eating at a fancy French restaurant with 17 knives and forks and 15 wineglasses anymore," adds Gail Simmons, *Top Chef* judge and special projects manager for *Food & Wine*. "Anyone can eat well if you learn tricks of the trade. Now when I'm out at dinner, I overhear strangers at another table discussing the acidity of a dish."

And larger societal trends may continue to drive America's fascination with food and the media that surrounds it. "The smaller the world becomes, the more similar it becomes," says *Bon Appétit's* Knowlton. "But as much as there is a Starbucks on every corner, food is one of the few things left that defines who we are. It gives us insight into a culture.

And that's not going away. In fact, we'll all probably have to work harder to keep up with it."

Where Do Foodies Come From?

By Cliff Bostock
Creative Loafing, October 25, 2012

Years ago, in my twenties, I regularly visited the only gay bar in Augusta, where I was living at the time. Surreal enough to appear in a Jean Genet novel, the Peacock Lounge was usually packed weekends with military people from nearby Fort Gordon, drag queens, druggies, drunks, and a few somewhat mainstream people. It was located in a cinder-block building, and a jukebox next to the tiny dance floor blared disco all night. Outside, police often recorded license plate numbers. I loved it. And hated it.

One summer evening, a guy asked me to follow him home. I was coming out at the time and rarely hooked up with strangers, but decided I'd give it a go. He was hot and appeared to be one of the stable customers (not to imply that I was). When we got to his house, he asked me to follow him to his basement.

The room was empty except for a blue tarp on the floor and a refrigerator. The guy stripped off his clothes, opened the refrigerator and removed several large containers of chocolate syrup and about six aerosol cans of whipped cream.

"Do you like mayo?" he asked, smiling. I told him I wasn't especially crazy about it.

He began spraying the whipped cream on the tarp and pouring the chocolate syrup on top of that. Then he put three pies on the floor in front of me. "I want you to smash these pies on me," he said, "starting with my face, then any place you want."

I was stunned, to say the least, but I was accustomed to being stunned in my journey out of conventional life. I grabbed the back of his head and planted a coconut cream pie in his face. Then he sunk to the tarp and began rolling around in the gooey mixture.

"Come on. Get naked and join me," he said. I declined.

"That's OK," he said. "Just watch."

It quickly became apparent that my presence was quite secondary to his experience on the tarp. That is typical of a fetish in the purest sense of the word. A fetish, first described in the early language of psychoanalytical theory, is an inanimate object that provokes intense sexual desire. There is nothing unusual about fetishes. A common example is a man who gets excited by wearing female underwear. For many who wear leather, the erotic appeal of the clothing far surpasses attraction to its wearer. There are also fetishes that focus on parts of the body. Foot fetishism is very common.

Later, I learned that my Augusta friend's fetish is referred to as gunge. It is also the only explicit food fetish I've encountered and, even so, the gunge mixture can contain anything slimy—motor oil instead of olive oil, for example.

According to the hugely controversial *Diagnostic and Statistical Manual of Mental Disorders,* fetishes are not classified as pathological unless they interfere with day-to-day life. That's all well and good, but most people still publicly regard them as perversions, even though the average person's sex life is crazy as hell, almost always a kind of mad, metaphorical representation—a waking dream—of everything going on in the person's life.

The use of food in sex play is not strictly fetishistic since it usually intensifies desire rather than becoming the sole object of desire. This, too, is quite common and rarely talked about, at least until recently. But the practice has been represented in many movies such as *Tampopo* (1985) and *Like Water for Chocolate* (1992). We watch them and maybe get stimulated. But most people would never suggest over the dinner table that seeing a beautiful woman peel and eat a fig evokes the desire to perform cunnilingus, as Alan Bates does in *Women in Love* (1969). In our repressed culture, something's not sexy if there is not a pinch of shame in the brew.

For convenience's sake, I'm referring to all these behaviors as fetishes. The big question is, how does a fetish begin in the first place? Freud's explanation for male fetishists—he never looked at women in this regard—has long been jettisoned. He attributed fetishism, like so much else, to castration anxiety. (It's complicated.) Those succeeding him in the psychoanalytical movement produced all kinds of related explanations. Post-Freudians observed that as the mother withdraws from the child, the kid naturally projects mama's attraction on an inanimate object, a "transitional object" like a teddy bear, which it eventually outgrows. In the case of adult fetishism, the need for such an object has not been outgrown.

> **What is true to anybody with minimal powers of observation is that foodies do indeed pursue the perfect foods and potions with obsessive zeal, always endeavoring to increase pleasure. We are, after all, a consumer society, so it's not surprising that oral gratification has become a national obsession.**

You don't have to take these explanations literally to appreciate them. They're all basically about being nurtured and one's orientation toward love. Don't we all tend to fixate on the "comfort food" our mamas made us? An example of an extreme food-related fetish that demonstrates this explicitly is feederism. In this case, erotic stimulation derives from feeding a mate to get her fat. The two mates can also feed one another. Attend a "stuffie" party if you want to check it out.

A broader way of looking at a food fetish psychoanalytically is to call it oral fixation. Freud designated five stages of psychosexual development: the oral, the anal, the phallic, the latent, and the genital. Each of the stages is characterized by some kind of pleasure. One may become fixated during the early stages because the signature conflict of giving up the particular pleasure and moving to the next stage goes unresolved, creating emotional distress. In the oral stage, the pleasure is sucking, biting, and swallowing. Fixation can result in two personality types, according to Freudians:

"The Oral receptive personality is preoccupied with eating/drinking and reduces tension through oral activity such as eating, drinking, smoking, biting nails. They are generally passive, needy and sensitive to rejection. They will easily 'swallow' other people's ideas.

"The Oral aggressive personality is hostile and verbally abusive to others, using mouth-based aggression."

This feels a little like astrology, but again, it's unnecessary to take Freud literally (and he admitted that he was more of an artist than a scientist later in life). What is true to anybody with minimal powers of observation is that foodies do indeed pursue the perfect foods and potions with obsessive zeal, always endeavoring to increase pleasure. We are, after all, a consumer society, so it's not surprising that oral gratification has become a national obsession. (Think *Top Chef* and the endless blather of the Food Network.) And lest you dismiss the notion of oral-explosive personalities, consider the personae of many judges and competitors on TV shows. For that matter, consider the mean mouths of us critics.

And then there is the growing cult of foodie purists who are so picky in their consumption of healthy foods that they end up malnourished, with an eating disorder called orthorexia nervosa. Dr. Steven Bratman identified the condition in 1997 as a "fixation on righteous eating." The disorder is dominated by middle-class, well-educated men and women over thirty.

Except for obviously extreme food fetishes and fixations that result in malnourishment or obesity, most psychologists today dismiss any notion of fetishes being pathological. So what if my Augusta friend got off by rolling around in slime? Is it that different from people who roll from one restaurant to the next, stuffing their mouths and groaning with pleasure?

Of course, the latter mostly don't see themselves expressing a psychosexual thrill. To do so would violate the puritanical—dare we say "hypocritical"—values of Americans who can't buy enough porn to peruse after Sunday church services. Sorry, but licking your fingers, rolling your eyes heavenward, moaning, and talking endlessly about some esoteric dish you inserted in your oral orifice in your quest for ever kinkier food is a clear expression of sensual desire and its fulfillment. It's too parallel to the usual sexual interaction to call it unrelated. Hell, spicy food even adds the note of pain that often precedes *la petite mort*.

Now, don't be self-conscious about this. Become a recumbent Roman at the banquet table. Hedonistic eating can be a good thing. Don't deny your own desire and use your mouth to condemn the unabashedly lascivious. Eat and lick. Chocolate, after all, has charms to soothe the savagely tempting breast.

Cliff Bostock holds a Ph.D. in depth psychology, and a clinically oriented M.A. in psychology. He is in private practice, principally as a life coach specializing in creativity and the imagination.

3

Big Food Business

(Photo by Mario Tama/Getty Images)

People crowd a Whole Foods store in Manhattan, New York.

The Dilemma of Mass Food Production

The "big food" business is a nebulous concept meant to encompass the many large and powerful companies involved in industrial food production, processing, manufacturing, distribution, and retail sales. In general, the entities lumped into this category—such as Yum! Brands, Nestlé, Monsanto, Kraft, and DuPont—are massive conglomerates divided into many different subsidiary companies, brands, and peripheral businesses. Modern agribusiness, which includes the commercial and industrial production and harvesting of crops, as well as the development of agricultural chemicals, is another major facet of the big food industry.

The big food industry is usually associated with the mass manufacture of products that are sold through the major grocery store chains and through legions of fast-food restaurants around the country. The products of the big food business also constitute the majority of what ends up in bulk-food and restaurant supply retailers; therefore, it also represents the majority of what people eat at any restaurant.

Big food businesses, like any other type of business, attempt to maximize profits while minimizing costs. Achieving these goals requires balancing complex factors that affect supply, demand, and profit margins. For example, food businesses must market their products to the changing tastes of consumers and must constantly try to stay ahead of consumer trends while finding ways to reach into new areas of the potential customer base. Food businesses must also attempt to limit their overall expenditures while continuing to offer products that are competitive in price and that meet the wants and needs of consumers.

The effort to reduce costs has led to the adoption of policies and procedures that some consumers might consider irresponsible, dangerous, destructive, and even immoral. In journalist Upton Sinclair's 1906 book *The Jungle*, which was intended to illuminate the struggle of working-class Americans, Sinclair describes details of the meatpacking industry's procedures and practices, including allowing large amounts of animal waste and the bodies of dead rodents to be included in sausages and other processed meats. Sinclair's book led to the first widespread public outrage over practices that were then common in the large-scale food-processing industry. More than a century later, the debate over the benefits and hazards of mass food production continue and have become more intense, with a growing international awareness of the related ecological, economic, and health-oriented issues that surround the industry.

Ecological Destruction and Animal Cruelty

The big food industry is responsible for a massive amount of ecological destruction around the world, primarily in the form of converting forests, grasslands, wetlands, and other ecosystems for farming or livestock husbandry. The large-scale conversion of ecosystems constitutes only the first step in a complex degradation process. Large, single-crop farming operations degrade the quality of the soil, making it impossible to utilize the same habitat for farming other crops. Additionally, processing botanical products or raising livestock contributes to the production of greenhouse gasses and, therefore, to climate change. In many respects, the mass agriculture industry may be more of a contributor to climate change than the fossil fuels industry because the greenhouse emissions produced by agriculture are compounded by the direct destruction of botanical ecosystems that would otherwise produce oxygen and buffer climate change.

While some animal-rights activists believe that it is ethically or morally wrong to kill any animal for any reason, many critics assert that the large-scale meat and poultry producing companies are guilty of far more heinous ethical and moral violations. Animals raised for meat or other products in large facilities are often kept in conditions considered by many to be unnecessarily cruel, and the slaughtering practices used by many companies have been designed with little or no regard for the potential pain and suffering of the animals. Numerous books, documentary films, and articles have explored the way that animals are treated and killed in the process of industrial meat production.

Health and Wellness

Another concern raised by many opponents of the big food industry is the possible health risk surrounding the pesticides, fertilizers, and hormone treatments used by companies involved in agricultural production. To give one example, Monsanto Corporation's bovine growth hormone, which is fed to cattle to increase their growth and, therefore, meat production, has been found to be carcinogenic and has been banned throughout the European Union, though it is still widely used in the United States.

In addition, companies such as Monsanto produce genetically modified crops that grow larger and are hardier than traditional varieties. One example is Monsanto's "Roundup Ready" soybeans, which are resistant to herbicides and therefore allow farmers to use herbicides on the rest of the plants in a soybean plot without killing the crop. Surveys have found that a majority of American consumers object to the use of genetically modified crops for a number of reasons, including suspicion that genetically modified varieties could have unforeseen impacts on health. In addition, the introduction of genetically modified varieties makes it difficult for farmers offering normal crop varieties to compete in the market, thereby creating a monopoly for companies marketing altered strains. In the United States, more than 90 percent of soybean farms now use Monsanto's herbicide-resistant soybean seeds.

Another common criticism of the big food industry is that it supports and promotes products and eating habits that lead to overeating and obesity and discourage consumers from choosing healthier options. The damaging physical and psychological effects of obesity have been well documented, and many studies have found that the big food business' marketing and advertising strategies are directly correlated with obesity rates.

For instance, the big food companies market unhealthy products directly to children, thereby getting young consumers accustomed to eating habits that are more likely to lead to obesity or other diet-related health problems in adulthood. Research conducted at the University of Missouri–Kansas City indicated that children are more likely to favor food associated with recognized logos and brands, even before they can read or understand the messages presented in food advertisements. Consumers find this alarming because many companies use these marketing strategies to direct children toward nutritionally inferior products, such as processed and fast food.

Other studies have shown that eating certain foods, especially candy and foods with high sugar content, can have an addictive effect on the human brain. Children who begin eating these foods at a young age may therefore experience a type of addiction to the effects of eating unhealthy snack food. As the child ages, it becomes more difficult for the individual to shift his or her eating habits to favor healthier diet options.

The relationship between big food and poor diet is more complex than simply offering products that are unhealthy. Big food companies also spend millions of dollars to lobby against legislation aimed at supporting healthy diet choices. For instance, in the past decade, many states have debated applying specific taxes to the sale of sodas and other sugary beverages. Proponents of these legislative measures argued that a "soda tax" may reduce the sale of unhealthy beverages while simultaneously constituting a significant economic benefit for cities and states. Meanwhile, soft-drink manufacturers have spent millions to lobby against beverage taxes, thereby undercutting, in the minds of some critics, efforts to address the growing obesity problem in the United States.

Economic Concerns

Some opponents of the big food industry also contend that major food manufacturers undermine international workers and farmers by creating a market in which those offering traditional agricultural products cannot compete. The marketing and economic dominance of big food companies has reduced wages for agricultural workers and marginalized workers at many different levels of the industry.

In addition, while the mass food industry constitutes a significant source of employment for millions of workers worldwide, economic analyses have shown that food-industry workers are more likely to live at or below the poverty line. The median income for food industry workers is below $20,000 annually, and those working in the factories and agricultural processing facilities earn significantly less than the median wage. While wages are generally tied to industry profits, studies have shown that workers earning the lowest levels of income work for large companies that are highly profitable. Among the highly profitable companies that typically pay below-average wages are a variety of food-service and production companies like Yum! Brands, the parent company of KFC and Taco Bell.

Attempting to Avoid the Big Food Industry

Given the large number of potential concerns regarding the big food industry, it is perhaps not a surprise that there are consumer movements around the world attempting to avoid supporting big food companies at various levels. This movement has increased in the twenty-first century, especially among affluent populations where consumers earn sufficient income to afford the often more expensive alternatives to processed and mass-produced foods.

Though many consumers may want to reduce their dependence on, or support of, the major food companies, it is often quite difficult to avoid supporting the big food industry, even if only indirectly. For instance, consumers opting for a vegetarian diet may find themselves opting for soy products, as soy milk is a common substitute for cow's milk and tofu is a common meat replacement for many vegetarian and vegan chefs. However, purchasing soy products supports the soy farming industry, and 90 percent of the soy produced by soybean farmers is used to produce feed for the commercial animal husbandry industry. In addition, many of the companies marketing tofu products in the United States and Europe are owned by parent companies that also own meat-production companies.

Many health-conscious consumers have also shifted toward the "organic food" market, hoping to purchase products that do not support, among other practices, genetically altered products, hormone-enriched meats and vegetables, and other chemical methods used to enhance crop production or reduce pest infestation. As the organic-food market has grown in popularity, the big food manufacturers have successfully adjusted to the market, marketing mass-produced "organic" products for the market or buying out companies that offer healthy or environmentally friendly products. Bear Naked and Kashi brand products, for instance, are produced by Kellogg Company, a prominent producer of mass-manufactured processed foods.

While the push for healthier and "ecologically friendly" foods has caused the major food manufacturers to produce healthier alternatives, in many cases companies have simply altered their advertising and marketing strategies rather than significantly altering their products. The term *organic,* for instance, is not always tied to specific industry standards, and many companies offer products marked as organic that are not significantly different, in terms of nutritional quality, from other mass-produced foods.

Many consumers trust chains such as Whole Foods Market to offer products that meet a certain standard in terms of nutritional, environmental, and social consciousness. In many cases, the brands offered at Whole Foods and similar markets and those offered through large grocery chains differ only in marketing strategy. Supporting alternative grocery chains does support organic agriculture, but to a lesser degree than purchasing from farmers markets and other alternative vendors that are not part of the big market food industry. However, though large corporations are attempting to dilute the public demand for healthier options, the evolving ecological and health consciousness of consumers around the world has continued to expand the market for alternative agricultural products and ethical and humane means of production.

Justifying the Big Food Business

Given the many obvious drawbacks of large-scale food production, it may seem obvious that many consumers would wish to withhold their support from the industry and perhaps seek out alternatives. For those who believe the industry is more bad than good, and who would like to see big food companies become a thing of the past, the question remains, what justifies the continued existence of the big food business and how would the loss of these companies affect society?

Any lobbyist or politician seeking to justify his or her support of the big food corporations need go no further than simply asserting that the industry employs more than 20 million workers in the United States, and millions more around the world, in addition to the economies of thousands of agricultural countries. The political catchphrase "too big to fail" certainly applies to big food, which supports so many workers, in so many categories, that the decline of the industry would require economic and sociological shifts so massive that they can scarcely be quantified.

Putting aside economic dominance, the existence of the big food industry in the United States, and all of the detrimental practices, policies, and procedures that have come to be a part of the industry, are partly the result of the fact that the food business is part of a free market, capitalist system. The seeming disregard for health and welfare, environmental integrity, and the economic stability of the working class are hallmarks of all industries operating for profit and are the result of thousands of individual, minor decisions aimed only at cutting costs and increasing profitability.

This does not mean that the big companies are not capable of adopting more ethical and environmentally responsible practices, but only that doing so often reduces the company's ability to compete in the budget-food market. From a financial perspective, companies benefit from selling products in as many market categories as possible, but competing in some areas requires the willingness to participate in business practices that come at a high environmental and sociological price.

The central message is that changing the nature of the food industry is a difficult and complex challenge that will take many years to achieve and will require participation from people at every level of society. In addition, simplistic consumer boycotts and "organic" shoppers, though important to the overall goal, will do little to address the factors underlying the detrimental facets of the industry. When examining the faults of big food (or the petroleum industry or the medical industry), humanity must determine how to protect the public within a system that places financial gain ahead of social welfare.

Food Co-ops Brace for Arrival of Giant Rivals like Whole Foods, Trader Joe's

By John Miller
Canadian Press, September 6, 2012

The Boise Co-op eliminated thousands of slow-selling items, sweeping away the claustrophobic effect that accompanied too many offerings. The Wheatsville Food Co-op in Texas is opening its second store after forty years.

And in California, the Davis Food Co-op turned to a designer to revamp its look.

It's no coincidence food cooperatives across the US are making big changes. Many are preparing for the arrival of a Whole Foods or Trader Joe's, two organic- and specialty-food industry giants that are opening new stores nationwide.

Some co-ops are even dispatching camera-toting, intelligence-gathering crews to poach ideas from the big guys.

With demand for organic, natural and specialty food continuing to outpace other segments in the grocery industry, co-ops say they must improve their stores, identify trends and appeal to a changing audience as the competition moves in.

Whole Foods Market Inc. aims to triple stores to 1,000, including in Boise and Davis, Calif.; German-owned Trader Joe's is expanding, too, with a 19 city "coming-soon" list.

"Co-ops had it easy for years" when customers had few other places to go, said Robynn Shrader, head of the 125-member, 164-store National Cooperative Grocer's Association. "It's more complicated being a retailer today."

The modern co-op movement dates back to the 1970s, when customer-owned food stores—including in Boise, Davis, Calif., and Austin, Texas—were organized to provide an alternative to national grocery chains. Despite typically higher prices, shoppers often feel as if they're buying more than groceries, that they are supporting a lifestyle.

They emphasize community roots and, though they've evolved from when nearly everything came in big bulk bins, they still stock an average of 20 percent local products, compared to 6 percent at conventional stores, according to a study released in August by Shrader's group. About 80 percent of co-ops' produce is organic, compared to 12 percent for conventional grocers.

Over the years, demand for natural, organic foods has only grown. The Organic Trade Association reports 2011 sales rose 9 percent to $31.4 billion.

Brent Hueth, director of the Center for Cooperatives at the University of Wisconsin–Madison, said he'd expected an increasingly crowded landscape of organic purveyors, including from conventional stores, to be tougher on co-ops.

That hasn't materialized. "Demand is growing faster than supply," Hueth said. "It's not saturated yet."

Even so, some co-ops have been hurt. In West Des Moines, Iowa, for instance, the Tall Grass Grocery Co-op closed in August, a year after opening and a month after Whole Foods' arrival.

At the 40-year-old Davis Food Co-Op in Davis, sales slipped 7 percent after Trader Joe's October 2010 opening, forcing wage freezes and retirement-plan cuts, manager Eric Stromberg said.

Though revenue has recovered, Whole Foods opens in October in this university town near Sacramento, so additional austerity measures are planned to navigate another dip.

"Honestly, the emotion I felt was anger," he said. "I worked really hard to give our employees good benefits. And I hate to see that nibbled away."

The Davis co-op is going on the offensive, too, enlisting a store designer who also works with Whole Foods to spiff up the place. Stromberg isn't bashful about "shoplifting" ideas from his bigger rivals.

"The goal is you walk away with at least one good idea we can use in our store," he said, describing how one crew was politely asked to leave a San Francisco Bay–area Whole Foods.

Whole Foods, which boosted second-quarter profit a third to $117 million and whose stock is valued at $18 billion, won't say when it hopes to crest the 1,000-store mark.

But Joe Rogoff, Whole Foods' Seattle-based manager for Northwest stores, insisted the Austin-based retailer isn't trying to muscle out smaller rivals. Rather, he hoped it turns on a whole new audience to natural, organic food.

One indicator for a new market's potential is a successful co-op, said Rogoff, a co-op volunteer in Sonoma, Calif., in the 1970s. "I hope they stay vital," Rogoff said. "They represent . . . the foundations of where we come from."

Trader Joe's didn't return phone calls and emails seeking comment.

In Boise, Ben Kuzma hired on as the local co-op's general manager in 2011, just as the store in the capital city's oldest neighborhood was about to be drenched by a wave of competition.

Two regional chains, Spokane, Wash.–based Huckleberry's and Denver's Natural Grocers arrived this year, while Whole Foods opens its 35,000-square-foot store a mile away in November.

So far, Kuzma said 2012 revenue growth has been cut in half, to about 3 percent, for a store that last year grossed $26 million. The impact could be even more significant when Whole Foods opens and lures curious shoppers away.

A veteran of California, Maine, and Arizona co-ops, Kuzma said looming competition forced him to cram a three-year store transformation into just one.

> **At the 40-year-old Davis Food Co-Op in Davis, sales slipped 7 percent after Trader Joe's October 2010 opening, forcing wage freezes and retirement-plan cuts, manager Eric Stromberg said.**

He joined the National Cooperative Grocers Association in February to take advantage of the group's national buying power. The company has also adopted new accounting standards and boosted employee training.

Other changes are more visible: Fast-growing organic pet supplies now have a separate storefront.

And Kuzma hired a chef to remake the deli—and abandon use of an outside supplier, Sysco Food Services, for prepared items. Kuzma wanted to use the organic food sold elsewhere in the store in the "grab-and-go" section because customers probably figured the store was doing that anyway.

"It's more honest," Kuzma said. "I felt like we weren't walking the walk."

In Austin, the Wheatsville Food Co-op opened in 1976, four years before Whole Foods Market got its start across town. Whole Foods now has more than 300 locations, while Wheatsville stuck with a single store.

That's changing. It plans a second location amid increasing competition: Whole Foods has three stores, including its flagship; popular gourmet grocer Central Market is down the street. Trader Joe's is coming, too.

Like the Davis co-op, Wheatsville hired a designer.

"We're looking at what makes people want to shop at Whole Foods and Trader Joe's, and trying to bring pieces of it to our next location," brand manager Raquel Dadomo said.

Monsanto, Genetic Engineering, and Food

By Betsey Piette
Workers World, October 15, 2012

Part 1 covered the hazards of genetically modified crops and the role of Monsanto in pushing them worldwide. "Monsanto, genetic engineering and food" can be found at workers.org.

Along with DuPont and Syngenta, Monsanto controls 47 percent of the worldwide proprietary seed market.

Today farmers buying Monsanto patented seeds must agree not to save the seeds for replanting or sell seeds to other farmers. Each year farmers must buy new seeds as well as more Roundup weed killer from Monsanto.

A farmer who attempts to reuse or cull seeds is likely to receive a visit from Monsanto "seed police." Monsanto's seed patents, which make it illegal for farmers to reuse genetically engineered seeds, apply even if GE seeds end up in fields by accident. Over a third of US cropland is already contaminated with genetically modified organisms (GMOs).

According to the Organic Seed Growers and Trade Association, Monsanto seed police investigate more than five-hundred farmers every year. Since the mid-1990s, Monsanto has sued 145 farmers for patent infringements; an additional seven-hundred farmers settled disputes with Monsanto out of court.

Traditional seeds are disappearing. In the 1990s most seed companies were purchased by pesticide manufacturers who saw a potential profit in monopolizing both aspects of farm production.

The problem is global. With the assistance of the World Bank's structural adjustment policies, agriculture in India was laid open to Monsanto GE seeds in 1998. Peasant farmers in India, while paying higher prices to plant GMO seeds, hoped to reap the higher yields Monsanto promised. But instead Indian farmers ended up buying greater quantities of pesticides. The GE seeds also required more water to grow.

Farmers became dependent on Monsanto to buy seeds for the next year's crops, further increasing their poverty and indebtedness. Since the introduction of GE seeds in India an estimated 200,000 farmers have committed suicide—unable to overcome their new impoverishment.

In 2009, Monsanto's GM maize failed to produce kernels for South African farmers, leaving some with 80 percent crop failure. The company compensated large-scale farmers, but gave nothing to small-scale farmers who had been given "free" packets of seeds. (Natural Science, April 19)

From Super Seeds to Super Weeds

The increased use of Roundup Ready seeds has led to a 20-fold increase in the use of Monsanto herbicides. According to the US Department of Agriculture (USDA), in 1994, farmers applied 4.9 million pounds of glyphosate on soybean crops. By 2006 (last available data), they used 96.7 million pounds. (Mother Jones, July 18)

Planting GMO seeds hasn't always produced the crop yields promised by Monsanto, but farmers are increasingly "harvesting" something they never planned for—super weeds!

As a result of Roundup Ready seeds overuse, a massive amount of "super weeds" now affect around fifteen million acres of US agricultural crops. Super weeds are also being documented in Australia, Argentina, Brazil, Chile, Europe and South Africa. Around a dozen super weeds, including giant ragweed, have become resistant to spraying with Roundup weed killer, even at twenty-four times the recommended dose. (BBC World Service, Sept. 18)

GE crops have also increased cumulative pesticide use—about 400 million pounds since 1996—as insects become more resistant. Just as DDT (dichlorodiphenyltrichloroethane) use led to the evolution of resistant pests and the need for even more toxic pesticides, GMO seeds today have "joined the pesticide treadmill," says food activist Jill Richardson, with the Organic Consumers Association. (PR Watch, Aug. 28)

While repeated use of Roundup weed killer has been linked to a reduction in the Monarch butterfly population, because it destroys their milkweed habitat, other insect populations are increasing, having become pesticide resistant due to wider use of Bacillus thuringiensis (Bt) seeds.

When simply sprayed on crops, the insecticidal protein Bt breaks down quickly. But genetically engineered Bt seed crops retain the chemical in every cell. As of 2012, 67 percent of corn and 77 percent of cotton in the US are being grown from Bt seeds. A 2010 study found Bt in 93 percent of maternal blood and 80 percent of fetal blood sampled.

Increased pesticide use has been linked to widespread amphibian decline over the last thirty years and also declining bee populations. Combined with a return to arsenic applications in agricultural fields, it puts rural communities, farm workers and the general population at greater risk.

Arsenic Still Kills

Since the nineteenth century, arsenic could be found in many common pesticides, including calcium arsenate preferred for cotton field use. This dangerous practice continued until the 1950s. While many farm children died from exposure, farmers overlooked arsenic's lethal nature because it was effective against some hard-to-kill pests.

It's not known how many African-American farm workers, the dominant labor force in cotton fields, died from exposure. By the 1930s, over one-hundred million people in the US showed symptoms of arsenic and lead poisoning, but the USDA still supported its use. (Contributor Network, Sept. 20)

In 2006, the US Environmental Protection Agency banned the use of arsenical pesticides, including MSMA (monosodium methanearsonate) on food as well as cotton fields. However, in 2009, claiming that weeds affecting cotton fields had become glyphosate resistant, cotton farmers successfully lobbied the EPA to again allow MSMA use indefinitely.

A study published by *Consumer Reports* found high levels of arsenic in rice products, including baby food (issue dated November 2012). Rice with the highest concentrations of arsenic came from south central US states with a history of MSMA use on cotton crops.

"Monsanto Protection Act"

Just how dangerous GMO products may be to human health is unknown. "The [Food and Drug Administration] has not conducted a single independent test of any genetically engineered product. The agency simply accepts the testing completed and provided by biotechnology corporations like Monsanto," wrote Dr. Joseph Mercola in *Natural Society.* (Sept. 14)

The Pesticide Action Network charges that "the USDA has been 'speed approving' the latest creations coming from Monsanto, reducing the approval time and subsequently the ability to measure the true effects." Earlier this year, requests for twelve new genetically engineered crops were submitted to the USDA for approval. Nine are under a new fast-track process that requires no independent studies.

This speed-up resulted from industry backlash following legal challenges to the deregulation of Roundup Ready alfalfa and Roundup Ready sugar beets. In both cases the courts required the USDA to complete a more extensive Environmental Impact Statement prior to deregulating crops, instead of an Environmental Assessment that limited the level of public involvement and shortened the time allowed for response. The courts also ruled that the crops in question could not be planted during the appeals process.

The USDA has since completed EISs for both crops and approved their deregulation, despite massive public opposition. But this was not good enough for the industry giants, who got the 2013 agriculture appropriations bill amended to include a rider, Section 733, referred to as the "farmer assurance provision." Food Democracy Now! calls Section 733 the "Monsanto Protection Act."

If the bill passes with this rider, any farmer requesting to plant a GMO that had been removed from the market after USDA regulation would have to be granted a permit to do so, even if the crop's safety was in question or under review.

The 2012 Farm Bill was also amended to limit the time and scope of future reviews of GE crops by requiring only EA, not EIS, reviews, and mandating that the USDA complete the reviews in 18 months. The provision forbade the USDA from spending money for a broader environmental impact study on a GMO.

The USDA has since completed EISs for both crops and approved their deregulation, despite massive public opposition. But this was not good enough for the industry giants, who got the 2013 agriculture appropriations bill amended to include a rider, Section 733, referred to as the "farmer assurance provision." Food Democracy Now! calls Section 733 the "Monsanto Protection Act."

Monsanto Plagued by Rachel Carson, Now Rats

This government rubber-stamping of GMO permits has not lessened the heat on Monsanto.

In September, while Congress was busy rewriting legislation to protect Monsanto and Dow, French scientists released a study that found rats fed on Monsanto's GMO corn or exposed to Roundup Ready seeds suffered tumors and multiple organ damage. (Reuters, Sept. 12)

Gilles-Eric Seralini and colleagues at the University of Caen fed rats a diet containing NK603—a Roundup Ready seed variety—or gave them water with Roundup weed killer at levels permitted in the United States. The rats died earlier than those in the control study.

The rats fed the GMO diet also suffered tumors, as well as severe liver and kidney damage. The study tracked the animals throughout their two-year lifespan. Given that three months is only the equivalent of early adulthood in rats, Seralini noted that his lifetime rat tests provided a more realistic view of the risks than the ninety-day feeding trials typically used for GMO crop approvals.

Just as Rachel Carson's early call for action against the environmental hazards of DDT was ridiculed by its producer Monsanto, it is not surprising that the company was quick to dismiss the French findings. Monsanto took issue that the "strain of rats [in the study] is very prone to mammary tumors." Seralini responded that he used the same rat strain that Monsanto did to get government authorization in its ninety-day trials.

The FDA approved Monsanto's use of recombinant bovine growth hormone (rBGH) in cows after only a ninety-day test using small animals. Wisconsin geneticist William von Meyer noted, "But people drink milk for a lifetime." (Vanity Fair, May 2008)

Monsanto is facing more challenges. In July, the Organic Seed Growers and Trade Association asked a US Appeals Court in Washington to reverse a dismissal of the association's 2011 lawsuit to invalidate Monsanto's GMO seed patents and prevent the company from suing farmers whose crops became contaminated by airborne GMO seeds.

Hawaii is a global center for open-air field testing of experimental GE crops grown for export. As a result, a majority of food is being imported to the islands as the biotech industry takes over valuable agricultural lands and water.

Monsanto operates about 8,000 acres for GE seed production there, yet no environmental impact studies have been done. In June protesters demonstrated outside the company's headquarters on Oahu to demand that Monsanto leave Hawaii and that GMO foods be labeled. Similar protests were held on Maui and Kauai. Organizers vowed more protests until Monsanto leaves the islands. (Eco Watch, July 5)

Monsanto and other companies spent over $45 million to defeat California's Nov. 6 ballot initiative to require labeling of foods containing GMOs. But the fight is far from over.

California's Prop. 37 campaign put the spotlight on GMOs' potential threat to human health and the environment, suggesting that the same companies that lied about DDT, Agent Orange, PCBs and other toxic chemicals just might not be trustworthy when it comes to telling the truth about the dangers of genetically modified foods.

Is the Junk Food Industry Buying the WHO?

By Tom Philpott
Mother Jones, November 1, 2012

The US Food and Drug Administration is notorious for bowing to food-industry interests at the expense of public health. Consider the case of trans fats—whose damaging effects the FDA ignored for decades under industry pressure before finally taking action in 2006, a story I told here. Then there's the barrage of added sweeteners that have entered the US diet over the last two decades, while the FDA whistled. This week, Cristin Kearns Couzens and Gary Taubes, who have been writing hard-hitting pieces on the dangers of excess sweetener consumption for a while, have a blockbuster *Mother Jones* story documenting how the FDA rolled over for the food industry on added sweeteners.

As evidence of harm piles up, the industry is only accelerating its effort to keep government action at bay. Back in April, a Reuters investigative report found that the food industry had "more than doubled" its annual lobbying spending under Obama and had successfully pursued a strategy of "pledging voluntary action while defeating government proposals aimed at changing the nation's diet."

But the food industry isn't satisfied with just keeping the US safe for its junk products. As a new Reuters report shows, the industry is also actively seeking influence at the global level by cozying up to the World Health Organization, the public-health arm of the United Nations. The WHO is most known for its efforts to fight communicable diseases like malaria and AIDS. But the UN has recently charged it with focusing on chronic, diet-related ailments like heart disease and type 2 diabetes.

At the same time, though, the global economic slowdown has meant tighter UN budgets—and fewer resources for fighting what the WHO calls "NCDs"—noncommunicable diseases. According to Reuters, the WHO has to trim its overall 2012–13 budget by 12 percent because of less funding—but it cut an out-of-proportion 20 percent from the Geneva headquarters' chronic-disease budget. WHO's Geneva headquarters now devotes just 6 percent of its budget to fighting these diet-related diseases—even though they "cause 63 percent of premature deaths worldwide," Reuters reported.[*]

As budgets shrink, the WHO is increasingly "relying on what it calls 'partnerships' with industry, opting to enter into alliances with food and beverage companies rather than maintain strict neutrality," Reuters reported. "The strategy differs

---

dramatically from WHO's approach to interacting with the tobacco industry—companies with which it is unwilling to partner."

At the organizational level, that doesn't mean accepting industry funds—Geneva-based WHO and five of its regional outposts have been barred from taking cash from the food and soda industries. But as the agency's funding dwindles and Western-style maladies like heart disease and diabetes spread to the developing world along with processed food, Reuters showed, the WHO is increasingly pushing industry-friendly, "voluntary" approaches.

And one regional office, the Washington-based Pan American Health Organization (PAHO), operates under different rules than the WHO's other regional offices—and it has begun accepting industry lucre, Reuters reports:

> $50,000 from Coca-Cola, the world's largest beverage company; $150,000 from Nestle, the world's largest food company; and $150,000 from Unilever, a British-Dutch food conglomerate whose brands include Ben & Jerry's ice cream and Popsicles.

The Pan-Am office is expected to exert serious influence over how Mexico handles its diet-related health crisis. Mexico is a flashpoint in the global diet-related health crisis—it has the globe's highest overweight rate, 69.5 percent (slightly edging out the US rate of 69.2 percent), and it's a lucrative market for the soda industry. Here's Reuters:

> [Mexicans] drink an average of 45 gallons of Coca-Cola products a year. That's almost eight times more than the world average and 70 percent more than Americans, who are the second biggest soda drinkers in the world.

And cash isn't the only thing the Pan-Am office is taking from Coke and other sugary-foods providers; it's also soliciting policy advice. In the appeal to businesses to joint the Pan American Forum on Non-Communicable Diseases, the Pan-Am office lists "avoid regulation," "reinforce the positive connection between their brand and healthy, active living," and "reduce risk and avoid future litigation" as "benefits of membership." So far, Coca-Cola, Kraft, Unilever, Nestle, and drug giant Merck have heeded the call.

Such footsie with industry doesn't always stop the WHO's Pan-Am office from taking stances that contradict industry interest. In 2011, the office convened a panel of "government officials, consumer advocates, and experts"—note the absence of industry reps—to come up with policy recommendations on how member countries should respond the targeting of children in junk-food ads. The result: "perhaps the world's toughest plan to restrict junk-food marketing to children," Reuters reported. The report repeatedly cited Mexico as the site of particularly blatant marketing practices: "marketing [that] aims to forge emotional connections with children and to provide fun and excitement to stimulate brand loyalty, notably through the use of cartoons," for example, and "marketing of unhealthy foods [that] often involves giveaways and contests."

The report called on each member nation to institute a regulatory ban on all marketing of junk food to kids. "[S]elf-regulatory and voluntary approaches are too

> *As budgets shrink, the WHO is increasingly "relying on what it calls 'partnerships' with industry, opting to enter into alliances with food and beverage companies rather than maintain strict neutrality," Reuters reported.*

limited to meet the objective of reducing exposure sufficiently to reduce risk to children," the report stated. Released in May 2011, the PAHO expert panel called on governments to act on its recommendations "in a time frame of no more than eighteen months"— that is, by right about now. But according to Reuters, "PAHO has yet to even formally present its report to the Mexican government."

Why not? A Mexican member of the expert panel told Reuters that PAHO health officials "do not want to have any kind of conflict with the industry."

And the junk-food industry is pretty powerful in Mexico. Vicente Fox, the country's president from 2000 to 2006, rose to that position after serving as president of Coca-Cola's Latin American unit. Fox's successor as Mexico's president, Felipe Calderon, has also been cozy with the sugary soft-drink giant. He has pushed a voluntary approach to the obesity problem, and applauded Coca-Cola's ever-expanding grip over his nation's beverage habits. Here's Reuters:

> Calderon had appeared with Coca-Cola chief executive Muhtar Kent at the World Economic Forum in Davos, Switzerland, in January [2012]. Kent said Coke would invest another $1 billion a year to grow the Mexican market. Calderon praised the plan for adding jobs. Coke has plans to double its sales in Mexico within a decade.

Brushed-aside expert panels, voluntary approaches—all of this is depressingly familiar to anyone who has observed the US government's attempts at reining in Big Food. Not only is processed junk food going global, but so are the tactics used to keep it free of any government restriction.

Correction: An earlier version of this story failed to clarify that the calculation for the portion of the WHO budget that is allocated to chronic diseases only applies to the Geneva headquarters; the organization was not able to provide a breakdown of its overall budget.

Organics "Thrown Under the Bus" in Farm Bill Extension, Say Industry Advocates

By Cookson Beecher
Food Safety News, January 6, 2013

"We've been thrown under the bus." That's how some organic farmers and advocates are describing the government's "eleventh-hour" decision on January 1 to extend the 2008 farm bill for nine months instead of enacting a new 2012 farm bill.

Their dismay is based on how organics fared when the 2008 farm bill was extended until September 2013 (Section 701). Pure and simple, mandatory funding for a variety of organic programs written into the 2008 farm bill didn't qualify for automatic inclusion into the farm bill extension.

That outcome is in contrast to the proposed Senate and House versions of the 2012 farm bill, hammered out last summer, that had included funding for all of the organic programs (except for one in the House version).

One reason for extending the 2008 farm bill was that there just wasn't enough time to enact a 2012 farm bill, especially in light of all of the frenzied work Congress was putting into keeping the nation from toppling over the tax side of the fiscal cliff. The other factor was that House leadership worried about possible infighting over cuts to food stamps and subsidy programs.

Lost Programs

Among the organic programs that weren't included in the extension of the 2008 farm bill are those that fund organic research and extension, cost share to become certified as organic, and an organic data collection system—the same sort of data collection system that has long been a mainstay for conventional agriculture and that qualified to receive continued funding.

Organic farmers say that these programs have helped them be more productive and better at marketing their goods to meet the growing demand for their crops, milk, meats and other products.

"This is a huge loss for the organic sector," Barbara Haumann, spokesperson for the Organic Trade Association, told *Food Safety News*. "The cuts are severe. It will impact farmers who use safer practices and could discourage some farmers because of the loss of cost-share for certification."

USDA's cost-share programs make certification more affordable for small- and mid-sized organic farmers and handlers by reimbursing them for as much as 75 percent—up to a maximum of $750 a year—for their certification costs. Eligible costs include application fees, inspection fees, travel for certification inspectors, and even postage.

Created in 2002, the National Organic Certification Cost Share Program was designed, in part, to recognize the public benefits of organic agriculture to environmental stewardship, according to the USDA. The program received $22 million in mandatory funding over five years in the 2008 farm bill.

Turning to research, Haumann said that the 2008 farm bill marked an important step forward for organic research. She called the loss of that funding "a real blow."

"Cooperative Extension (a nationwide network that operates through certain universities in each state to provide research-based information to agricultural producers, among others) was working with organic farmers," she said. "It wasn't that long ago, that there was no funding for organics. We don't want to lose ground."

USDA's National Institute of Food and Agriculture, the federal partner in the Cooperative Extension System, provides federal funding to the system.

In the 2008 farm bill, the Organic Agriculture Research and Extension Initiative was funded at $18 million for fiscal year 2009 and $20 million for fiscal years 2010–12, plus a $25-million-per-year authorization for appropriations

According to the National Organic Coalition, USDA research programs have not kept pace with the growth of organic agriculture in the market place. Compared to the amount of research dollars going to other sectors of the industry, organics gets significantly less proportionately when looking at the nearly 4 percent of total US food retail market it represents.

"As our economy struggles to rebuild, organic agriculture is a bright spot that is clearly part of the solution," said Steven Etka, legislative coordinator for the National Organic Coalition.

Organic farmer Anne Schwartz, owner of Blue Heron Farm in Western Washington, told *Food Safety News* that Washington State University alone has 150 research projects focused on organic and sustainable farming, including a thirty-acre showcase organic farm.

"We've made an impact," she said, referring to strides organic producers have made. "But right now research is funded at the federal level. When we lose federal funding for that, we're in trouble, and they know it."

Pointing to another program that lost funding in the nine-month extension, Haumann said that the Organic Production and Marketing Data Initiative has been "a wonderful help" for organic farmers and businesses because it helps keep track of what organic crops or livestock are being raised and where and what their costs are.

"It helps producers and buyers make business decisions across the board," she said. "And it helps encourage investors when they see how much organics is growing."

The 2008 farm bill provided $5 million in mandatory funding for the collection and publication of the data.

As far as Haumann is concerned, organic agriculture "is not getting its fair share in the extension of the 2008 farm bill to encourage good practices that produce food that many families want to buy."

"A slap in the face and anti-people," said Schwartz referring not just to what the loss in funding means to the organic sector but also to the general public, which benefits from the environmental stewardship and the boost to regional economies, biodiversity, and food security that organic agriculture offers.

Ironic Twist

Instead of reforming US agricultural policy, as had been proposed in the Senate and House versions of the 2012 farm bill, the nine-month extension of the 2008 version includes $5 billion for subsidies and direct payments. These are payments typically doled out, farm bill after farm bill, to certain farmers (among them corn, soybeans, wheat and rice farmers).

In contrast, the House and Senate versions of the 2012 farm bill had called for eliminating the subsidies. The reasoning behind that proposed change was that the commodity farmers were doing well financially and didn't need them. Apart from farm policy, proposed cost-cutting measures in the farm bill were seen as a way to help fix the nation's budgetary woes. For example, the Senate bipartisan version of the 2012 Farm Bill called for cuts of $24 billion in spending.

After the 2008 bill was extended, US Senator Debbie Stabenow, chairwoman of the Senate Agriculture, Nutrition and Forestry Committee, made it clear that she wasn't pleased with the outcome, describing it as "a partial extension that reforms nothing, provides no deficit reduction, and hurts many areas of our agriculture economy."

As for why some of the organic programs weren't included in the extension of the 2008 Farm Bill, it all comes down to something called the "budgetary baseline." According to a Congressional Research Service Report, thirty-seven programs that received mandatory funds in the 2008 farm bill weren't eligible to continue receiving them because they didn't have what is referred to as a "budgetary baseline" beyond FY2012. If policymakers want to continue these programs in the 2012 farm bill, they will need to find offsets to pay for them.

No easy task, say organic advocates, who point out that any requests for new appropriations will be part of the national debate on spending cuts, entitlement reform and the debt ceiling. In addition, the 2012 farm bill will need to go through committee mark-up and onto the House and Senate floors before it can be enacted into law.

Even so, the Organic Trade Association has vowed to lead the

> *According to the National Organic Coalition, USDA research programs have not kept pace with the growth of organic agriculture in the market place. Compared to the amount of research dollars going to other sectors of the industry, organics gets significantly less proportionately when looking at the nearly 4 percent of total US food retail market it represents.*

direct-advocacy effort for these critical programs, according to a news alert sent out to members.

What About Food Safety?

Although food safety is generally thought of as keeping food free of dangerous pathogens such as E. coli, Salmonella, or Listeria, organic farmers and consumers view food safety from an additional perspective. For them, for food to be safe, it must also be free from pesticide residues and genetically modified organisms and cannot be raised using synthetic chemicals, compost that contains pathogens, or sewage sludge. Or, in the case of meat, poultry and fish, the animals, or fish, can't be treated with antibiotics or growth hormones.

These are just some of the standards that organic producers must meet to qualify for certification under USDA's National Organic Program, which allows them to sell their products bearing the agency's official organic seal. That seal gives them an important boost in the marketplace, where some consumers are more than happy to pay higher prices for food that has been raised organically.

Lisa Bunin, organic policy director for The Center for Food Safety told *Food Safety News* that organically grown food is the only food that is legally mandated to safeguard natural resources such as the soil and water, human health, animal welfare, and the environment.

As an example of that, a legal guide by the National Agricultural Law Center about the National Organic Program points out that legislation specifically says that the plant and animal materials must be managed by the producer "to maintain or improve soil organic matter content in a manner that does not contribute to contamination of crops, soil, or water by plant nutrients, pathogenic organisms, heavy metals, or residues of prohibited substances."

According to a fact sheet from the Organic Farming Research Foundation organic agriculture—a $29 billion industry in the United States in 2010 with more than 14,500 organic farmers in its ranks—is one of the fastest growing sectors of US agriculture. For ten years, the industry grew at an enviable average annual rate of 20 percent, and even during the recent recession, continued to enjoy positive growth.

It Rankles

The National Sustainable Agriculture Coalition, which represents family and smaller-sized farmers, rankled at the decision to extend the 2008 farm bill.

"The message is unmistakable—direct commodity subsidies, despite high market prices, are sacrosanct, while the rest of agriculture and the rest of rural America can simply drop dead," said the organization in a statement.

For Mark Kastel, co-founder of The Cornucopia Institute, a populist farm policy research group, the loss of funding for some critical organic programs in the extension of the 2008 farm bill goes beyond whether organic food is safer or more nutritious than conventionally grown food. While that debate is important, he pointed out that there's also this economic reality to consider: It (the extension) flies in the face of the free-market system the United States' economy is purportedly based on.

"It (the 2008 farm bill extension) undercuts where markets are going," Kastel told *Food Safety News*. "Instead, with this extension, we have the government giving more money (in direct payments) to commodity farmers even though they don't need payments now because they're doing well. They're ignoring what the consumers are voting for in the marketplace. It's assbackwards. It's undermining our capitalistic structure and free markets. We're having the government pick and choose the winners."

Kastel also pointed out that what organics receives in federal support is "peanuts" compared to the subsidies and other support that conventional agriculture typically receives through the nation's farm bills and agricultural policy.

Dissected Dreams: California's Engineered Cornucopia Falters

By Matt Black
Orion Magazine, March/April 2011

The yellow and black signs announcing the start of California's new water war began appearing in the spring of 2009: CONGRESS-CREATED DUSTBOWL. The Central Valley's most productive stretch of farmland, the immense Westlands Water District, had seen its water supply cut by 90 percent to forestall the ecological collapse of the Sacramento Delta, the largest estuary on the Pacific coast and a crucial source of water for wildlife and humans. All along Interstate 5, the state's main north-south highway, the signs were soon ubiquitous. Parked atop patches of barren farmland, they announced what appeared to be a modern-day agricultural apocalypse: 200,000 acres of the nation's richest farmland out of production, unemployment above 40 percent in some towns, and bread lines stretching around the block.

Of course, the entire enterprise in the Westlands was likely to fail. Its folly seems painfully obvious today—turning a patch of semi-arid desert into farmland through the construction of a massive concrete river running in reverse, with water pumped uphill from the delta a hundred miles away. A creation of the same 1930s New Deal ambition that plugged the Colorado and Columbia rivers and brought electricity to much of the nation, California's Central Valley Project and its huge aqueduct are from a time of unbridled engineering confidence. Today such certainty, such faith in the power of bulldozers, concrete, and the draftsman's pen, seems unimaginably naïve and very nearly quaint—but its bequest is the modern American West.

These days the Westlands is home to the nation's largest and richest farms—some cover more than ten square miles and rake in millions of dollars each year—but it is also home to some of the poorest towns in California. The average farm worker in the Westlands makes about $10,000 a year. While its bonanza harvests serviced by a near-feudal labor system are a throwback to another time, it's no backwater. Each spring and fall, 90 percent of the nation's lettuce comes from these fields, as well as the majority of many other crops, from almonds and cantaloupes to tomatoes and pomegranates.

As I watch this ersatz abundance turn to dust, I'm left conflicted. When a group of farmers and politicians pose for news cameras in front of destitute housewives in a bread line, it feels outrageous. Don't they know that families here have relied on food handouts for years? Are they really using their workers' poverty—a poverty born of decades of exploitative wages—to get more subsidized water?

But on the way out of town, as dusk falls and the landscape rolls by, the stretches of brown stick in my eye like bits of dust blown in. To watch crops wither and see farmland turn to dust feels deeply wrong, like watching civilization's seams start to unravel. The Westlands might be a landscape imbued with an aura of corruption, but it is a human landscape, and once its thin green veneer is torn away, the makeshift community it supported—schools, homes, towns—is quickly reduced to an eerie tableau of dust storms and bouncing tumbleweed. At times such as this, the ecological havoc in the Sacramento Delta seems far away.

These days the Westlands is home to the nation's largest and richest farms—some cover more than ten square miles and rake in millions of dollars each year—but it is also home to some of the poorest towns in California. The average farm worker in the Westlands makes about $10,000 a year.

I stop by a friend's house, a Mexican migrant whom I've known on both sides of the border. His elderly parents, two of the sweetest people I have ever met, live in a remote Oaxacan village in a dirt-floor adobe house perched on the side of a mountain, scratching out a living on a small corn farm. Without the money their son sends them, about fifty dollars a month, both will soon be skipping meals. My friend tells me he hasn't had work in six months, and the only money coming in is from the tacos his wife sells out of the back of a broken-down catering truck parked in their driveway. Next to the truck, he's planted a sign: "No water, no life."

The Other Side of the Valley

By Barry Estabrook
Gastronomica, Winter 2011

By San Joaquin Valley standards, Tom Willey's farm is so puny that I sped past it without noticing. My mind had been swept away by the region's agoraphobia-inducing sense of infinite vastness. Ruler-straight byways traverse miles of almond trees planted on precise geometric grids like perfectly drilled soldiers. Those give way to tracts of grape vines trellised in parallel rows stretching to the horizon, followed by green oceans of lettuce, onions, tomatoes, and alfalfa running to the base of distant blue-gray mountains.

There is a gritty majesty to San Joaquin, the southern half of California's Central Valley. Route 99, the freeway that bisects it, thunders with the traffic of tractor-trailers that haul equipment in and agricultural products out 24/7. The geography beside the highway is marked by grain elevators and storage silos that soar like medieval turrets. Enormous piles of almond hulls (sold as cattle feed) rise in conical mounds as tall as five-story buildings. I passed warehouse after warehouse, each big enough to be an airplane hangar. Farm equipment dealerships broke up monotonous gray and whites with the yellow, green, orange, and scarlet hues of tractors, plows, combines, dump trucks, bulldozers, and Rube Goldberg contraptions whose purpose I could only guess, all seemingly designed to be operated by a race of giants.

On the surface, the San Joaquin Valley gives no hints that it is home to some of the most innovative food producers in the country. On a seventy-five-acre "patch," as Willey aptly calls it, T & D Willey Farms grows fifty different varieties of produce: "everything from artichokes to zucchinis." (More typically, his nearest neighbor raises a single variety of wine grape on 750 acres.) "Conventional farming approaches are just too brain-dead for me," he said, in the cluttered bungalow that serves as his head office. "As an organic farmer, you have to be out ahead of the game. You have to be studying insect ecology and soil microbiology. It's fascinating, challenging, and intellectually stimulating."

The governor of the local Slow Food chapter, Willey is a stubborn pioneer among a group of agricultural contrarians who are bucking the cycle of commodity production in the Central Valley—what he calls "producing food widgets." He ticked off other like-minded mavericks. Hidden in plain sight amidst huge industrial farms, they include a grower of the world's sweetest apricots; a rancher whose cattle spend their entire lives eating grass on pasture; a third-generation Japanese American rice-producing brother and sister team who still adhere to the standards of quality established by their grandfather; and a born-again factory-scale dairy farmer turned farmstead cheesemaker who has won the highest awards in the world.

Through their efforts, these outliers are fashioning a new paradigm for American agriculture, with farms that are large enough to distribute regionally and even nationally, but still small enough to grow food that has real taste. If alternative agriculture can take root in what many consider to be the heart of everything that is wrong with our broken, industrial food system, then it can flourish anywhere.

With his cascading white beard, faded jeans held up by suspenders, and ever-present baseball cap, the sixty-three-year-old Willey looks just like what he is: the granddaddy of sustainable agriculture. When he started out in the 1970s, Willey farmed with chemical fertilizers and pesticides, just like virtually everybody else in the area. But when he bought his own land in the early 1980s, he realized that he had to use more fertilizer and pesticide each season to replicate the yields of the previous year. He went organic in 1984. Willey's definition of sustainability also extends to his workers. He specifically designs his planting schedule and crop selections to generate a twelve-month harvest, giving his employees year-round work, rather than relying on temporary laborers who are the mainstays of Big Ag in California. "Farmworkers shouldn't be migratory," he explained. "They should be part of the community."

When the first American explorers came to the valley, they encountered a barren land of kangaroo rats and brown grasses. "The most miserable country that I have ever beheld . . . little better than a desert," wrote George Horatio Derby, an army topographer in 1850. Two decades later, Moses J. Church built a crude dam across the Kings River, introducing irrigation to the arid land. Now, thanks to clever hydraulic engineers and canny politicians, the Central Valley's 450-mile-long, mountain-rimmed trough of rich alluvial soil is watered by one of the world's most elaborate canal and aqueduct systems. It is home to four of the five biggest farming counties in the United States, according to the United States Department of Agriculture. "The world's richest agricultural valley," as the late University of California Berkeley geographer James J. Parsons called it, is a throbbing food-generating machine that pumps out poultry, beef, dairy products, and more than 250 different crops: oranges, lemons, apricots, peaches, plums, cherries, apples, figs, almonds, walnuts, pistachios, asparagus, avocados, grapes, onions, lettuce, artichokes, zucchini, and tomatoes, to list a sampling. According to the authors of *A Field Guide to California Agriculture*, Parsons also said that the valley was the most interesting place in the world—"if you happened to be wired for the complexities of agriculture."

Barely an hour north of Willey's farm, John Fiscalini introduced me to his vision of the future of dairying. Started by his grandfather, who emigrated from Switzerland in the 1890s, the farm is home to 1,500 cows. In a space that looked as sanitary as a hospital room, two Hispanic men in white cloaks were stacking slabs of blonde cheese curd in a stainless-steel trough. Within a few hours, the curd would begin the aging process in an adjacent room that was stacked to the rafters with rounds of cheddar. In breezy, open-sided barns, Holstein and Brown Swiss cows lay in clean stalls chewing their cud. Cleanliness and contented cows are the keys to producing quality milk and cheese, according to Fiscalini.

A decade ago, tired of having all the milk he took such care producing dumped into anonymous tanks with that of less-conscientious dairymen, the sixty-two-year-old Fiscalini decided to begin making farmstead cheese. He flubbed his first attempt at making a Fontina-style product. The brilliant, yellow result bore only a faint resemblance to Fontina, but customers loved it. Fiscalini has been replicating his error ever since, and San Joaquin Gold—a "gold medal mistake"—has become a popular seller in high-end grocery stores and grocery shops throughout the country and has won top honors in national competitions. Fiscalini has received even higher acclaim for his cloth-wrapped English-style cheddar, an extra-mature cheese that took first place in the 2007 World Cheese Awards in London.

At a time when other Central Valley dairies are cutting back or going out of business, Fiscalini has his eyes on expansion. He recently installed a system to reduce greenhouse gas emissions by converting manure into enough methane gas to fuel an engine that generates nearly three times as much electricity as his farm uses. He has drawn up plans for an underground cave and an expanded cheesemaking facility, complete with a visitors' center. His goal is to continue to grow that side of his business until every drop of the milk produced by the 1,500 cows on his farm is made into cheese, up from the current level of about 10 percent. He hopes that marketing Fiscalini Farmstead Cheese will encourage his two daughters who "don't like shoving their arm up a cow's rectum or getting their clothes covered in manure" to stay on the farm.

On the eastern side of the valley, beneath blazing sunshine and cloudless skies, with the gleaming white peaks of Yosemite in the background, apricot trees grow in neat rows around John Driver's house. Producing apricots that people genuinely like, Driver insists, is the only way a small grower like him can survive in competition with "the big boys."

"The world's richest agricultural valley," as the late University of California Berkeley geographer James J. Parsons called it, is a throbbing food-generating machine that pumps out poultry, beef, dairy products, and more than 250 different crops: oranges, lemons, apricots, peaches, plums, cherries, apples, figs, almonds, walnuts, pistachios, asparagus, avocados, grapes, onions, lettuce, artichokes, zucchini, and tomatoes, to list a sampling.

To find an apricot that would trump the rest, Driver, a plant geneticist in his late fifties who also grows walnuts and almonds, scoured the valleys of Central Asia. Nowhere else comes close to having the genetic variation found there. For more than a decade, Driver brought the seeds of ultra-sweet, intensely flavored specimens back to his orchards, seeking varieties that would flourish. By 2006 he had found trees that met his standards. Picked when fully ripe (unlike conventional apricots that are harvested green), Driver's apricots, branded as CandyCots, are sold in San Francisco's Ferry Plaza Farmer's Market and through Whole Foods Markets and specialty fruit stores in Los Angeles and New York.

Driver laid out several on his dining-room table. They were smaller than usual apricots—about the size of golf balls—and had deeply orange, almost persimmon-colored flesh. The intensity of their sweetness was an epiphany, with a bright edge and a complex background of floral and spicy flavors. "Frankly, most apricots sold are really bad," said Driver. "They are just decorations for the grocery store. I can't eat them, and consumers don't like them."

On the opposite side of the valley from Driver's orchards, Robin Koda and her brother, Ross, are going against the grain of industrial agriculture, literally. The Kodas have been successfully growing and milling artisanal rice near Los Banos for three generations. After their grandfather successfully developed a rice business in the 1920s and 1930s, the farm was stripped to nothing when he was forced into an internment camp during the Second World War. After the war, his sons rebuilt the operation. According to Robin, they developed the first commercially grown sweet rice in the United States and the first premium medium-grain rice, called Kokuho Rose.

"To most Americans, rice is just filler," said Robin. To change that attitude, the Kodas have had to master all aspects of the business: they are plant breeders, seed producers, farmers, millers, and marketers. When I visited, the fields were freshly plowed. Planting—mid May—was still weeks away. In a long, low building, hundreds of numbered paper bags were lined up on the floor, each topped by a few stalks of rice with the grains still attached. Every bag, Ross explained, represented a sample taken from the previous year's harvest. At the beginning of each season, he painstakingly examines each one, selecting only those that meet the exacting standards set down by his father, and grading each batch like a strict schoolmaster. If the grains are of uneven size, if there are too many broken grains, if overly white "chalky" grains are present—the sample fails and is discarded. Then he takes the best and grows them for three seasons in test plots until he has amassed enough seed to sow all of his fields. From an industrial farming perspective, Kokuho Rose is a loser: slow to mature, low yielding, and too tall. From a culinary perspective, it shines with subtle floral flavors. Martha Stewart has praised it as the best sushi rice on the market.

In the foothills of the Sierra Nevada, Seth Nitschke is raising beef cattle "the way God intended"—eating grass on pastures near the hamlet of Cherry Valley. Conventional cattle are shipped off to vast feedlots. Earlier I had driven past one near Coalinga owned by Harris Ranch: a black, muddy, fetid square mile packed with nearly 100,000 cattle, not a tree or blade of grass in sight.

"The way I do it is more expensive and takes longer, but the cattle get fat, and we produce a better product. The cows are not maxed out to all their livers can handle. We don't need hormones or antibiotics," Nitschke said. From the crown of his worn Stetson to the pointy toes of his boots, he is every inch a cowboy. A 1999 graduate in livestock management from California Polytechnic State University, he became familiar with the industrial side of meat production during a stint as a cattle buyer for Excel Fresh Meats, a division of agribusiness giant Cargill. He took a 180-degree turn five years ago when he decided to strike out on his own.

The day I was with him, Nitschke had a problem that the folks at the Harris feedlot never face: He couldn't find his cattle. We set off on his mud-spattered all-terrain vehicle, me holding on to the bucking contraption for dear life as we bounced over streambeds and blasted up steep hillsides of Mariposa Ranch, the 1,100-acre tract that he leases. Stopping near a copse of oaks, Nitschke cupped his hands to his mouth and issued an authentic moo. Within minutes, several dozen stocky, black cows emerged from the woods. "The real cowboys say that I'm producing 'hippie chow,'" Nitschke said. "But I have a whole lot of customers who love what I do, and I sleep well at night."

On my last day in the valley, I stopped into the Escalon Livestock Market, which bills itself as the strongest livestock market in the valley. Brawny pickup trucks and cattle trailers filled the parking lot, and the air was thick with the aroma of manure. A cacophony of bellowing and bawling and mooing came from the auction barn. In the theater-like auditorium, enormous Holstein cows were paraded one by one into a small corral while an auctioneer rattled along in a nonstop chant. I couldn't understand a word, but the rest of the audience, mostly cowboy-hatted professional buyers, did, and each cow had but a few seconds in the limelight before changing hands and being driven out to make way for the next animal on the block.

Out of my depth, I wandered outside and found myself at Escalon's weekly small-animal auction, where the atmosphere was more like a country fair, right down to the aroma of deep-fried food emanating from the snack bar. A crowd made up of suburban farmers, aging hippies, twentysomething back-to-the-landers, wide-eyed toddlers, Mexican women, youthful 4-H club members, and curiosity seekers strolled among cages of chickens, ducks, turkeys, quail, geese, and rabbits.

The contrast couldn't have been sharper or more typical of the paradox that is the Central Valley: two auctions, two different worlds—united only by their common connection to food production.

4

The Art of Food Writing

Melanie Acevedo

Everybody's a Critic

Food writing takes a variety of forms, from a memoir of a respected chef's life in the kitchen to the Internet critic who praises or pans a restaurant on a community review website. The quality and purpose of food writing varies greatly between sources. Some instructional books, such as Irma S. Rombauer's *Joy of Cooking* (1931), have sold millions of copies and have influenced the cooking and eating habits of generations, while a food columnist working for a small community newspaper or a budding food blogger might have an audience small enough to fit in a single restaurant.

Food writing is a multifaceted endeavor that spans the range of publishing outlets, from academic texts to newspapers and blogs, and there are thousands of individuals around the world either working as food writers or attempting to enter the field. Books about food, including cookbooks, historical texts, and memoirs, continue to garner high sales, ranking just behind self-help books and romance novels.

Food writing is also an evolving field, partially because of widespread changes in the way that humans view food. Modern food writers have come to embrace a more informed perspective on the ecological, sociological, and biological aspects of the food industry, and there is an increasing tendency to look more critically at commercial food production and to explore alternative methods of cooking and eating. In addition, the potential health-and-wellness issues surrounding food have developed into a strong subfield, producing hundreds of books and articles on subjects ranging from vegan dining to the health benefits of eating acai berries or flaxseed.

Another factor that has played a major role in the evolution of food writing is the growing dominance of Internet publishing and communication. When print publications were the rule, only a small number of writers had the potential to reach an audience, whereas the ease of access and democratic nature of the Internet has vastly expanded the space available to potential food critics, recipe makers, and others peripherally involved in the industry. Today, many of the respected critics and columnists who once published only in ink have adjusted to the technological revolution, producing web versions of articles, Facebook and Twitter posts, and blogs to supplement their columns.

Why Does Food Writing Matter?

Whether approached from an economic, historical, biological, or sociological perspective, it is easy to argue that food writing occupies an important place in American culture. Humans, like all animals, spend much of their lives concerned with food, in no small way motivated by the fact that organisms must eat to remain alive. Meeting daily food requirements takes up a considerable amount of time, especially given the modern options available concerning what and how to eat. If you add up the amount of time a person spends eating, cooking, food shopping, and thinking about food, researchers calculate that at least eight to ten years of an average seventy-year lifespan are spent dwelling on the subject.

From a historical perspective, many of the major events that have shaped human culture have hinged on the evolution of the food industry. Consider, for instance, George Orwell's assertion in *The Road to Wigan Pier* (1937) that World War I could never have occurred if not for the development of the first prepackaged food. In addition, food is intimately linked to many of humanity's cherished cultural rituals, from wedding cakes to the concept of "Sunday brunch." The way we eat plays a major role in determining the way our culture functions at any point in time.

Food writers sometimes write directly about the multifaceted role of food in history, culture, and society, but often focus on more proximate goals, examining a single recipe, restaurant, or dining trend. In both cases, a food writer functions as a documentarian, committing aspects of cultural and social development to record. A new trend in pasta preparation or the opening and closing of a neighborhood bistro is not only important to the immediate community but also may have greater significance to the way society is changing as a whole. Add to this the fact that the economic well-being of a restaurant or chef, or even a community, can hinge on the preferences of food columnists, and the importance of the food-writing industry becomes apparent on many levels.

Although food and food culture may be of central importance to human life, food writing is, at least in some sense, an unnecessary feature. Even in a small, remote village, food culture continues to evolve and change as recipes are passed down between families and friends. Food writing is second order, constituting an optional dimension to food culture in general. However, for those who have access to food writing, whether through books, articles, or the Internet, the experience of cooking and eating has the potential to be greatly enhanced.

What Makes a Good Food Writer

The best food writers are capable of addressing the complex relationship between food and culture without losing sight of the more immediate pleasures of cooking and eating. Writer Mark Kurlansky, for instance, in his book *Cod* (1997), explores the history and the ecological and social ramifications of cod fishing from ancient to modern times while simultaneously providing recipes that do not fail to communicate the more visceral appeal of cod as a dining option. In the same vein, writer Michael Pollan, author of books like *The Omnivore's Dilemma* (2006), explores the social and environmental aspects of our food choices but still manages to communicate the sensual pleasures that surround the experience of eating.

Another important category of food writing is the creation of cookbooks and recipe collections. These books, such as the groundbreaking *Joy of Cooking*, have a major influence on human culture, helping would-be cooks to improve their craft, sample cuisine from around the world, and expand beyond the bounds of what they were taught by parents or peers. A cookbook writer must balance providing enticing descriptions of dishes with offering clear and concise instructions, such that a reader with average skill can follow the recipe. The most successful cookbooks are those that introduce excellent food and complex recipes while remaining accessible to a range of readers.

Cookbooks and books on various types of cuisine may also be successful because they are written by (or based on the work of) famous food personalities, including television chefs like Rachael Ray, Wolfgang Puck, and Emeril Lagasse. The phenomenon of celebrity chefs has added a new dimension to the food-writing industry, as articles and books written by famous personalities gain disproportionate appeal compared to publications by chefs who are generally agreed to have more skill, but have not achieved celebrity status.

There are a smaller number of food writers who work as cooking instructors or professional chefs and who have gained renown within the food community for the quality of their cuisine and skill in teaching. An example is Madeleine Kamman, founder of the American School of Chefs and author of numerous volumes about cooking. Kamman is regarded as one of the world's top cooking instructors, and her books appeal to many aspiring chefs, though she has never achieved the popularity of television chefs such as Bobby Flay. Kamman's success as a writer stems from her tendency to teach students not only to replicate recipes or techniques but also to develop the capacity to think like a chef when confronted with challenges. Another author whose work has found an audience among many professional chefs and gourmands is Giuliano Bugialli, whose books on Italian cuisine are considered among the best on the subject. Like Kamman, Bugialli concentrates on teaching students to master the foundational skills that can be applied to any recipe.

Another category of food writers is the professional critic who publishes in newspapers, in magazines, and on websites. While some critics are professional chefs and/or hold degrees in cooking or food-related fields, many are professional journalists whose skills lie in their ability to describe the eating and dining experience for readers. Though they are generally adept with creative descriptions of food and ambiance, food critics also remain cognizant of their function as a news source, keeping diners aware of changes in their restaurant environment and also supporting the restaurant business by driving traffic and helping spread the word about new businesses.

Pete Wells, lead food critic for the *New York Times*, and Jonathan Gold, of the *Los Angeles Times*, are consistently ranked by peers, readers, and restaurateurs as two of the world's top restaurant critics. Though neither has any credentials to establish himself as having better "taste" than the average reader, both have demonstrated an ability to describe the details of a dining experience in a way that appeals to their audience.

The Role of Critics in Food Culture

Whether specifically qualified or not, food critics can have a dramatic effect on the success or failure of a restaurant, and many professionals and diners alike have questioned whether our society's faith in the role of the food critic may be misplaced. After a 2012 article in which critic Wells gave a scathing review of celebrity chef Guy Fieri's new restaurant in Manhattan, Fieri publicly attacked Wells, claiming that the reviewer had an "agenda" and did not deliver a fair review. In his own defense, Wells revealed much of his reviewing process, including the fact that he generally visits a restaurant on three separate occasions in an effort to get an accurate understanding of the food. In the case of Fieri's restaurant, Wells visited four times before committing to his opinions. In addition, Wells often takes the experiences of his friends and fellow diners into account before writing a review.

After years visiting and writing about restaurants, professional critics develop expertise that sets them apart from casual diners. In addition, food writers often research the history and culture of food for their articles, and this gives them a unique perspective from which to evaluate a restaurant. However, despite the qualifications of the critic, judging food is not a science, and every review is in part based on subjective opinion and personal taste. A review can be a useful guide, especially when a reader knows and trusts the opinions of a specific reviewer, but a wise eater will realize that a review is no substitute for firsthand experience.

Food Writing in the Internet Age

When considering the role of the food critic in the modern age, it should be noted that the public has taken on much of this role because of the prevalence of website reviews and community guides such as Yelp! In many cases, diners considering a potential restaurant take their cues from anonymous reviews posted on websites and in amateur food blogs that can be easily found through a basic Internet search. In addition, thousands of would-be food critics post their thoughts on everything from local restaurants to health-food trends and global food production.

Taken as a whole, the democratic participation in the Internet has brought about massive changes in the food-writing industry. Many professional critics, columnists, and cookbook authors now publish Internet versions of their work, or supplement their writing with blogs, Facebook, and Twitter participation. Public restaurant review sites have come to have a dominant influence in determining the dining habits of the general public and have had an equally significant effect on the economics of the restaurant industry. A new restaurant unlucky enough to receive only negative reviews on a popular review site in its first week may suffer from greatly reduced customer flow, at least until another reviewer comes along to balance the scales. Many restaurateurs have friends or colleagues post positive reviews on these same public review sites, eroding the reliability of the system.

The influence of the Internet and the subsequent expansion of the food-writing phenomenon has both positive and negative aspects. For one, aspiring food writers and chefs have a new and exciting platform through which to market themselves and their work. In addition, Internet recipe sites provide instant access to thousands of quality recipes, many of which would have been difficult or impossible to acquire before Internet research became the norm. Review sites also help many users avoid unfortunate dining experiences and continue to become more useful as thousands of new contributors add to these sites each month.

On the negative side, the influx of amateur food writing dilutes the field, often reducing the sales of professional cookbooks and making it more difficult for professional critics and columnists to find gainful employment. In addition, the anonymity and ease of posting one's opinions on the Internet increases the likelihood that an individual will publish a review colored by an unrelated bad mood or that a writer will misrepresent a recipe through some mistake that might have been caught by an editor in a professional setting. On any site that allows public commentary, from Facebook pages to community guides, some of those who post are motivated by a personal agenda, hoping to use the public space to demonstrate their expertise, intelligence, and wit. At first glance, this may be no different from what professional critics do, but the professional critics are tempered by editors and constrained by policies, such as visiting a restaurant numerous times before writing a review.

In terms of the history of food writing, the Internet and public participation in criticism is a relatively recent phenomenon, but most have already learned that Internet commentary should be treated as suspect by nature. Even though the public is now assuming a greater role in determining what is good or bad in the realm of food, the anonymous diner can never replace the expertise of a professional food writer.

Incredible Edibles

By Kim Honey
TheStar.com, July 28, 2008

It was time to kill the fluffy bunny. Mine had blond fur and little black eyes. It was cute, but I wanted to eat it.

The cooking demonstration began with instructions on how to dispatch the rabbit with one humane blow to the skull. I gathered its back legs into my fist, turned it upside down and held it out to the side. It started to wiggle and Gino Ferri, an expert in wild food, had to help me regain my grip.

"The point is if you're a cook and a chef, you have to do it the whole way through," says Ferri, director of Survival in the Bush, a wilderness survival school in Hanover, sixty kilometers south of Owen Sound.

I had mentally prepared by thinking about the fish I had caught as a kid and how I bashed their heads on the side of the boat, slit open their glistening bellies and gutted them. Fish may not have faces, but they do bleed.

The bunny part didn't faze me because I had eaten rabbit in a tiny Greek village where it arrived on a platter along with the charred head. It was the first time I had seen the eye sockets of the animal I was about to eat.

I calmed the rabbit by putting it on my chest. Ferri, who has a PhD in psychology, has seen soldiers who served in Bosnia almost break into tears at this point—even battle-hardened men are unnerved by the death of a defenseless animal.

As my right arm began its downward arc, thick stick in my left hand, I hesitated. In an instant and without thought, my killer hit turned into a tap on the temple. The rabbit wasn't even stunned.

I lost my nerve and handed it over to Ferri, who killed it with three sharp hits.

"I'm still tied up in knots every time I dispatch an animal," said Ferri, who makes sure every bit of the animal is used.

But eat we must, and if we eat meat, there will be blood.

For most of his sixty-three years, Ferri has been hunting and gathering wild food. After he immigrated to Toronto from Italy, "Anglo-Saxon" kids made fun of his family for gathering dandelion and chicory for salad. The Don River Valley was his playground, where he hunted pheasant with bow and arrow, snared rabbits and fished.

Now it's illegal to trap, snare or shoot a wild animal in Toronto and the city is overrun with cottontail rabbits. You can't walk out the back door without staring down a couple of haughty raccoons, and Lake Shore Blvd. is like Canada's Wonderland for geese.

When I took the food editor's job earlier this year, "local" food had become a cliché and the 100-mile diet was a hackneyed phrase.

As I idly observed the scourge of the city waddling along the waterfront one day, it suddenly occurred to me that we could probably eat them.

I realized the so-called locavores had skipped over the most fundamental victuals: the uncultivated plants and undomesticated creatures that share our urban spaces. What could be more local than nature's bounty?

Eating wild in the city presents a modern conundrum. Canada geese are not poisonous, but no one would suggest a bird that has been snacking on Wonder Bread in water not fit for humans would be good eating. Ditto plants that grow in contaminated soil. As Michael Pollan, the latest philosopher-king of food, says: "You are what you eat eats."

I began at High Park Nature Centre, where I learn garlic mustard (*Brassica spp.*) is a highly invasive plant that crowds out native species such as the trillium. I make a pesto with it, which is pungent and a bit on the bitter side, but definitely novel and delicious on pasta.

A few days later, Ferri arrives in Toronto bearing garden snails, wild leeks and wild oregano. After a wash in the *Toronto Star* test kitchen, the mollusks slowly high-tailed it toward the walls of the sink. My stomach did a flip, but I boiled them for an hour and sautéed them in garlic and butter. It was hard to choke them down. The image of them strolling around my sink turned me off, to be honest.

We made a trip to Sunnybrook Park at Eglinton Ave. and Leslie St. Within thirty minutes, just a few hundred meters from the parking lot, Ferri identified thirty-one edible wild plants, including wild spinach, chicory and shepherd's purse, most of which we would consider weeds.

He pulled up a plant to show me a tiny root the diameter of a pencil. A millisecond after he sliced it open, the unmistakable smell of carrot hit my olfactory lobes. I had no idea Queen Anne's lace is also known as wild carrot. My mouth watered, but he could tell the place had been sprayed in the past 5 to 10 years so he warned me off.

Ferri sounded sad. "You see the irony: Here we have all this food and we can't eat it."

That's when I decided on a trip to the country. Since it wasn't rabbit-hunting season, we had to settle for a farm-raised stand-in.

The bunny's body was warm when I cut off the head and feet, peeled off the skin like a glove, and gutted it. Then I butchered that rabbit like a straight-A anatomy student.

The firepit Ferri had built for the cooking demonstration was ready. We cut the rabbit in quarters, added some to a stew pot and put the rest into a foil packet with potatoes, wild leeks, carrots and potatoes.

> *I realized the so-called locavores had skipped over the most fundamental victuals: the uncultivated plants and undomesticated creatures that share our urban spaces.*

There was a rainbow trout to fillet and wild turkey to prepare. After burying it all underground for an hour, we dug it up for the feast, which we ate on the grounds of the Saugeen Valley Conservation Authority, just ten meters from the killing field.

The firepit rabbit was moist and succulent. The wild leeks were roasted perfection and enhanced the meat's mild flavor. No visions of live rabbits hopped through my head.

Ferri said hunter-gatherer diets were 70 percent plants. It is obvious the modern omnivore probably eats more meat than his forbears. I know we don't need to kill rabbits to eat, but why not eat rabbits?

As nutrition becomes a science, we continue to measure and analyze our diets. What we are missing is intangible. Food may fuel our bodies, but once energized, our ponderous brains will ruminate.

Eating is about what makes us feel good. Feeling good can be all about taste, but taste is heightened or depressed by what we think about food and why we feel the way we do.

I have learned it's a wild world out there.

Somewhere, not too far away, there's a pristine wild carrot with my name on it that would be sublime in a wild rabbit stew.

Should Food Critics Be Anonymous?
My Talk with Jonathan Kauffman

By John Birdsall
CHOW.com, July 30, 2012

The anonymous restaurant critic was an innovation of the 1960s, when consumer protection was as fashionable as giggly grass-smoking parties in suburban living rooms, and to our glassy eyes now, about as quaint.

The idea was that nobody dropping money in a restaurant should be treated like they didn't matter, so restaurant critics would pretend to be nobodies and report what happened. Mimi Sheraton was the *New York Times'* no-bullshit everyman; Gael Greene and Ruth Reichl wore disguises (though, come on, wouldn't a lady in sunglasses and a Carol Channing wig provoke more suspicion than she squelched?). But these days, anonymous critics stand a good chance of getting busted, either because Eater or some raging restaurant owner will out them, or else they'll win a Pulitzer and be photographed drinking Champagne from a clowny glass, or because they simply cannot spend a decade as a critic without everybody eventually getting to know their face.

Plus the demands on writers to make money means that sooner or later, tape is gonna roll—ask food and travel writer Brad A. Johnson, the one-time *Angeleno* critic who's about to host a TV reality show. If you're a younger writer, taking a critic's job means reverse-engineering a state of official anonymity, prorated from the time you took the gig, marked by swapping out your full-frontal avatar on Twitter for a less revealing one. These days, as Elvis Costello sang on an album called *Momofuku* that was somehow not about David Chang or Christina Tosi, there is no hiding place.

Village Voice critic Robert Sietsema might be the most famous of the anonymous left standing, but that hasn't stopped him from getting in front of a camera. Sietsema donned his now-shticky satanic half-mask to cook pasta in a 2010 CHOW video, in which he called himself one of the last anonymous restaurant critics "on the face of the Earth." That sounded sadly post-apocalyptic.

In May, Sietsema's post-apocalypse got a little lonelier, as one of American food writing's faceless holdouts outed himself. Jonathan Kauffman managed to hold on to his anonymity for more than a decade—Kauffman worked in the Village Voice Media stable as a food writer and critic for more than a decade, has a James Beard medal dangling on a wall somewhere, and like Sietsema, was one of America's last diligently anonymous critics. His final faceless gig was as critic and staff writer for *SF Weekly* in San Francisco, where Kauffman and I worked together (before that,

I succeeded him as restaurant critic at Oakland-based *East Bay Express*). Anony-mous no more, Kauffman's now San Francisco editor of TastingTable.com, an email newsletter with regional and national editions. He's got a fantastic San Francisco–focused food blog, too.

I invited Kauffman out recently. Over coffee, I asked him if it felt weird to finally reveal his face after more than a decade of paranoia, whether the age of anonymity is truly over, and if anybody outside the industry even cares about an old-fashioned thing like a food critic's ethics anymore.

Birdsall: So, you swapped out your generic Twitter avatar for a smiling headshot . . .

Kauffman: That was a strange moment.

Birdsall: Did you feel weirdly naked?

Kauffman: Exposed, yeah.

Birdsall: But did you also feel relieved not to have to hide anymore? The few times I went out to eat with you, before I took over your critic job at the *[East Bay] Express*, I think I inadvertently blurted out something about food writing—nothing that would ever have busted you, but I think you were really freaked out that I'd somehow exposed you.

Kauffman: *(laughs)* I totally was paranoid, I know! Kind of ridiculously so, and I would make fun of it myself. Sometimes I feel like that was being megalomaniacal, but other times I look at the fact that I lasted eleven years and I was never outed.

I think there's always been this tension with being anonymous. I think that anonym-ity made me a more fearless, honest critic. That doesn't mean it holds true for every-one—there are critics whose faces who are well known who aren't afraid to be brutally honest about a restaurant's failures (in Britain, particularly, where restaurant criticism is a blood sport). But for me, it seemed to be the condition that allowed me to write most frankly—keeping readers, instead of people in the industry, in mind.

Birdsall: But being known—even if it's just having some Facebook photos out there, and not being exactly sure if anybody in a restaurant recognizes you—couldn't that make you a more responsible critic, in a way? More likely to temper your judgments, since you'd be personally more answerable? Less likely to lob bombs at a restaurant, or deliver cheap shots while hiding behind anonymity?

Kauffman: Sure, if that's the type of person you are, and those are the kinds of checks that are going to keep you fair rather than nasty. Even in the age of Facebook, JPEGs, and critic-busting blogs, what I think is even more important than actual anonymity of the Michelin guide kind is the *practice* of anonymity: Making reservations and paying under other names, keeping a low profile, not attending public events, keeping personal relationships with restaurant people to a minimum. Restaurant critics often have more in common, interest wise, with industry people than the general public does. We're both insiders in one way or another. But it's easy for those shared interests to feel like alliances, which may sway reviews independently of the actual dining experience.

Birdsall: But the whole job model for a critic changed at some point in the last ten years—didn't it?—when the restaurant critic couldn't just be this purely isolated, purely anonymous writer anymore. They also had to do food journalism, even do their own research for the restaurant review, like calling up to check the hours and staff names. There used to be paid assistants or interns to do stuff like that, but the economics changed.

Kauffman: Well, I always had to have a secondary column, a reported column—that was always part of our responsibilities. So there was a certain amount of reporting I always had to do. I just chose my stories differently so I didn't have to talk with chefs so I could try and break scoops. That just wasn't who I was.

Also, frankly, the practice of anonymity can be a marketing tool for a restaurant critic. I certainly have had numbers of people in the industry tell me that my devotion to it earned their respect. Outside the industry, well—whether anonymity has benefited me as a writer in the long run, since many general readers don't pay close attention to bylines, who knows? Guess I'll find out soon enough.

The Food Movement, Rising

By Michael Pollan
NY Review of Books, August 19, 2010

1. Food Made Visible

It might sound odd to say this about something people deal with at least three times a day, but food in America has been more or less invisible, politically speaking, until very recently. At least until the early 1970s, when a bout of food price inflation and the appearance of books critical of industrial agriculture (by Wendell Berry, Frances Moore Lappé, and Barry Commoner, among others) threatened to propel the subject to the top of the national agenda, Americans have not had to think very hard about where their food comes from, or what it is doing to the planet, their bodies, and their society.

Most people count this a blessing. Americans spend a smaller percentage of their income on food than any people in history—slightly less than 10 percent—and a smaller amount of their time preparing it: a mere thirty-one minutes a day on average, including clean-up. The supermarkets brim with produce summoned from every corner of the globe, a steady stream of novel food products (17,000 new ones each year) crowds the middle aisles, and in the freezer case you can find "home meal replacements" in every conceivable ethnic stripe, demanding nothing more of the eater than opening the package and waiting for the microwave to chirp. Considered in the long sweep of human history, in which getting food dominated not just daily life but economic and political life as well, having to worry about food as little as we do, or did, seems almost a kind of dream.

The dream that the age-old "food problem" had been largely solved for most Americans was sustained by the tremendous postwar increases in the productivity of American farmers, made possible by cheap fossil fuel (the key ingredient in both chemical fertilizers and pesticides) and changes in agricultural policies. Asked by President Nixon to try to drive down the cost of food after it had spiked in the early 1970s, Agriculture Secretary Earl Butz shifted the historical focus of federal farm policy from supporting prices for farmers to boosting yields of a small handful of commodity crops (corn and soy especially) at any cost.

The administration's cheap food policy worked almost too well: crop prices fell, forcing farmers to produce still more simply to break even. This led to a deep depression in the farm belt in the 1980s followed by a brutal wave of consolidation. Most importantly, the price of food came down, or at least the price of the kinds of foods that could be made from corn and soy: processed foods and sweetened beverages and feedlot meat. (Prices for fresh produce have increased since the 1980s.) Washington had succeeded in eliminating food as a political issue—an objective dear to most governments at least since the time of the French Revolution.

But although cheap food is good politics, it turns out there are significant costs—to the environment, to public health, to the public purse, even to the culture—and as these became impossible to ignore in recent years, food has come back into view. Beginning in the late 1980s, a series of food safety scandals opened people's eyes to the way their food was being produced, each one drawing the curtain back a little further on a food system that had changed beyond recognition. When BSE, or mad cow disease, surfaced in England in 1986, Americans learned that cattle, which are herbivores, were routinely being fed the flesh of other cattle; the practice helped keep meat cheap but at the risk of a hideous brain-wasting disease.

The 1993 deaths of four children in Washington State who had eaten hamburgers from Jack in the Box were traced to meat contaminated with *E.coli* 0157:H7, a mutant strain of the common intestinal bacteria first identified in feedlot cattle in 1982. Since then, repeated outbreaks of food-borne illness linked to new antibiotic-resistant strains of bacteria (campylobacter, salmonella, MRSA) have turned a bright light on the shortsighted practice of routinely administering antibiotics to food animals, not to treat disease but simply to speed their growth and allow them to withstand the filthy and stressful conditions in which they live.

In the wake of these food safety scandals, the conversation about food politics that briefly flourished in the 1970s was picked up again in a series of books, articles, and movies about the consequences of industrial food production. Beginning in 2001 with the publication of Eric Schlosser's *Fast Food Nation*, a surprise bestseller, and, the following year, Marion Nestle's *Food Politics*, the food journalism of the last decade has succeeded in making clear and telling connections between the methods of industrial food production, agricultural policy, food-borne illness, childhood obesity, the decline of the family meal as an institution, and, notably, the decline of family income beginning in the 1970s.

Besides drawing women into the work force, falling wages made fast food both cheap to produce and a welcome, if not indispensible, option for pinched and harried families. The picture of the food economy Schlosser painted resembles an upside-down version of the social compact sometimes referred to as "Fordism": instead of paying workers well enough to allow them to buy things like cars, as Henry Ford proposed to do, companies like Wal-Mart and McDonald's pay their workers so poorly that they can afford *only* the cheap, low-quality food these companies sell, creating a kind of nonvirtuous circle driving down both wages and the quality of food. The advent of fast food (and cheap food in general) has, in effect, subsidized the decline of family incomes in America.

2. Food Politics

Cheap food has become an indispensable pillar of the modern economy. But it is no longer an invisible or uncontested one. One of the most interesting social movements to emerge in the last few years is the "food movement," or perhaps I should say "movements," since it is unified as yet by little more than the recognition that industrial food production is in need of reform because its social/environmental/public health/animal welfare/gastronomic costs are too high.

As that list suggests, the critics are coming at the issue from a great many different directions. Where many social movements tend to splinter as time goes on, breaking into various factions representing divergent concerns or tactics, the food movement starts out splintered. Among the many threads of advocacy that can be lumped together under that rubric we can include school lunch reform; the campaign for animal rights and welfare; the campaign against genetically modified crops; the rise of organic and locally produced food; efforts to combat obesity and type 2 diabetes; "food sovereignty" (the principle that nations should be allowed to decide their agricultural policies rather than submit to free trade regimes); farm bill reform; food safety regulation; farmland preservation; student organizing around food issues on campus; efforts to promote urban agriculture and ensure that communities have access to healthy food; initiatives to create gardens and cooking classes in schools; farm worker rights; nutrition labeling; feedlot pollution; and the various efforts to regulate food ingredients and marketing, especially to kids.

It's a big, lumpy tent, and sometimes the various factions beneath it work at cross-purposes. For example, activists working to strengthen federal food safety regulations have recently run afoul of local food advocates, who fear that the burden of new regulation will cripple the current revival of small-farm agriculture. Joel Salatin, the Virginia meat producer and writer who has become a hero to the food movement, fulminates against food safety regulation on libertarian grounds in his *Everything I Want to Do Is Illegal: War Stories from the Local Food Front.* Hunger activists like Joel Berg, in *All You Can Eat: How Hungry Is America?*, criticize supporters of "sustainable" agriculture—i.e., producing food in ways that do not harm the environment—for advocating reforms that threaten to raise the cost of food to the poor. Animal rights advocates occasionally pick fights with sustainable meat producers (such as Joel Salatin), as Jonathan Safran Foer does in his recent vegetarian polemic, *Eating Animals.*

But there are indications that these various voices may be coming together in something that looks more and more like a coherent movement. Many in the animal welfare movement, from PETA to Peter Singer, have come to see that a smaller-scale, more humane animal agriculture is a goal worth fighting for, and surely more attainable than the abolition of meat eating. Stung by charges of elitism, activists for sustainable farming are starting to take seriously the problem of hunger and poverty. They're promoting schemes and policies to make fresh local food more accessible to the poor, through programs that give vouchers redeemable at farmers' markets to participants in the Special Supplemental Nutrition Program for Women, Infants, and Children (WIC) and food stamp recipients. Yet a few underlying tensions remain: the "hunger lobby" has traditionally supported farm subsidies in exchange for the farm lobby's support of nutrition programs, a marriage of convenience dating to the 1960s that vastly complicates reform of the farm bill—a top priority for the food movement.

The sociologist Troy Duster reminds us of an all-important axiom about social movements: "No movement is as coherent and integrated as it seems from afar," he says, "and no movement is as incoherent and fractured as it seems from up close." Viewed from a middle distance, then, the food movement coalesces around the recognition that today's food and farming economy is "unsustainable"—that it can't go on in its current form much longer without courting a breakdown of some kind, whether environmental, economic, or both.

For some in the movement, the more urgent problem is environmental: the food system consumes more fossil fuel energy than we can count on in the future (about a fifth of the total American use of such energy) and emits more greenhouse gas than we can afford to emit, particularly since agriculture is the one human system that *should* be able to substantially rely on photosynthesis: solar energy. It will be difficult if not impossible to address the issue of climate change without reforming the food system. This is a conclusion that has only recently been embraced by the environmental movement, which historically has disdained all agriculture as a lapse from wilderness and a source of pollution. But in the last few years, several of the major environmental groups have come to appreciate that a diversified, sustainable agriculture—which can sequester large amounts of carbon in the soil—holds the potential not just to mitigate but actually to help solve environmental problems, including climate change. Today, environmental organizations like the Natural Resources Defense Council and the Environmental Working Group are taking up the cause of food system reform, lending their expertise and clout to the movement.

But perhaps the food movement's strongest claim on public attention today is the fact that the American diet of highly processed food laced with added fats and sugars is responsible for the epidemic of chronic diseases that threatens to bankrupt the health care system. The Centers for Disease Control estimates that fully three quarters of US health care spending goes to treat chronic diseases, most of which are preventable and linked to diet: heart disease, stroke, type 2 diabetes, and at least a third of all cancers. The health care crisis probably cannot be addressed without addressing the catastrophe of the American diet, and that diet is the direct (even if unintended) result of the way that our agriculture and food industries have been organized.

Michelle Obama's recent foray into food politics, beginning with the organic garden she planted on the White House lawn last spring, suggests that the administration has made these connections. Her new "Let's Move" campaign to combat childhood obesity might at first blush seem fairly anodyne, but in announcing the initiative in February, and in a surprisingly tough speech to the Grocery Manufacturers Association in March, the First Lady has effectively shifted the conversation about diet from the industry's preferred ground of "personal responsibility" and exercise to a frank discussion of the way food is produced and marketed. "We need you not just to tweak around the edges," she told the assembled food makers, "but to entirely rethink the products that you're offering, the information that you provide about these products, and how you market those products to our children."

Mrs. Obama explicitly rejected the conventional argument that the food industry is merely giving people the sugary, fatty, and salty foods they want, contending that

> *Viewed from a middle distance, then, the food movement coalesces around the recognition that today's food and farming economy is "unsustainable"— that it can't go on in its current form much longer without courting a breakdown of some kind, whether environmental, economic, or both.*

the industry "doesn't just respond to people's natural inclinations—it also actually helps to shape them," through the ways it creates products and markets them.

So far at least, Michelle Obama is the food movement's most important ally in the administration, but there are signs of interest elsewhere. Under Commissioner Margaret Hamburg, the FDA has cracked down on deceptive food marketing and is said to be weighing a ban on the nontherapeutic use of antibiotics in factory farming. Attorney General Eric Holder recently avowed the Justice Department's intention to pursue antitrust enforcement in agribusiness, one of the most highly concentrated sectors in the economy. At his side was Agriculture Secretary Tom Vilsack, the former governor of Iowa, who has planted his own organic vegetable garden at the department and launched a new "Know Your Farmer, Know Your Food" initiative aimed at promoting local food systems as a way to both rebuild rural economies and improve access to healthy food.

Though Vilsack has so far left mostly undisturbed his department's traditional deference to industrial agriculture, the new tone in Washington and the appointment of a handful of respected reformers (such as Tufts professor Kathleen Merrigan as deputy secretary of agriculture) has elicited a somewhat defensive, if not panicky, reaction from agribusiness. The Farm Bureau recently urged its members to go on the offensive against "food activists," and a trade association representing pesticide makers called CropLife America wrote to Michelle Obama suggesting that her organic garden had unfairly maligned chemical agriculture and encouraging her to use "crop protection technologies"—i.e., pesticides.

The First Lady's response is not known; however, the President subsequently rewarded CropLife by appointing one of its executives to a high-level trade post. This and other industry-friendly appointments suggest that while the administration may be sympathetic to elements of the food movement's agenda, it isn't about to take on agribusiness, at least not directly, at least until it senses at its back a much larger constituency for reform.

One way to interpret Michelle Obama's deepening involvement in food issues is as an effort to build such a constituency, and in this she may well succeed. It's a mistake to underestimate what a determined First Lady can accomplish. Lady Bird Johnson's "highway beautification" campaign also seemed benign, but in the end it helped raise public consciousness about "the environment" (as it would soon come to be known) and put an end to the public's tolerance for littering. And while Michelle Obama has explicitly limited her efforts to exhortation ("we can't solve this problem by passing a bunch of laws in Washington," she told the Grocery

Manufacturers, no doubt much to their relief), her work is already creating a climate in which just such a "bunch of laws" might flourish: a handful of state legislatures, including California's, are seriously considering levying new taxes on sugar in soft drinks, proposals considered hopelessly extreme less than a year ago.

The political ground is shifting, and the passage of health care reform may accelerate that movement. The bill itself contains a few provisions long promoted by the food movement (like calorie labeling on fast food menus), but more important could be the new political tendencies it sets in motion. If health insurers can no longer keep people with chronic diseases out of their patient pools, it stands to reason that the companies will develop a keener interest in preventing those diseases. They will then discover that they have a large stake in things like soda taxes and in precisely which kinds of calories the farm bill is subsidizing. As the insurance industry and the government take on more responsibility for the cost of treating expensive and largely preventable problems like obesity and type 2 diabetes, pressure for reform of the food system, and the American diet, can be expected to increase.

3. Beyond the Barcode

It would be a mistake to conclude that the food movement's agenda can be reduced to a set of laws, policies, and regulations, important as these may be. What is attracting so many people to the movement today (and young people in particular) is a much less conventional kind of politics, one that is about something more than food. The food movement is also about community, identity, pleasure, and, most notably, about carving out a new social and economic space removed from the influence of big corporations on the one side and government on the other. As the Diggers used to say during their San Francisco be-ins during the 1960s, food can serve as "an edible dynamic"—a means to a political end that is only nominally about food itself.

One can get a taste of this social space simply by hanging around a farmers' market, an activity that a great many people enjoy today regardless of whether they're in the market for a bunch of carrots or a head of lettuce. Farmers' markets are thriving, more than five thousand strong, and there is a lot more going on in them than the exchange of money for food. Someone is collecting signatures on a petition. Someone else is playing music. Children are everywhere, sampling fresh produce, talking to farmers. Friends and acquaintances stop to chat. One sociologist calculated that people have ten times as many conversations at the farmers' market than they do in the supermarket. Socially as well as sensually, the farmers' market offers a remarkably rich and appealing environment. Someone buying food here may be acting not just as a consumer but also as a neighbor, a citizen, a parent, a cook. In many cities and towns, farmers' markets have taken on (and not for the first time) the function of a lively new public square.

Though seldom articulated as such, the attempt to redefine, or escape, the traditional role of consumer has become an important aspiration of the food movement. In various ways it seeks to put the relationship between consumers and producers on a new, more neighborly footing, enriching the kinds of information exchanged in the transaction, and encouraging us to regard our food dollars as "votes" for a different kind of agriculture and, by implication, economy. The modern marketplace would have us decide what to buy strictly on the basis of price and self-interest; the food movement implicitly proposes that we enlarge our understanding of both those terms, suggesting that not just "good value" but ethical and political values should inform our buying decisions, and that we'll get more satisfaction from our eating when they do.

That satisfaction helps to explain why many in the movement don't greet the spectacle of large corporations adopting its goals, as some of them have begun to do, with unalloyed enthusiasm. Already Wal-Mart sells organic and local food, but this doesn't greatly warm the hearts of food movement activists. One important impetus for the movement, or at least its locavore wing—those who are committed to eating as much locally produced food as possible—is the desire to get "beyond the barcode"—to create new economic and social structures outside of the mainstream consumer economy. Though not always articulated in these terms, the local food movement wants to decentralize the global economy, if not secede from it altogether, which is why in some communities, such as Great Barrington, Massachusetts, local currencies (the "BerkShare") have popped up.

In fact it's hard to say which comes first: the desire to promote local agriculture or the desire to promote local economies more generally by cutting ties, to whatever degree possible, to the national economic grid. This is at bottom a communitarian impulse, and it is one that is drawing support from the right as well as the left. Though the food movement has deep roots in the counterculture of the 1960s, its critique of corporate food and federal farm subsidies, as well as its emphasis on building community around food, has won it friends on the right. In his 2006 book *Crunchy Cons*, Rod Dreher identifies a strain of libertarian conservatism, often evangelical, that regards fast food as anathema to family values, and has seized on local food as a kind of culinary counterpart to home schooling.

It makes sense that food and farming should become a locus of attention for Americans disenchanted with consumer capitalism. Food is the place in daily life where corporatization can be most vividly felt: think about the homogenization of taste and experience represented by fast food. By the same token, food offers us one of the shortest, most appealing paths out of the corporate labyrinth, and into the sheer diversity of local flavors, varieties, and characters on offer at the farmers' market.

Put another way, the food movement has set out to foster new forms of civil society. But instead of proposing that space as a counterweight to an overbearing state, as is usually the case, the food movement poses it against the dominance of corporations and their tendency to insinuate themselves into any aspect of our lives from which they can profit. As Wendell Berry writes, the corporations will grow, deliver, and cook your food for you and (just like your mother) beg you to eat it. That they do not yet offer to insert it, prechewed, into your mouth is only because they have found no profitable way to do so.

The corporatization of something as basic and intimate as eating is, for many of us today, a good place to draw the line.

The Italian-born organization Slow Food, founded in 1986 as a protest against the arrival of McDonald's in Rome, represents perhaps the purest expression of these politics. The organization, which now has 100,000 members in 132 countries, began by dedicating itself to "a firm defense of quiet material pleasure" but has lately waded into deeper political and economic waters. Slow Food's founder and president, Carlo Petrini, a former leftist journalist, has much to say about how people's daily food choices can rehabilitate the act of consumption, making it something more creative and progressive. In his new book *Terra Madre: Forging a New Global Network of Sustainable Food Communities*, Petrini urges eaters and food producers to join together in "food communities" outside of the usual distribution channels, which typically communicate little information beyond price and often exploit food producers. A farmers' market is one manifestation of such a community, but Petrini is no mere locavore. Rather, he would have us practice on a global scale something like "local" economics, with its stress on neighborliness, as when, to cite one of his examples, eaters in the affluent West support nomad fisher folk in Mauritania by creating a market for their bottarga, or dried mullet roe. In helping to keep alive such a food tradition and way of life, the eater becomes something more than a consumer; she becomes what Petrini likes to call a "coproducer."

Ever the Italian, Petrini puts pleasure at the center of his politics, which might explain why Slow Food is not always taken as seriously as it deserves to be. For why *shouldn't* pleasure figure in the politics of the food movement? Good food is potentially one of the most democratic pleasures a society can offer, and is one of those subjects, like sports, that people can talk about across lines of class, ethnicity, and race.

The fact that the most humane and most environmentally sustainable choices frequently turn out to be the most delicious choices (as chefs such as Alice Waters and Dan Barber have pointed out) is fortuitous to say the least; it is also a welcome challenge to the more dismal choices typically posed by environmentalism, which most of the time is asking us to give up things we like. As Alice Waters has often said, it was not politics or ecology that brought her to organic agriculture, but rather the desire to recover a certain taste—one she had experienced as an exchange student in France. Of course democratizing such tastes, which under current policies tend to be more expensive, is the hard part, and must eventually lead the movement back to more conventional politics lest it be tagged as elitist.

But the movement's interest in such seemingly mundane matters as taste and the other textures of everyday life is also one of its great strengths. Part of the movement's critique of industrial food is that, with the rise of fast food and the collapse of everyday cooking, it has damaged family life and community by undermining the institution of the shared meal. Sad as it may be to bowl alone, eating alone can be sadder still, not least because it is eroding the civility on which our political culture depends.

That is the argument made by Janet Flammang, a political scientist, in a provocative new book called *The Taste for Civilization: Food, Politics, and Civil Society*. "Significant social and political costs have resulted from fast food and convenience foods," she writes, "grazing and snacking instead of sitting down for leisurely meals, watching television during mealtimes instead of conversing"—40 percent of Americans watch television during meals—"viewing food as fuel rather than sustenance, discarding family recipes and foodways, and denying that eating has social and political dimensions." The cultural contradictions of capitalism—its tendency to undermine the stabilizing social forms it depends on—are on vivid display at the modern American dinner table.

In a challenge to second-wave feminists who urged women to get out of the kitchen, Flammang suggests that by denigrating "foodwork"—everything involved in putting meals on the family table—we have unthinkingly wrecked one of the nurseries of democracy: the family meal. It is at "the temporary democracy of the table" that children learn the art of conversation and acquire the habits of civility—sharing, listening, taking turns, navigating differences, arguing without offending—and it is these habits that are lost when we eat alone and on the run. "Civility is not needed when one is by oneself."

These arguments resonated during the Senate debate over health care reform, when *The New York Times* reported that the private Senate dining room, where senators of both parties used to break bread together, stood empty. Flammang attributes some of the loss of civility in Washington to the aftermath of the 1994 Republican Revolution, when Newt Gingrich, the new Speaker of the House, urged his freshman legislators *not* to move their families to Washington. Members now return to their districts every weekend, sacrificing opportunities for socializing across party lines and, in the process, the "reservoirs of good will replenished at dinner parties." It is much harder to vilify someone with whom you have shared a meal.

Flammang makes a convincing case for the centrality of food work and shared meals, much along the lines laid down by Carlo Petrini and Alice Waters, but with more historical perspective and theoretical rigor. A scholar of the women's movement, she suggests that "American women are having second thoughts" about having left the kitchen. However, the answer is not for them simply to return to it, at least not alone, but rather "for everyone—men, women, and children—to go back to the kitchen, as in preindustrial days, and for the workplace to lessen its time demands on people." Flammang points out that the historical priority of the American labor movement has been to fight for money, while the European labor movement has fought for time, which she suggests may have been the wiser choice.

At the very least this is a debate worth having, and it begins by taking food issues much more seriously than we have taken them. Flammang suggests that the invisibility of these issues until recently owes to the identification of food work with women and the (related) fact that eating, by its very nature, falls on the wrong side of the mind–body dualism. "Food is apprehended through the senses of touch, smell and taste," she points out, which rank lower on the hierarchy of senses than sight and hearing, which are typically thought to give rise to knowledge. In most of philosophy, religion, and literature, food is associated with body, animal, female, and appetite—things civilized men have sought to overcome with reason and knowledge.

Much to our loss. But food is invisible no longer and, in light of the mounting costs we've incurred by ignoring it, it is likely to demand much more of our attention in the future, as eaters, parents, and citizens. It is only a matter of time before politicians seize on the power of the food issue, which besides being increasingly urgent is also almost primal, indeed is in some deep sense proto-political. For where do all politics begin if not in the high chair?—at that fateful moment when mother, or father, raises a spoonful of food to the lips of the baby who clamps shut her mouth, shakes her head no, and for the very first time in life awakens to and asserts her sovereign power.

Food Anthropology and Happy Mediums

By Dana Staves

Whisks & Words: A blog about a writer who cooks, June 1, 2012

Today, my ENG 110C students will be turning in their Food Anthropology paper. When I came up with this paper, I was looking for a way to transition them from narrative to more analytic styles, dropping into profile and description along the way. The Food Anthropology paper is essentially a profile paper—a portrait of a food. But I wanted them to take it one step further.

Rather than have them write a portrait of an apple or some similar whole food, I asked them to pick a highly processed food that is readily available to them, one that is the product of years of scientific and technological innovation. Once they choose the food, they should begin drawing its genealogy, drawing a lineage back to its original roots. What food was the original base for Chee-tos or Dippin' Dots? Where did Go-gurt come from? How did we get to Choco-tacos?

I'm excited to see what they're going to come up with, but in anticipation of their writing this paper, I prepared a lecture last week on kitchen history, on the innovations that have come into play over the last two hundred years to make our current ways of cooking possible. I used a cookbook my sister gave me, *The Old-Time Name-Brand Cookbook,* as my source, and I drew out a history of cooking for my students. (I should mention, for any of my teacher friends who might be reading, that this is a traditional English Composition class, utilizing traditional rhetorical modes and focusing on grammar, writing process, etc., but we use food as our entry point on all assignments. It's awesome.)

In drawing up a simple history for my students, I got to thinking about our current food movement. If we look at our culinary history in waves, especially over the last two-hundred years, we can see moments of great inspiration, moments when somebody saw a need and developed a product to make life easier. Powdered gelatin was packaged and sold in smaller amounts by a Mr. Knox because he watched his wife spend six hours making calves' foot jelly. Who knows what his inspiration was? The conclusion was: there has to be an easier way. The mid- to late-nineteenth century is full of small stories like these, stories where somebody came up with a product that is now a household name. These stories led to what we have come to understand as processed foods. But back then, "processed foods" wasn't an evil term. It was a relief, an answer to tasks that took hours (even all day) and several people to make it happen.

If you think about it, our daily food routines can be done rather economically and efficiently. Get up. Make coffee (which has been pre-ground for us) in a coffee maker in our homes. Grab a _____(banana, granola bar, Pop-Tart, Breakfast-on-the-Go pouch, whatever), and head to work. Either go out to lunch at a restaurant, or eat a lunch you brought from home. Perhaps a sandwich on bread that was made and packaged for you, with pre-packaged peanut butter and jelly. Perhaps a microwavable meal, one that has been flash-frozen to maintain freshness. Head home. Order a meal to be delivered to you, or cook it yourself: perhaps chicken breasts, pre-butchered for you, etc. You get my point.

> *I've begun doing some things the slow(er) way. I like to get fresh, seasonal produce from farmer's markets. I make my own bread.*

I say all this not as judgment. That Breakfast on the Go pouch is mine. This is the world we live in, and this is what we traded in for. Before World War II, before the subsequent wave of the feminist movement, which made it possible for women to transition out of the home and into the work force, food preparation was done the slow way, the homemade way, the way that took a lot of time and left little energy leftover for a woman to have independent hobbies, jobs, etc. In that way, I'm thankful for the little pouch of nuts and freeze-dried berries covered in yogurt; I'm glad I can choose when I'll spend an entire day covered in flour and cooking grease and end the day with tired feet and an achy back.

In my presentation to my students, I recounted a fact from the aforementioned cookbook, about the release of *The Boston Cooking School Cookbook* by Fannie Farmer. This cookbook includes instructions for precise measuring, a new idea back then, based on the idea that cooking could be standardized and made fool-proof. I have a second edition copy of this book, its pages old and yellowed and smelling magnificent. In the poultry chapter, there are instructions for plucking and cleaning the bird, removing its head and guts, etc. I read this aloud to my students and asked them what they preferred: the Fannie Farmer way of the early twentieth century, or the Harris Teeter way, cleanly wrapped in cellophane. They chose cellophane. No surprise.

After World War II, these innovations in cooking took a nasty turn. Flavor enhancers and preservatives came into play. I have a theory (possibly entirely unsupported) that the scientific community in America was on a high after their developments in chemical (nuclear) warfare in World War II. If they could evaporate an enemy city, they could surely make bread last longer and apple pie filling taste more appley. What was originally a beautiful "American dream" moment of innovation—see a need, develop a product—grew and morphed and deviated into a science of manipulating our food for the utmost in convenience, nutrition, etc. Eventually, the artificial became more normal than the real.

Enter the slow food movement. I have been mulling over all of this since I made that presentation last week. On Friday, I went to pick up my bag of CSA goodies, and in it there was a bag of fresh shelled May peas. We had just opened our bag from the previous week that morning; there was no way we'd be able to get to both bags this week. So I decided to freeze the May peas, the fresh ones, for a later date. I did some Internet research on how best to freeze them, and I began boiling a large pot of water so that I could blanch them, kill off any bacteria, then halt the cooking process in a bath of ice water, before sealing them up and tossing them in the freezer. While I was at it, I went ahead and trimmed beet greens from our bunch of beets, cleaned the leaves, and put them in a bag for ready use. I washed our blackberries and put them away in Tupperware so they wouldn't leak in the refrigerator. I felt quite old fashioned, like an essay by MFK Fisher, one where she recounts the image of her grandmother, mother, and cook making jam from fresh summer strawberries, preserving fruit over and over during the summer so they would have it when they wanted it come mid-winter (when fruit like that would be unavailable).

I've begun doing some things the slow(er) way. I like to get fresh, seasonal produce from farmer's markets. I make my own bread. Amanda and I are looking for ways to cut down on meat consumption so that we can afford to buy ethically raised meat rather than meat from scary unethical operations. I have a beautiful idea that one day I'll find someone who will trade me freshly laid eggs in exchange for something I could offer—bread? Baked goods? Mint from my herb garden?

I think we are quick to condemn processed foods, and rightly so. The processed foods we are most acquainted with are hardly real food, and it becomes difficult to trace those foods back to their roots, to perform my students' Food Anthropology exercise on common snack foods, breakfast foods, and even things that are to pass for dinner. But after preparing for that lesson last week, it's hard for me to condemn it completely. I'm thankful that I can get chicken that doesn't still have feathers and a head on it. I'm happy that my sugar comes in a bag, granulated for me, rather than me having to break off chunks from a block of sugar hanging from the ceiling. I'm stoked that I can turn on my oven to a precise temperature and not have to guess at it, stoking a fire and raising the temperature in a guessing game of baking. So in some ways, I'm thankful for that history, for early food processors.

I'm also thankful for fresh May peas, resting in my freezer, waiting for me to eat them later, when I'm ready. And homemade bread sitting on my counter. For urban chickens and farmer's markets and the group of people who decided to make this into a slow jam, to look for a way back. I'm thankful today for happy mediums.

Comfort Me with Gnocchi

By Sara B. Franklin

Leitesculinaria.com, February 29, 2012

I met M on a farm just outside Boston on a rainy day in June. It was the summer before my senior year of college, and I was trying my hand at farming. I'd always had a knack for books, though I was itching to spend some time outdoors, coaxing something real from the ground. M was a handsome, painfully shy twenty-three-year-old with a slight scar beneath the curve of his left eyebrow. He wore an army green felt hat that cast a shadow over his strong, deeply tanned face and dark eyes. His shoulders were slender yet muscled, and I caught myself glancing at his chest beneath his threadbare t-shirt and instantly regretting my decision that morning to wear baggy hiking pants and a curve-concealing turtleneck fleece. He was one of the assistant growers for the season. In other words, he was my boss.

That first day he barely spoke to me. I left the farm intrigued, knowing little more than he was originally from Uruguay and had recently moved to the tiny milling town of Waltham, Massachusetts.

My second day on the farm, M and I moved a pile of wooden posts from behind a crumbling red barn in a remote corner of the property. The posts, which had been left untended for more than a year, were infested with ants. When I climbed into the cab of the truck next to M—on whom I'd already developed a crush—I realized with horror that a few ants had crawled up my shorts. I squirmed in my seat. M turned to me, a smile playing at the edge of his lips.

"What's going on?" he asked, amused.

"I think I have ants . . . in . . . my pants . . . ." I stuttered while wriggling and forcing a half smile as the little buggers pinched. He guffawed and turned his gaze back to the rutted farm road. An awkward silence ensued.

I desperately wanted to change the topic, to not come off as a complainer. "There's an Edward Hopper exhibit about to open at the Museum of Fine Arts," I blurted out. "Any interest in going?"

Ours was a relationship built on, and measured by, 29ths. Our first date, to see that Hopper show, took place on June 29th. A month later, for his birthday on July 29th, I wrapped a used copy of Hemingway's *A Moveable Feast* in newsprint. And come August 29th, we were camping together, announcing to our coworkers in neighboring tents that we were, officially, an item. The 29th became the box on the calendar that we marked in bold red.

It was also the day we marked with a ritual of a different sort, something softer and more fleeting. In M's native Uruguay, the 29th of each month is El Dia de Ñoquis, or the Day of the Gnocchi, a custom that Uruguayans still fervently, almost obsessively observe. The tradition began in the late nineteenth century, when nearly everyone was paid on the first of the month. By the time the end of the month came around, wallets had typically grown thin and pantries bare. Uruguay being a country where conviviality is practiced with as much devotion as religion, the situation was spun into a celebration in which families and friends gathered and flour, potatoes, salt, and eggs created a thrifty, filling meal. Given the belief that diners who slip a coin under their plate can expect the next month to be filled with prosperity, it was a lucky meal as well.

M and I fervently played up the double celebration of private anniversary and cultural ritual on every single one of our shared 29ths. Whether for luck or just for kicks, it's hard to say. On those days, we'd peel a pile of potatoes, boil them until soft, and press them through the ricer. As M's hands were sufficiently calloused and practiced to withstand the still-steaming starch, he'd mix the potatoes into a mound of flour along with a few eggs and some salt and gently knead until a pale yellow dough formed. I still remember my first time, how he gingerly showed me how to separate the amorphous lump of dough into logs, cut them into pieces just so, and, with a graceful, delicate turn of his fingers, deftly roll each one of the pillowy little dumplings along the curved tines of a fork before placing it on a semolina-dusted baking tin. He was endlessly patient in the kitchen, in stark contrast to my hurried and often slapdash cookery, and his tenderness with the dough resulted in gnocchi so light, so airy they bordered on indefinable.

Six months under our belts, we marked our anniversary with a gnocchi supper, as was our custom. It was December 29th, and our relationship seemed as though it was going strong. If you think about it, this made sense according to *Dia de Ñoquis* logic regarding luck. That same logic intimated that the new year, a leap year, ought to be unusually lucky. February was typically a wash for gnocchi revelers, whereas this year afforded an extended month in which to squeeze an extra celebration as well as an extra entreaty for good things to come.

Sure enough, things seemed to be going well that year, at least at first. M had lined up a better-paying farm gig for the following spring, and I was spending my winter break traveling with my best friend, Anna, eating my way through the Pacific Northwest before returning for my final semester of school. But by the second week of February, it became obvious that my

> *We still mustered the courage to celebrate the end of each month, raising a tattered flag in honor of our custom, just as we'd always done. M would race home from the farm on his bicycle and burst through the door to our room, sweaty and exhilarated, a goofy grin on his face. "Baby, it's gnocchi day!" he'd gasp.*

mom, who'd been battling pancreatic cancer for more than three years, didn't have the strength to rebound from yet another round of treatment. Her doctor recommended we stop the chemo. I immediately dropped out of school and, on Valentine's Day, moved home to the suburbs of New York to care for her. A month later, my mother passed away.

Left suddenly without the structure of class or caretaking, I found myself filled with an urgent need to flee the shadows of sickness and death. I packed what was left of my life into the car and I moved back north with M to a ramshackle apartment in Amherst.

I'm not quite sure what I expected to happen in that creaky wood-paneled house with the tiny galley kitchen. I think I was hoping that by playing house with M—establishing a routine built around cooking, laundry, and making the bed—I would reclaim some sense of stability and home. Instead, I found myself more and more confused. From within the thick, sucking muck of grief, M seemed inaccessible and far away. And rightly so—he was wholly unfamiliar with this sadder, weakened version of me. It became impossible for me to distinguish my sadness about the cracks spreading in our relationship from the ache of missing my mother. The harder he and I fought to find one another, the farther apart we seemed to drift.

What kept us hanging on during those long months were the hours we spent together in the kitchen, our shared love of the rituals surrounding food: The unmistakable aroma of onions caramelizing in butter; the satisfaction in mincing garlic cloves; the simple effort of whisking olive oil, vinegar, and mustard for salad dressing; and, on the 29th of each month, the shared act of making gnocchi.

We still mustered the courage to celebrate the end of each month, raising a tattered flag in honor of our custom, just as we'd always done. M would race home from the farm on his bicycle and burst through the door to our room, sweaty and exhilarated, a goofy grin on his face. "Baby, it's *gnocchi day!*" he'd gasp. (As though I hadn't been counting down to this day, too.) Then he'd lift me from my desk chair where I'd been writing and squeeze me in one of his almost-too-tight hugs. I'd follow him into our stuffy, closet-sized kitchen, where we were kinder, softer to one another. Suddenly we'd be transported back to the early, weightless days of our love.

The next day, without fail, we'd snap back to our distant shores.

The following January, it was time for M to make a pilgrimage to Uruguay. He hadn't seen his father and half-sisters in five years, and I decided I wanted to go with him. In my imagination, the trip would be filled with tears, reunions, and an extensive, confusing web of relatives who would soothe the aching loss in my own family. M's loved ones did, indeed, welcome me, and I allowed myself to fall into the easy rhythm of lazy days at the beach and long, lively meals at night.

On the 29th of that month, M and I showed up on his grandmother's doorstep with plastic bags bulging with ingredients for gnocchi. Together we quietly moved through the motions of prep. Relatives peered in the kitchen, observing our teamwork. As I rolled dumplings down the tines of a fork, I was having trouble imagining a life without this monthly ritual, without M. I wasn't sure I could bear another loss. As I arranged the gnocchi on a pan, readying them for cooking, I thought, if we could prepare such beautiful meals together, perhaps we had the mettle to tough it out after all.

That night the gnocchi were sublime, the best we'd ever made, light and bathed in a rich Bolognese. The wine flowed freely. We all lingered into the night, sipping whiskey long after the dishes had been cleared.

That was our last Gnocchi Day.

It had become clear to me that our private rituals, however beautiful and steadfast, were never going to be enough to fill the glaring void in my own life. Nothing would. I needed time and space to heal. It was time to let go. Our luck had run its course.

It's been three years since M and I parted ways, and just as long since I've rolled gnocchi. These days my faith in luck has dwindled, although things are actually looking promising. My love of food has turned into something of a livelihood. I've a new lover, one who seems better versed in the ways that loss sculpts us. And while I'm wary of false starts, I'm thinking this year, in which we're once again granted an extra day tacked onto the end of this month, is going to be better than the last few have been. Although just to be certain, come February 29th, I may have to set my big stockpot to boil, pull out my pasta board, and make some gnocchi.

My Mom Couldn't Cook

By Tim Junod
Esquire, March 21, 2011

I cook for my family. To put it another way: I am my family's cook, and so I cook almost every night. I cook three hundred days a year, and have cooked three hundred days a year for *years*. I cook for the three of us—for my wife, my daughter, and myself—and before there were three of us, I cooked for the two of us. I am a husband who cooks for his wife, which makes me a man who cooks for his woman and now his women, which in turns makes me a man who to some extent cooks *like* a woman: out of love and generosity, yes, but also out of service, out of duty. I cook because it's my job. I don't get many days off from cooking. I don't *take* many days off cooking, because I only like to eat at restaurants that serve food better than my own, or that serve Mexican food or sushi. Hell, I don't even take days off from cooking when I go out for days on the road, because before I leave I prepare my family food to be eaten in my absence. I cook so that there is no absence. I cook so that I am always there, even when I'm gone, even when I die, and my cooking translates in my daughter's memory as, simply, this: time.

This is not to say that my cooking is selfless. It is anything but, because in order to endure cooking like a woman I have to cook like a man—which is to say, for myself. The food I cook for my family is the food I like to eat. The food I like to eat is the food I cook for my family. I cook out of hunger, and so, to the degree that I am selfless as a cook, I am also despotic and fanatical. I do everything myself, make everything myself, from salad dressings to chili powder. I do not ask for help and I do not consider shortcuts. I want to take time, not save it, aware of the paradox born of my driven dedication, aware that if the time I spend at the stove is time given to my family, it is also time taken away.

This, however, is not a story of my cooking, or the odd combination of freedom and thralldom it confers. It's the story of what—or who—inspired my decision to be my family's cook, gave me the will to do it, and made it both a practical and, apparently, a psychological necessity. It is the story of my mother—of my mother's cooking.

My mother, Frances Junod, was not just a mother, not just a mom. She was a dame. She was a broad. She was a beauty from Brooklyn who wore fantastic hats, when they were in style, and furs, even when they were not. She went through her entire life as a Harlowesque platinum blonde, and I never knew the real color of her hair. She liked go to the track, and she liked to go out to restaurants. She did not like to cook. That she did it anyway—that she had no choice—owed itself to generational expectations, and to the fact that if my mother was a doll, in the Runyonesque sense of the word, my father was a guy, a pinky-ringed sharpie who spent many nights going to the New York City restaurants my mother longed to frequent, but who, on nights when he came home, loudly expected food on the table. So my mother put food on the table. She was my family's cook. She cooked three hundred nights a year.

She cooked for my father, and, when he was away, which was often, she cooked for me and my brother and my sister, and then, when they, both ten years older than me, left home, she cooked for me. She cooked me spaghetti with butter and cheese. She cooked me hamburgers, "pan-fried" without added fat on a hot, salted cast-iron skillet, until they formed a hard crust. She cooked me scrambled eggs, made idiosyncratic by the addition of a teaspoon of water. She cooked me shell steaks sprinkled with salt and Ac'cent—MSG—and she cooked chicken parts lathered in a sweet-sour sauce called Saucy Susan and she cooked me chicken or veal cutlets bought "scallopini" style at the supermarket and coated in Progresso Italian-Style breadcrumbs. For dessert she made Junket or Jell-O or My-T-Fine chocolate pudding. Except for Friday nights, when she served a cold meal—what she called a "platter" of cantaloupe slices, cottage cheese, and tuna fish salad—she never cooked for herself, to satisfy her own hunger.

It took me a while to figure out that she hated cooking, and a while—much—longer to figure out that she hated cooking because she couldn't cook. For one thing, she was my mother, and mothers were supposed to know how to cook. For another, I was her child, and so for most of my childhood she was the only cook in the world. I had to like her cooking, and I did, as long as she observed the Mashed Potato Rule. The Mashed Potato Rule, simply stated, is this: There is no such thing as bad mashed potatoes as long as they're actually potatoes, mashed. We had mashed potatoes a lot when I was a kid—I can still see the blood and, better, the clear juices from the pan-fried hamburger running into them on my plate—and it didn't matter that they were lumpy and grainy and that my mother had no talent for making them; they were *Edenic* so long as she did. I loved them, as I loved her. That she was not the kind of mother who made everything from scratch, the way the mothers of my Italian friends did; that for her the words "homemade" and "gourmet" were virtually interchangeable, to be pronounced with the same dreamy covetousness she employed when she pronounced the word "Paris" or "Aruba" or some other exotic destination she knew she'd never visit; that the only vegetables I ever ate came not from a field but rather from a can (LeSeur) or a freezer pack (Jolly Green Giant); that she favored convenience foods to the extent that I came to fear them, and cringe at commercials for the Pillsbury Doughboy: all this was not forgiven but simply forgotten when the mashed potatoes were potatoes, mashed. But while on my plate they formed the barrier between the battleship-gray lamb chops and the olive-drab green beans, in my heart they formed the barrier between the discovery that my mother hated cooking and the altogether different discovery that my mother hated cooking so much that she even hated cooking for me.

See, I had figured that my mother hated cooking for the obvious reason that she hated cooking for my father. She could never satisfy him. Indeed, she hated cooking for him so much that he kept their marriage intact by absolving her of the responsibility—by taking her with him to Roosevelt Raceway, where they ate at the Cloud Casino, while I stayed home and panfried a shell steak in the salted pan and made spaghetti with butter and cheese. But I was absolved of responsibility as well. I was in high school, stoned and rapacious and suddenly free to be disloyal, by which I mean I was suddenly free to tell the truth. Like most human beings, I grew up making the connection between food and love; what I began to realize when I started cooking for myself was that the more necessary connection was between food and honesty. My parents were both charmingly dishonest people; my father's lies were such that he couldn't admit them except to urge me to develop, like him, "a little larceny in your soul," but my mother could, since most of her lies were about food. "Oh, I'm a terrible fibber," she'd say, and then blithely assert that the Mott's applesauce she'd doctored with lemon and cinnamon was "homemade" or that she'd spent "hours over a hot stove" cooking the package of frozen Banquette fried-chicken drumsticks on our plates. She'd say this with a knowing cackle that served simultaneously as an admission of guilt and as a warning that we must never say that she was guilty. Food was love, all right, and we had to tell my mom that we loved her by buying into her "fibs" about it. To do otherwise was not only to make her cry but also to risk the wrath of my dad, who was as fearsome in his defense of my mother as he was in his attacks upon her. And so dinnertime became an exercise in swallowing a fiction that everybody knew was untrue, and the story that was repeated over and over and over again in my family (the other enforced fiction in my family being the fiction that the story you were hearing for the hundredth time was a story you'd never heard before) was the time my mother made a huge vat of her "homemade" applesauce for my brother's wrestling-team dinner and my brother ate the whole thing in order to spare my mother the knowledge that nobody else did.

I was still in high school and living at home when my mother first broke the Mashed Potato Rule: when the mashed potatoes she served started tasting like the mashed potatoes that were served in my high school cafeteria; when it was clear that, in fact, they were neither mashed nor potatoes. From another perspective: I was in high school when I first broke the rule that if food was to be love then so was the obligation to accept my mother's untruths about it. Me: Ma (I always called her Ma), what's with the potatoes? My mother: What's wrong with the potatoes? Me: They're not potatoes. My father: Just eat the potatoes. Your mother slaved over a hot stove to make those potatoes. Me: They're not potatoes. They came from a box. My mother: So what if they come from a box? They're still potatoes. Me: They're not potatoes! My mother: *You can't tell the difference.*

And with that my mother uttered the signal words of my culinary existence, which happened to be the signal words of my familial existence as well. I could tell the difference, and I spent the rest of my life proving that I could. My mother, for her part, spent the rest of her life trying to prove that I couldn't. I refused to eat the potato flakes that she served me, or the potato buds, or the potato powder, and my mother refused to admit that they were potato flakes and potato buds and potato powder. I mean, she would hide the box. She would peel a potato and put the peelings on top of the garbage, and the box of French's at the bottom. I used to think that she should have used her ingenuity just to mash the damned potatoes, while using my own ingenuity to find the box and to produce it, with prosecutorial flourish.

> *Like most human beings, I grew up making the connection between food and love; what I began to realize when I started cooking for myself was that the more necessary connection was between food and honesty.*

"Come on," my father said, "enough's enough. Just eat the potatoes. You're breaking your mother's heart." But enough was never enough, because just as my mother had come to the conclusion that *It's not worth it*, I was coming to the conclusion that *It is*. The only thing left to be decided was the matter of what that mysterious "it" might be, and the only thing we both understood was that a lot more was at stake than the authenticity of my mother's "mashies."

My mother was a good mother. I was a good son. My mother was a betrayed woman—I think I knew that, from an early age—and so I was careful never to betray her, as she, by instinct, never betrayed me. But now I felt betrayed, and I betrayed her in return, by learning to cook. No: by cooking. No: by marrying a girl who had no interest in cooking, and cooking for her. No: by cooking for my wife as I wished my mother had cooked for me. No: by cooking as my father would have cooked, had he taken up the toque—by cooking unyieldingly, despotically, ball-bustingly, hungrily, not just selflessly but also selfishly, as an assertion of prerogative. When my mother came to visit, I made her chop, according to specification. "How's this?" she'd ask, showing me the cutting board of haphazardly chopped broccoli, and when I'd say she had to chop it smaller, finer, more uniformly, she'd say, "You're some pain in the ass" or "What a pill." I was perversely proud of her exasperation, perversely proud to be addressed in terms heretofore reserved for my old man. A pill? I had never been a pill before. I had always been, in my mother's estimation, "a good egg," but now I'd become a pill by insisting that my eggs taste good. My mother wasn't college-educated, but she wasn't stupid, either. She knew what was going on. When, much later, I wrote a flattering profile of my father for a magazine, she dismissed it tersely: "Don't forget who raised you, kid." But my cooking—my decision to cook—was a rejection of the way I'd been raised, a rebuke of the way she'd raised me. I had been on my mother's side, but now, unforgivably, I was on my father's, by taking my mother's job.

And yet hunger won out, as it always does in human affairs. As I learned to cook, I eventually learned what to cook for my parents—what made them hungry and satisfied their hunger at the same time, without carrying an implicit *statement* meant to divide or offend them. It was pot roast. On Sunday nights after they moved near us, we'd have them over for Sunday supper—a term that seemed the province of a family not my own—and I'd serve the one meal that, as any novice cook knows, obeys its own variant of the Mashed Potato Rule: there's no such thing as a bad pot roast as long as you put enough stuff in the pot and you roast it long enough. But my mother didn't know. Because she'd become too old and uncertain to chop, she'd watch me do the work and laugh to herself, as was her habit: "What are you laughing at, Ma?" "Nothing. Just laughin'." But she was interested not just in what she still regarded as my folly but in what made my folly *worth it*—what made the food good. There was a word that my mother used in restaurants, used, indeed, almost any time she was eating food she didn't have to cook, and that was "de*licious*," as in, "Hey, Ma, how's that pork chop?" "De*licious*." She said it with a combination of relief, wonder, and her own kind of hunger, which was the hunger to be free—to be what she was when she first married my father: a pampered beauty, a spoiled child. Now she used it, admitted it, in regard to my pot roast, and she wanted to know why. "What kind of meat do you use?" she'd always ask, and when I wondered why she wanted to know, she said, "Well, it's always so tender." And that's how I knew what I wasn't supposed to know all along: my mother didn't know how to cook. She didn't know the rule that can get you through just about any meal, the rule that's even more fundamental than the one governing the preparation of mashed potatoes: If it's tender, cook it fast over high heat; if it's tough, cook it slow over low. I used to wonder why my mother hated cooking so much. I used to wonder why she cooked salmon fillets for two hours and pot roast for one. I thought for a long time that it was because she was a bad cook, because she rejected cooking as a way of rejecting us, because she was, at heart, a liar. Now I understood that she hated cooking because she didn't know how to do it and so had no idea how a meal might turn out. I understood that she simply wasn't cut out for it, and yet, because she was part of the postwar suburban vanguard, she knew she was going to be judged on it—and so she *demanded* to be judged on it, meal after awful meal. Hence, the fibs; hence, the lies. She was as innocent of culinary knowledge as the housewives of her era were supposed to be innocent of sexual knowledge, and once I figured that out, I came to the same conclusion I came to when I figured out the extent of my father's infidelities: they were in over their heads. They were more unhappy than I ever allowed myself to know. They deserved the love they got, and the forgiveness they didn't.

Did she forgive me? Did she forgive me for being a pill and a pain in the ass—for taking my father's side? I know damned well she never thought of it that way. I was her, after all, and I was a good egg. But that's how I thought of it, and I can tell you that the narrative arc of a life is more unforgiving than a mother could ever be. After my father died, my mother went into assisted living—or, to be more precise and unsparing, I put her there. She flourished, though food was an issue. "Ma, eat something." "I'm not hungry." "C'mon. The food's not bad"—and to prove it, I'd eat large platefuls of it, including the mashed potatoes that were neither mashed nor potato. "It stinks," she'd say, and that was that. One day, in her ninety-second year, she simply stopped eating, and when she went to the hospital for intravenous fluids, she suffered a stroke that deprived her of her ability to feed herself. I had a conversation with her gerontologist, in which he told me the way she would die, in which he told me that unless she was fed via feeding tube she would die of the complications of malnutrition—of hunger. He didn't want to give her a feeding tube. Neither did I, versed as I was in the letter and spirit of her living will and her medical directives. But I never asked her about it. I never told her that we planned for her to die. I simply went every day, and tried to spoon-feed her cottage cheese that dribbled from her mouth like sand. I even cooked for her—the spaghetti with butter and cheese that was the first food I ever loved; the pot roast that was the last food she called delicious. I was the family cook, which meant that I was driven to preserve my family by making them care about something they had to do: eat. But my mother didn't have to care anymore. She didn't even have to eat. The family cook, I fed her tenderly to the last, and she starved to death.

5

Open for Business

Ghislain & Marie David de Lossy

A restaurant is one of the most challenging of all business ventures, yet as many as a thousand new restaurants open each year in the United States.

The Ins and Outs of the
Restaurant Business

It is generally accepted within popular culture that a restaurant is one of the most difficult businesses to own and operate. According to the popular mythos, more restaurants fail than almost any other type of business. The question is, why should this be the case, given the fact that the restaurant is one of the most important institutions in human culture?

Outside the common wisdom that "people have to eat" there is also the fact that restaurants provide a foundation for community cohesion, they often anchor retail neighborhoods and pave the way for other businesses, and they provide a community with food, the central necessity of biological existence and one of the primary sensual pleasures of life. The popularity of restaurant culture can also be expressed in the statistics of the industry, with more than 1 million restaurants operating in the United States, collectively bringing in more than $600 billion in annual sales.

Though the restaurant occupies a unique and important place in society, the success or failure of a restaurant, or any other business, depends on a variety of interrelated factors, many of which are difficult to control from a business owner's or manager's perspective. The fortunes and failures of the restaurant industry are tied, for instance, to the larger economic shifts that affect consumer preferences and spending patterns.

For many chefs and restaurant owners, the success or failure of a restaurant is about more than the economic equations balancing expenses and profits. The restaurant is also a human institution, and involvement in the industry is—for many owners, workers, and chefs—a matter of lifestyle choices. Ultimately, the success of a restaurant or any other business is also a psychological experiment, attempting to find balance between all the complex factors of the business to achieve personal, often emotional, goals.

Restaurant Failure

The common wisdom says that approximately 90 percent of restaurants fail during their first year in business. This statistic has been widely repeated in popular culture, even appearing in advertisements for the NBC reality series *Restaurant: A Reality Show*, which debuted in 2003. Professor H. G. Parsa, of the Cornell School of Hotel Administration, conducted an investigation into this commonly held belief by analyzing restaurant trends in a variety of American cities and found that only about 30 percent of restaurants fail in their first year, which is similar to the rate of failure for many other types of retail businesses.

Given Parsa's investigation, it seems that perhaps a fledgling restaurant is no more likely to fail than a fledgling clothing store, and yet the perception of the 90 percent failure rate endures. The willingness to believe this foreboding statistic may be partially because the arrival and disappearance of a restaurant from a community is more obvious, in many cases, than other types of businesses. A person may go years or decades without purchasing flowers from a local florist, for example, but the average consumer patronizes a local restaurant far more often.

In addition, there may be greater popular understanding, or at least awareness, of the difficulties inherent in the restaurant business than other types of enterprise. People understand, for instance, that a restaurant must continually purchase new stock, because its product is highly perishable. Also important are the restaurant-themed reality series that have brought the economics of the restaurant business to the forefront of popular culture and often actively encourage the idea that restaurants are one of the most difficult types of businesses to own and operate.

According to Parsa, the banking industry is one of the primary perpetuators of the 90-percent myth, using this "economic analysis" to restrict lending to restaurants. This creates a situation where prospective restaurateurs are unable to obtain sufficient start-up capital from banks, therefore leading to a greater number of failed restaurants and feeding into a self-perpetuating cycle. Industry analyses indicate that a lack of start-up capital is one of the primary reasons that restaurants go out of business after their first year.

Major Factors Affecting Restaurant Success

In part, the fortunes of the restaurant industry are determined by larger economic trends that affect consumer spending. In 2013, for instance, industry analysts estimate that the economic recovery in the United States has reduced disposable income for many categories of consumers, leading to reduced revenues for restaurants across the board. Economic conditions that reduce disposable income often affect restaurants less than some other categories of retail businesses because even in strained economic conditions, many consumers consider food and drink to be more important than a mere luxury.

Federal, state, and local legislation can also have a negative effect on restaurant success, sometimes in profound ways. For instance, the Patient Protection and Affordable Care Act, which is intended to expand healthcare coverage to employees working at least thirty hours per week, is expected to have a negative effect on hiring in the restaurant industry. However, the full impact of this legislation remains to be seen, and some analysts believe that the healthcare expansion may stimulate many industries in the long term.

In addition, restaurant success differs regionally, as some states or cities simply provide a far more favorable environment for restaurants than others. In Philadelphia, Pennsylvania, for instance, antiquated liquor laws and increased taxation for independent businesses create a highly unfavorable environment for the restaurant industry that is only partially offset by the size of the city's population. In states or cities with smaller dining populations, a minor increase in wage or business taxes can be fatal to a restaurant operating within a limited budget.

On a related level, regional and urban planning can have a significant positive or negative effect on restaurants in an area. A freeway expansion can bring potential customers to businesses, but also reduces foot traffic in the area immediately surrounding the freeway. Urban planning can create new retail or dining areas, expanding opportunities for restaurants, but can also restrict traffic or residential expansion, thereby limiting customer volume for restaurants in a newly restructured area. At the same time, the construction needed to complete an urban design project can restrict access to existing businesses.

Other factors that can have broad effects on the restaurant industry are natural disasters and widespread climatic variations that affect the availability, quality, and price of food. The North American drought of 2012–13, for instance, has had a significant impact on the food industry, limiting access to certain products and raising the price of others. Similarly, hurricanes and tsunamis may limit the availability of certain types of seafood, and shortages of certain species can continue for years after a hurricane or tsunami has occurred.

A final major factor that affects restaurants around the world is the flux in consumer preferences and trends. In 2013, US restaurants are in the process of adjusting to an increase in the demand for sustainable, organic, and/or local food offerings, a trend that has had a major impact, especially on independent restaurants. The full effect of this trend remains to be seen because it is difficult to know to what extent and in what form these preferences will become a permanent part of American dining habits.

Sustainable and local food options often come at an increased price and are subject to limited availability in comparison to mass-produced food products. The "slow food" movement, for instance, promotes the consumption of products that are both locally obtained and representative of the local ecosystem. A restaurant that attempts to offer cuisine in keeping with the slow food ideal will need to completely restructure its menu over the course of a year, as various local products come in and out of availability. In addition, a regional drought or deluge can cause availability of local goods to plummet, with a devastating effect on restaurants trying to concentrate on this type of cuisine.

A new restaurant opening in the midst of current consumer trends is better able to offer cuisine that is in vogue, while older established restaurants often have a more difficult time adjusting. A restaurant that serves traditional hot dogs or hamburgers, for instance, might find that its cuisine is increasingly frowned upon based on current standards of nutrition and sustainability. Overall, consumer trends lead to major shifts in the broad demographics of the industry as the cuisine of the previous generation is replaced by restaurants offering newer selections. By the same token, if current trends change, or if suddenly hot dogs become a chic way to break with the mainstream dining habits, the new generation of restaurants may find themselves suddenly outside the popular sphere.

Immediate Factors Affecting Restaurant Success

In addition to large-scale factors, there are many variables that affect the success of a restaurant on a more immediate scale. Many restaurants fail because they lack adequate capital at the beginning of the business, and their cash flow is never sufficient to make up for the lack of start-up money. As mentioned earlier, this is exacerbated by the fact that the lending industry, in some cases, adheres to inaccurate statistics regarding the viability of a restaurant as an investment opportunity.

In other cases, business owners simply underestimate the amount of money they believe they need to start a successful restaurant. The first year of business is critical, and few new businesses turn a significant profit until they have become established. Restaurants lacking the financial capital to survive revenue fluctuations in the first year may find themselves out of business before the restaurant can build an adequate customer base.

The location and design of a restaurant are also critical factors that have a major effect on success. Restaurants that establish themselves in an up-and-coming area, in conjunction with a number of other retail establishments, may have a significant advantage, building on the growth of a city or town as a whole. Establishing a restaurant in a "pioneer" area has pitfalls as well, however, as customer flow is often slow to arrive in these areas, and many potential customers may avoid the restaurant because it may be located in what has traditionally been perceived as a less desirable part of town.

The design of a restaurant is so important that there are marketing and architectural specialists who concentrate solely on building restaurants. Thoughtful design can increase customer flow and is a major factor in establishing the mood and atmosphere of a dining area. Poor design choices can adversely affect customer satisfaction and are precipitating factors in many restaurant failures. The name of a restaurant also plays a role in customer recognition, and restaurant names often follow local or even national trends. Analyses of restaurant names indicate that the most successful names are short and memorable.

Choices regarding location, start-up capital, design, and name are all part of the overall concept of a restaurant, and it is in the conceptual stage where many restaurants plant the seeds of success or failure. Analyses of restaurant trends suggest that customers like restaurants that can be defined in terms of genre or cuisine, and successful restaurants are often able to create an overall feel that communicates this concept to its customers. Restaurants that are poorly conceived, attempting to offer elements of many different restaurant genres, often have less success than those that concentrate on a single idea and attempt to exemplify that concept.

Ultimately, the fortunes of a restaurant depend to some extent on leadership and entrepreneurial aptitude. Poor management and customer service are factors that lead to the decline of many restaurants and can offset any advantages in terms of cuisine, location, or overall concept. Successful restaurants are often owned and/or operated by individuals who are comfortable with the "restaurant lifestyle," which often includes long hours and a preponderance of minor problems and issues that must be solved on a weekly, daily, and hourly basis. Successful restaurateurs must be amenable to change, but they must also avoid chasing trends at the expense of maintaining their overall concept because customers respond best to a mixture of stability and adaptability. The personalities of the managers and employees are extremely important factors in overall success or failure, both in terms of customer satisfaction and longevity.

Measuring Success in the Restaurant Industry

For industry analysts, the success of a restaurant often boils down to profit and economic stability, but for those who own and operate restaurants, success is far more difficult to quantify. For instance, some restaurateurs are concerned primarily with their cuisine and start restaurants because they want to bring a new or quality cuisine option to the dining community. For these restaurateurs, substituting quantity for quality or offering inferior ingredients to save money may not be an acceptable option, though these options are common among successful restaurants in many facets of the industry.

Other restaurant owners are primarily interested in the human element of the business, and view their restaurant as a part of a neighborhood or community. For those interested in the community/social function of their restaurant, success may be measured partially in the number of neighbors or customers who come to view the restaurant as an important facet of their community. Many restaurant owners cooperate with family or friends to establish their businesses, and for these individuals, the ultimate success of the restaurant must take into account the way the experience has benefited their family.

The fastest road to success in the restaurant industry is to aim for mass appeal, offering cuisine, prices, and design that appeal to the largest number of consumers. Another good bet is to follow the hottest new trends in food, and restaurants that do this successfully often have a rapid rise to financial success early in their operation. The far more difficult path is to offer a cuisine with integrity and individuality, opting for providing a high-quality, rather than hip, dining experience. For those who choose this road, the path to financial success may be steeper, but ultimately more lasting and more satisfying.

Dinner for Schmucks

By Alan Richman
GQ, September 1, 2011

Sooner or later, depending on how long it takes to get a reservation, you'll end up having a bad time at what is supposed to be a good restaurant.

When that happens, you might be startled by how upset you become. It probably won't be the food that's to blame. You can always shrug off a tough steak, since the chef didn't mean to disappoint you. But everyone takes poor service personally. Get a bad table and you'll wonder if the hostess finds you unworthy. Find yourself with a disrespectful server and you'll feel worse, because you're expected to tip.

Now and then, poor service is the result of a restaurant having an unfortunate day. Maybe the chef snapped at your waiter and made him sulk. Maybe the front of the house, as it's called, is short-staffed because a waiter called in sick.

More than likely, poor service is inherent, caused by a staff with lackluster spirit or a manager with a lax attitude. Here in New York, with our restaurants tumbling into informality, a guest can easily become a casualty of incompetence. We've entered the post-service era, where fewer and fewer restaurateurs still stand watch.

Which brings me to M. Wells, a metal-clad diner as shiny as a magpie's trinket, situated on a corner in Queens as dead-drab as one of the borough's countless cemeteries. A little more than a year ago, the diner was an abandoned shell, and now it symbolizes the renewal of Long Island City as surely as the MoMA PS1 art museum and the Silvercup film studios. I don't know what a burger once cost at the derelict diner that became M. Wells, since I never ate there, but I'm betting it was about $2.99. M. Wells sells one for $42, proof that gentrification is thriving in Queens.

Walk in and you might presume that you've stumbled on a formulaic re-creation of the diner genre, but you'd be wrong. M. Wells is not a faux-old-fashioned spot with black-and-white shakes and brassy waitresses to put you in your place. It's not retro-romantic, with votive candles, arugula salads, and flourless chocolate cake.

My experience there was like no other. The motto is "All's well at M. Wells." I assure you it is not.

The proprietors are Hugue Dufour and Sarah Obraitis, husband and wife. He is from Montreal, where he was a partner at Au Pied de Cochon, a modern legend that might well have launched lowbrow-made-highbrow dining. The restaurant's most enduring accomplishment was the uplifting of *poutine*, a dish usually found in rural Quebec dives that consists of fries, cheese curds, and brown gravy. Au Pied de Cochon added seared foie gras and was besieged with praise. M. Wells calls itself, oddly, a Quebeco-American diner. It specializes in freakishly appealing combinations, some brilliant and some frivolous, most unkempt but a few artistic. It also offers inspired pastry classics. The pineapple upside-down cake, as it's made here, is clear evidence that this dessert deserves enshrinement alongside Babe Ruth and FDR as an icon of twentieth-century America.

Dufour is a quirky presence. On one of my early visits, he wore fleur-de-lis-patterned pants while sitting on one of his counter stools, drumming his fingers, looking anxious. Obraitis, who is from Queens, runs the front of the house with considerable charm and little attention to detail. Or maybe the chipped plates, distracted staff, and badly washed glasses are intended to enhance an unceremonious ambience. She is totally relaxed, seemingly everywhere, talking to everyone, a wonderful hostess but a less than attentive supervisor.

My editors and I first went there for dinner because we had heard that it was exceptional, which is certainly true of the atmosphere, part raucous frat boys on a bus, part tranquil middle-aged women in cute shifts, plus a whole lot in between. Queens is not a destination for residents of other boroughs, other than those en route to airports, but M. Wells appears to be changing that.

We were happily stunned by a gargantuan meat-loaf sandwich stabbed through its heart with a serrated knife, and by a *côte-de-boeuf*-and-fried-soft-shell-crab combo plate, the meat a showcase of succulence, massive and mouthwatering, while the poor crabs had to settle for burial under a mound of rare flesh, drowning in animal blood. It was cuisine and carnage combined.

I assumed Obraitis and Dufour didn't know I was a critic, even when I showed up for a second meal. The first dish I ate could not have been better—escargots and marrow set in the trench of a bisected shinbone. The marrow enriched the escargots, and the escargots gave heft to the marrow, which is usually perceived as little more than quivering fat. Topping it all were minute, crunchy breadcrumbs. The beef tartare was a bit too moist and much too chunky, precisely as it was intended to be. The cooking here has two styles: a little too much or a lot too much.

I admired the M. Wells interpretation of Caesar salad, which has smoked herring substituting for anchovies. It did have one flaw, in that the herring obliterated the flavor of the grated Parmesan. (Anchovies, magically, don't do that.) Porchetta Sierra was a spin on *vitello tonnato*—slices of rare, rosy, roasted veal covered with a mild tuna sauce. Dufour's version was half-good: The mackerel-mayonnaise sauce was wondrously clever, but it couldn't save the dry, overcooked pork beneath it. If you admire audaciousness over achievement, both preparations could be described as intriguing. Then came the greatest pineapple upside-down cake of my life.

So I was practically bounding when I approached Obraitis to ask if I could set up an interview with her and her husband. She seemed delighted and immediately agreed—and added that she knew who I was, even if I had made my reservation using a pseudonym. She promised to get back to me within a few days.

The days passed. I didn't hear from her. I called the restaurant and left a message. I e-mailed her at an address recommended by the fellow who answered the phone: write@mwellsdiner.com. I have my share of detractors, but Obraitis had given no indication that she wished to avoid me.

I've been reviewing restaurants for more than twenty years, almost always for *GQ*. Unlike other critics, I'm not particularly interested in disguises—camouflage seems so World War II. When I'm reviewing, I always hope to eat like an anonymous patron and be treated as such. That means not being noticed, but people in the restaurant business make fun of me whenever I claim I'm not recognized. They say I always am. To answer the question most asked, I don't know if my photograph is on any kitchen wall. If it is, I hope it's above the pastry station.

Restaurant reviewing, as you probably suspect, is a nice way to make a living, although spending your waking hours overstuffed is not as much fun as you might think. Being recognized isn't so delightful, either. The food does not improve for a critic once he is known, although service tends to change dramatically. Consider a world where you are perceived to be captivating and where each word you speak is deemed to be of dazzling import. Whatever you desire—clean plates, crisp napkins, warm rolls—is yours for the asking. Restaurants occasionally send out extra dishes to people like me, which is something we don't desire, yet it would be churlish to refuse the gesture, to insist that unordered entrées be taken away. Perhaps I'm naive, but I don't think of these offerings as bribes; they're more like an opportunity for the chef to show off.

When I'm on assignment, I pay for every meal. In case you're wondering, now and then a restaurant owner who has known me forever refuses to give me a check. When I'm not working, I take it—and always leave an oversize tip, in cash. When I am working, we battle until I am permitted to pay. I always try to be truthful and candid in my evaluations, which has cost me dearly. The great chef Jean-Georges Vongerichten, who long ago invited me to eat with his parents in Alsace, no longer speaks to me because of a story I wrote.

This is the ethical core of who I am and what I do, yet the ethics of food writing don't end there. I'm also extremely aware of my behavior in restaurants. I try to be diplomatic and considerate. Never in my professional life has anyone in the restaurant business questioned my conduct. Not until I ate my third meal at M. Wells.

Finally, eight days after our first meeting, Obraitis wrote and asked if the story was still possible. I wasn't surprised or offended by the delayed response. Wizened journalists have learned to suppress such reactions. Anyway, M. Wells felt like a restaurant still in training, even if it had been operating for nearly a year, and I wasn't expecting efficiency. I figured I'd get my story done.

I wrote back to her on a Sunday morning, cheerily telling her we were on. I told her I already had made a reservation at M. Wells for the following Tuesday evening and was thinking of having the Peking duck. She replied, "You would absolutely adore the Peking duck, but we need 48 hours to get it ready." Hmm. In my business we don't expect excellent math skills from the folks we write about, either.

We later spoke on the phone and arranged a future dinner date for me, her, and her husband. She seemed pleased with my choice of restaurants, a small Cantonese seafood palace in Manhattan's Chinatown. We would do the interview there.

Tuesday night arrived. My 6 P.M. reservation was for four persons: myself, two other journalists, and a woman in the restaurant business. The doors opened promptly, and we were amiably sent off to the right. On my second visit I had been seated to the left of the front door at a long wooden communal table set with Mexican religious candles. That's by far the more comfortable section of the long, narrow diner space. The right side has cramped booths, a majority of the counter stools, and heat rising from cooking surfaces.

The two men were across from me, the woman next to me. I sat on the outside, which gave me the best view of the room. We ordered wine and bar snacks, smoked mussels and *papas bravas*, potatoes that are a specialty of Spanish tapas restaurants. The wine, a rosé, was crisply excellent. The mussels were superb: plump, fresh, oily, and lightly smoked. The potatoes were bland despite the supposedly spicy tomato sauce.

Our waiter, a young fellow, never returned. We sat amid the detritus of our snack course—soiled plates, crumpled napkins, empty glasses. At least forty-five minutes went by. My friends were unhappy, one of them vocally. I pleaded for patience. When I'm working, I always wait as long as it takes to get whatever service the restaurant is capable of providing. That's part of being a critic, a way of evaluating whether it's well run or not.

This time I realized my guests were becoming far too restless, not just from the lack of attention but also from the heat, the stickiness, the dearth of space. I finally got the attention of a young waitress. She came over and said, unconcerned, "Do you know what you want?" I admit that her brusqueness caused me to snap. I replied, "We knew what we wanted forty-five minutes ago." She did not respond. Perhaps she deserves credit for remaining unruffled, although I think a more likely explanation is that she didn't give a damn. She took our order. We ate.

The best dish of this meal was the massive, underpriced ($9) blue-cheese salad with monstrous chunks of cheese and hunks of candied walnuts as big and burnished as jeweled Fabergé eggs. Lee Perkins Tuna, a kind of overdressed sashimi, fell flat, dead on arrival, and the *pommes de terre fondantes*, spuds with veal demi-glace and summer truffles, were both overly rich and inexplicably flavorless. The barbecued short ribs consisted of caramelized meat on prehistoric-size bones, not bad eating but not much of it, a rarity for an establishment that likes to send out an avalanche of food. These are splendid bones for your dog, if you own a very big dog.

Then came the banana-cream pie, textbook perfect. That's the pie I want smashed in my face when I play for the Yankees and hit a walk-off home run.

Nothing else of significance happened during that dinner. What stands out is the heat and the long waits. During our meal, Obraitis came by to say that she and her husband had to leave to attend an event and were looking forward to seeing me in a few days. I felt the same, although I didn't enjoy the food as much as I had at the first two dinners, and the service was dreadful. In order to get a check, I had to wave to our elusive waitress.

Late the next afternoon, an e-mail arrived from Obraitis. This is what it said:

> I am a bit distressed by the feedback I received after your visit last night. Either you had despicable service or you guys were in an awful mood. It seems we couldn't make you happy, several servers heard you complain and ask for more attention. One of those servers, a female, received a hardy pat on the ass from you. Totally unacceptable in our world. I don't know what to think or how to proceed. But I must relay my worry.

I sat numb, experiencing the kind of paralysis a person feels when he picks up the phone and learns of a ghastly accident or a horrific illness. I was being accused of sexually harassing a member of a restaurant staff. After a few minutes, I wrote back, and this is what I said:

> Absolutely, 100 percent untrue. I just went bone-cold when I read that. In all my years going to restaurants, I have never done that and never been accused of doing that. I would not do that. Who in the world told you that? I will be happy to come to your restaurant tonight and confront that person, face-to-face. It's a lie.
>
> I will comment quickly on the other stuff. First, I thought one of the men in my group was totally out of line with his mouth and his comments. I just couldn't get him to shut up. Second, we had two servers. A young kid, practically a boy, who brought the bar snacks and then forgot about us for 45 minutes, and a taller woman (blonde, wearing yellow?) who took over. Yes, I said something to her about nobody taking our order for 45 minutes, but that was the extent of my comments about service.
>
> But it simply isn't important compared to that accusation. I assure you it never happened, not by me.

That indictment from Obraitis was wickedly reckless—unless, of course, she had witnessed me doing such a thing, which she had not. She did not ask for my account of what occurred after she and her husband left the restaurant. Under other circumstances, I might have dwelled on the illogicality of the first part of her message. Here was a restaurant proprietor blaming guests for being in a bad mood because they were treated hideously. But at the moment, it didn't get my attention. The accusation was way too momentous.

I think all of us, men and women, fear the false allegation, being put on trial for something we did not do. For a man, a charge of sexual harassment is nuclear, because we are always perceived as guilty. It's damned if you do and damned if someone says you did.

People who have dealt with me in restaurants know I didn't do this. I'm far from beloved as a critic, but I've never been accused of pawing a waitress. Think about it. Would a critic who is dining in a restaurant where he has been recognized do something like this? It seems too stupid to be believed, and I don't think anybody considers me brainless.

I was left breathless, not only by the accusation but by the offhand manner in which it was delivered. Something this damning should be treated with the utmost seriousness. And of course, the complainant has to be identified—the ugliness of an anonymous accusation is beyond measure.

Eventually I decided there could be only two explanations for Obraitis's e-mail. The first assumes that the waitress really did make a complaint. One of my companions put forth a theory: The waitress created a fabrication to deflect attention from the appalling job she had done.

There's another possibility, my theory. I wonder if Obraitis made it all up in order to intimidate me, stop a restaurant critic from writing an unflattering review. Either one of these scenarios is possible. It could have been the waitress fearing for her job or Obraitis fearing for her restaurant. I asked my three friends for their recollections. The first guest, a man, said, "I didn't see any of the behavior that Sarah is alleging. I find her comment ridiculous."

The second guest, another man, called it "absurd—I witnessed nothing untoward on your part." He went on to say how "bizarre" it was "that we, the patrons, are somehow to blame for not having a good experience. An experience that consisted of dirty dishes and glassware, lack of utensils when plates are served or careless thrusting of utensils, huffy attitude, and all-around eye-rolling. I guess that's the whole hipster restaurant proposition: Service is for stiffs."

The woman added, "I was sitting beside you for the entire meal and did not see you touch anyone. I walked behind you when we left the restaurant and didn't see you touch anyone. It's sickening that someone would make this up and direct it at you. It crosses a line. They treated us badly, were not sorry about it, and then decided to attack you further with untrue accusations. It's the worst restaurant experience I've ever had."

Three days later, I got another e-mail from Obraitis, the last one. The first thing she said was that she and her husband were canceling our dinner plans and no longer wished "to pursue the interview." I remember thinking how disconnected she was from reality, that after making such a terrible denunciation, she could think that I would be interested in eating with her. I did not speak or write to her again.

That last e-mail from her contained slightly more details on the alleged incident. Obraitis wrote, ". . . apparently upon requesting your check you tapped one of our female servers inappropriately." I suppose she's backing off somewhat by adding the word "apparently" and by changing the "hardy pat on the ass" to a simple tap.

I've reported what occurred at M. Wells. I believe I have been accurate. I do think the "hipster restaurant" mentality mentioned by one of my friends is partly to blame for what occurred. There is a reason why serious restaurants

> *I always try to be truthful and candid in my evaluations, which has cost me dearly. The great chef Jean-Georges Vongerichten, who long ago invited me to eat with his parents in Alsace, no longer speaks to me because of a story I wrote.*

train people working for them to be polite and attentive. After my three dinners at M. Wells, I am reasonably certain that thorough schooling has never taken place there.

Critics like me deserve some blame for the current proliferation of impossibly low service standards in so many casual New York restaurants. We tend not to censure lackadaisical conduct, thinking this is what customers want and that we would appear out of touch if we disapproved. In fact, the article I was planning to write most likely wouldn't have dwelled on the egregious manners I'd encountered.

I wish I had never been so forgiving in my reviews of New York restaurants. I should long ago have paid attention to this disastrous decline in service. Casualness in restaurants does not automatically make customers feel more relaxed. It often has the opposite effect. Remember how tense my friends became when we received no attention at M. Wells.

I appreciate an atmosphere lacking formality. I love Momofuku Ssäm Bar in Manhattan and Schwa in Chicago, both unpretentious and unfussy—but also attentive. They employ people who know how to take orders, fill glasses, clear plates, drop checks. Neither neglects customers. These days, too many new restaurants do. Their motto might as well be Too Cool to Care.

Well-run restaurants recognize that thoughtful service enhances an evening out, and that a bit of formality might be required in order to reach that goal. Customers these days tend to confuse discipline and manners with arrogance. Perhaps they are remembering the excess stuffiness of decades past. That hardly exists any longer. Arrogance today is exhibited by inconsiderate servers who do almost nothing for customers other than slap plates down in front of them and expect a generous tip. Arrogance is a restaurant believing it can prosper without looking after its customers.

I will tell you what else is extraordinarily self-defeating: We empower popular restaurants, and M. Wells is very much one of them. All we care about is accessibility, getting through the door. Such restaurants are rarely held accountable, no matter how uncaring they might be. I doubt that the people who operate these sought-after spots ask themselves if they are treating their customers properly. They are not obliged to do so.

There is one thing more to say. It is not charitable, so I don't suppose it will reflect well on me. I do not forgive the people at M. Wells for what they have said. I wish there were some way they would not get away with it. I'm pretty certain they will, and I will always be sorry for that.

Chef Q & A: Thomas Keller

By Becky Paskin
The World's Best 50 Restaurants, March 30, 2012

Revered the world over, innovative chef Thomas Keller is probably the most awarded chef in history, with a Legion of Honour, several James Beard awards, Michelin stars and two stints as the S.Pellegrino World's Best Restaurant for The French Laundry in California. Reputed to be somewhat of a perfectionist, the talented chef invests much time into training and mentoring his staff to ensure standards remain impeccably high across his six-strong stable of restaurants, which include Per Se in New York.

You recently ran a pop-up version of The French Laundry at Harrod's in London as your first foray in the UK. How was the experience for you?

The pop-up was extraordinary. It was an amazing event more so because of the historical aspect of it—it's never been done before by us or Harrods. Most pop-ups are done in someone else's restaurant space on the fly for a commercial purpose but this was done just the opposite to resemble a restaurant that already existed. We did an amazing job of replicating it. When you're on the fifth floor of Harrods you don't have a lot to work with, but we tried to make the space resemble the real thing as much as possible. We even had astro turf for the garden space. It's kind of corny but it's an attempt and we couldn't put real grass up there. It's kind of Disney-esque but a lot of things are staged in department stores—people go to look at the windows because of the staging. So the concept fit well within the environment we operated in.

It was also incredible when you just think about the different groups of individuals that were part of that process, none of whom had ever worked together before. We had chefs and dining room staff who came from all of our restaurants who don't typically work together; working with the Harrods team who we've never worked with before and also a third team of 14 servers from the UK put together especially for the event. How these different groups of people came together for me was one of the proudest moments I've had.

Were you pleased with the reviews The French Laundry pop-up received?

I never expected any reviews—I thought it was a bit strange for magazines and newspapers to review a restaurant that was not permanent and sold out from the time we opened so people wouldn't have a chance to make a reservation, but we got one from every major newspaper in London. To try and compare our restaurant to others already in London was a bit awkward for me. There was one newspaper that said the pop-up was the best restaurant in London. I've got colleagues there like Gordon (Ramsay), Heston (Blumenthal), Marcus (Wareing) and Jason (Atherton), and it was just a slap in their face to review a restaurant that's not even permanent or one that anybody can get into, and try to qualify it in comparison to restaurateurs and chefs who have made their careers in London. Writing a story I get it, but to give it three, four or five stars—there's no point.

Would you ever like to do it again?

No, we've been thinking about touring The French Laundry for several years, and I don't know if it would be The French Laundry or not, but it's already been done before. Paul Prudhomme already did it in 1983 so it's nothing new. Everything's been done before.

Where does your desire to continuously break new ground come from?

I'm a one off person and once I've done it I don't necessarily want to do it again.

The French Laundry dropped out of the S.Pellegrino World's 50 Best Restaurants list for the first time last year—after previously being named number one on two occasions. What did that mean to you?

It bothered me for a moment but we are not defined by other people. We don't live for an award; it's just not who we are. The awards we receive are wonderful—to be the first chef to have back to back wins was extraordinary; it was a very proud moment. To be the only chef ever to have two restaurants on the list let alone in the top ten is an extraordinary accomplishment, but it's not about me; it's about the team we have and with that credit comes a sense of responsibility not to the award but to the guests and each other. That's the cause. Our culture and society get caught up in this idea of awards and it deteriorates and diminishes the reason to do things. I have fifteen James Beard awards for everything but they are just sitting on the shelf. I'm the only chef to win the Wedgewood award, the only American chef to have three Michelin stars and the only male American chef to have been given the Legion of Honour in my profession. Was I proud to be a part of those things? Yes, but how can they define who I am? I can't let that happen. At the end of the day, who really cares? I want to think about what I'm doing tomorrow, because we are going to come to work knowing we are going to do a better job than we did yesterday.

How has The French Laundry developed in the past year?

The French Laundry is one of those unique restaurants that develops every day. We change our menu every day and by doing that we continue to build on what we did yesterday. The nuances of what we do continue to develop but part of the important thing we do is working with our suppliers and making sure that we continue to support them, give them what they need and continue to progress as well, because when they become better so do we. Cooking is a very simple equation: it's about ingredients and execution, and if we are not supporting the people who supply us those ingredients then they are not going to be able to do what we need them to. If we can bring those two elements together through support in significant ways then we should have a successful evening. At the end of the day it's a sport franchise, a baseball team, and it's about making sure you have the right individuals in that team to perform at a high level and ensuring they have the right tools they need to perform.

You're a very busy man, how do you divide your time between your restaurants and still maintain standards?

It's not about me, it's about the team I have working for me and their commitment, determination and desire to work at very high standards. If you hire the right individuals, train them and mentor them and give them the tools they need, then they will be able to perform at a very high level and that's the most important part for me. It's not about any one person.

You made an advert for American Express lately that ran during the Super Bowl—how did you get involved with that?

It was nice to move outside of my normal scope of work and experience something else, like making Spanglish or Ratatouille. American Express has been a great partner of ours so when they asked me to become part of their new membership effect programme I was happy to help.

What are you looking at in terms of expansion?

Nothing right now, but there are opportunities everywhere and it's a matter of having the time. It's easy to open restaurants but it takes a lot more to maintain them. Someone's always writing a letter suggesting somewhere to open. In 19 years I've opened six restaurants—that's one every three years. That's quite conservative when you compare me to some of my colleagues who have opened three times as many restaurants than I have in half the time.

What's been your ultimate lifetime goal?

I've achieved more than I could ever dream of. My goal was just to have one restaurant one day and I failed that three times before I got The French Laundry. My goal now is that my restaurants today have what they need. It's an interesting time to be in the restaurant business. When I started out there were no celebrity chefs in America, or even the world outside of France. There was no respect for food so when I started cooking it was simply about the act of cooking and not about becoming famous. I decided to become a chef after cooking for three years and I was then enlightened by a chef who showed me that we cook to nurture people and make them smile. That's the moment I became a chef—because I realized that I'm a nurturer at heart. I want to make people happy and what better way to do that than feed them. If I wasn't a chef I'd be a doctor or a teacher—something where you can have a positive impact on people.

> *Cooking is a very simple equation: it's about ingredients and execution, and if we are not supporting the people who supply us those ingredients then they are not going to be able to do what we need them to.*

What's in the future for Thomas Keller?

My partners ask me what's my exit strategy, but as a chef I don't have one. I won't be a chef all my life but the one greatest thing that's happened to our profession in the last thirty years is chefs have been liberated from being in the kitchen all the time. The last generation of chefs who were in their kitchens died in their kitchens. Chefs work really hard to reach a level in their career where they hopefully have a successful restaurant and work it with determination and desire, but at some point they reach an age where they can no longer physically do that. In older generations chefs didn't have options—they physically stayed in their restaurants and started to diminish. And most of those guys would have trained and mentored the next generation who would have gone on to eclipse them. Today if we are lucky enough and have a little bit of talent and are in the right place at the right time with the right idea then we are given opportunities to do other things that liberate us. We can now establish a culture and business that continues to perpetuate the ideals and standards that you begin with and evolve into a place that is better than you ever thought it would be. And that for me is what I want to do. None of my restaurants have my name on it—what would happen if I wasn't here, or I sold it, or died? It would cease to exist and what kind of legacy is that? There's no place I'd rather be more than in the kitchen and I'm not ready to sit back just yet.

Have people eclipsed you in terms of skill?

Yes, I don't know about everybody but quite a few have and my job is to make sure that when youngsters come into our restaurants, whether it's in the kitchen or dining room, that they have the knowledge and training that's going to help them be better in their next position. If I hire the right individual and mentor that person then they are better than me. I'm proud of them all.

You have a reputation amongst those that have worked with you in the past for being somewhat of a perfectionist. Do you think your reputation is accurate?

I never think anything's perfect because if you get to the point where you think something's perfect you soon realize it's not. You can never achieve true perfection. That's one of the things that drives us—how do you make it better? We use green tape in our kitchens to tape things down and between 1994 and 2004 we used to rip the green tape off the roll. But when we opened Per Se in 2004 one new member of the team was taping down the pass for the first time and he took a pair of scissors and cut the tape. It was monumental because no-one had never done it before. For an entire decade no-one had the thought to cut the green tape instead of tearing it.

So while we are always striving for precision and perfection none of us thought to cut the green tape. You look at something forever and it's hard to see how to improve simple tasks. From that point on we've always cut the tape. It's now become an extension of The French Laundry—you'll see it at a lot of restaurants.

Charity Case: Can a Restaurant That Gives All Its Profits Away Succeed in D.C.?

By Jessica Sidman
Washington City Paper, November 1, 2012

Not many restaurant opening parties kick off with a PowerPoint presentation.

But during last week's debut of the U Street NW corridor "philanthropub" Cause, founders Nick Vilelle and Raj Ratwani stood before the crowd in suits with microphones in hand.

"I never thought I'd be using graphs in a bar," Ratwani told about 50 people. He pulled up a slide showing that younger people eat out more than others, then another that showed they also donate less to charity. "Coming from a cognitive psychology background, what I want to do is integrate these two, and that's exactly what we're going to do with this bar concept."

Cause will operate like any other bar: You come in, buy drinks, eat food. The restaurant pays its staff and its bills. And then it does something completely unheard of in the restaurant industry: It gives 100 percent of the profits to charity.

At the opening, Ratwani quickly acknowledged to the crowd of nonprofit reps, friends, and media that he and Vilelle have no restaurant experience. "Two psychologists trying to start a restaurant? I'm sure everybody knows the statistics about the failure rate of restaurants."

That's where The Light Horse owner and restaurant vet John Jarecki came in. Now the managing director of Cause, he told the audience that Ratwani, a friend of a friend, first approached him about opening a bar five years ago. "I said, 'Well, what experience do you have?' And he said, 'None.' So I said, 'Do me a favor, take what money you had for opening this bar, and flush it down the toilet. You'll thank me in five years.'"

Ratwani and Vilelle came back to Jarecki a year ago and pitched a more developed business plan. The idea struck a chord with Jarecki, whose family members are heavily involved in nonprofit causes. "I said, 'This is amazing. We've got to do this. Let's paint ourselves into a corner and make this happen, because it needs to happen.'"

What happens next is an experiment. As far as the founders know, no one has ever done anything like it.

But the idea seems to be a product of our time: Social enterprises—revenue-generating businesses with social or environmental goals—are the hot new model in philanthropy. Toms Shoes, for example, has become the poster child for profit with a purpose, giving away a pair of shoes to a child in need with every purchase. The company has donated more than two million pairs of shoes, while remaining one of the most popular consumer footwear brands. Cause wants to accomplish something similar in giving back while giving people what they want. But whether the do-goody concept can work in the unrelenting, fickle restaurant industry has yet to be seen.

Vilelle and Ratwani believe D.C. is the perfect guinea pig. The city has one of the largest concentrations of nonprofits in the country, and a significant population of well-to-do young professionals. Cause's founders may be the first to acknowledge the high failure rate of restaurants, but they still believe they can make their idea work.

The plan was hatched about five years ago over beers at Clarendon Ballroom. Vilelle had just come back from a Peace Corps stint in Togo, and Ratwani was working on his cognitive psychology Ph.D. at George Mason University.

Looking around, they saw all the cash that young professionals were spending on drinks. "This money!" Vilelle remembers thinking. "What it could do in my village is just mind-boggling." Meanwhile, Ratwani was searching for a way to give back, but he didn't have much money or time, especially working up to 80 hours a week on his dissertation.

"You always find time to grab a beer, is one thing I noticed," Ratwani says. He and Vilelle thought a restaurant and bar would be a fun, easy way for people to give to charity by doing something they already do. They tossed the idea back and forth over a few years before getting Jarecki and his partner at The Light Horse, Dave Pressley, on board.

Cause will choose between three and six small local and international organizations to benefit each quarter. The groups go through an application process and are vetted by a five-person advisory board of volunteers with backgrounds in law, finance, and nonprofits. The chosen organizations are listed on the menu, and when guests receive their bill they'll check a box for which group to support. Servers are also trained to give information about the groups in the same way they might tell you what's in the African chicken groundnut stew. But Cause's founders don't want the charity angle to be in your face. "We don't want a 'Do you want to round up for breast cancer?' situation. We don't like those, because you feel like an asshole saying 'No,'" Vilelle says.

Cause is not a nonprofit. Selling food and alcohol makes it difficult to qualify for tax-exempt status with the IRS; those sales would likely count as what the IRS calls "unrelated business income" and be taxed anyway. Also, Cause is not carrying out any charitable activities itself. Although it misses out on some of the tax benefits of a nonprofit, operating as an LLC gives Cause the flexibility to donate to causes (or other social enterprises) that might not be registered 501(c)(3)s, Vielle says.

Eventually, if it becomes possible, Cause may become a "B Corp" or for-benefit corporation, a new designation popping up in some states (though not yet D.C.) for businesses that have a mission for social good.

Cause still aims to have the level of transparency that's legally required of nonprofits. Vilelle and Ratwani believe the only way to satisfy critics who think they're taking big salaries or using charity as a gimmick is to be up-front about their financials. So Cause will post all its salaries and expenses on its website at the end of each quarter. Screens near the restrooms will also visually display the numbers.

Start-up costs have been minimal. Cause opened with $100,000 in debt, very little compared to most restaurants, which often spend at least half a million dollars to open. The restaurant raised $23,576 from the crowd-founding site Indiegogo to help with build-out of the space. Other costs were offset by pro bono legal, graphic design, and PR work. Chef Adam Stein will share his time between The Light Horse and Cause, so Cause won't have to pay him a full-time salary.

> *Vilelle and Ratwani believe the only way to satisfy critics who think they're taking big salaries or using charity as a gimmick is to be up-front about their financials. So Cause will post all its salaries and expenses on its website at the end of each quarter.*

Ratwani doesn't plan to take a salary for now (he has a full-time job as a senior research scientist for MedStar Health), and Vilelle says he will only pay himself for the hours he works in the restaurant and the jobs he does. So if he buses tables for a night, he'll pay himself a busboy's wage.

Cause plans to pay down its debt to private investors over about five years. That way, it will be able to give to charity from day one. Financial Foods co-founder Adam Williamowsky, who consults with D.C.-area restaurants on development and investment, says most full service restaurants take four years to pay off investors. First-time restaurateurs typically don't pay back anything in their first year.

Cause is also protecting itself against a common source of financial trouble for restaurants: the lease. Rents can jump significantly when a lease ends, forcing restaurants out. But in this case, Cause is its own landlord. A group of Cause investors purchased the property at 1926 9th St. NW for $930,000. By owning the building, they're able to subsidize the rent for the restaurant at about 20 percent below market value. Cause's founders say the building's investors will still make money from the rent, but less than they would otherwise.

Ultimately, Cause will still need to draw a crowd if it wants to stick around. Williamowsky says sustaining any business—nonprofit, restaurant, or otherwise—always boils down to providing a quality product. For Cause, that means not just supporting great organizations, but also quality food and service.

Just to break even, the restaurant will need to bring in about $1 million a year. According to the National Restaurant Association, the average profit margin for restaurants is 4 to 6 percent. Jarecki says he's projecting a profit margin between 10 to 20 percent (revenues of $1.1 to $1.2 million). Williamowsky says the full-service restaurants he's worked with in the area see profit margins between 8 to 14 percent, on average. Successful fast-casual spots can do better than 20 percent.

Cause's goal is to give away $100,000 in its first year. "Some people say we're crazy," Vilelle says. "But I think we've done a lot to keep our overhead low." If it's successful, Vilelle and Ratwani want to open up other locations across the country, and possibly internationally.

The duo think the exposure they're giving nonprofits may ultimately be more valuable than their donations. By simply going out, thousands of people will at least learn about the organizations, and Cause's founders hope some will later donate or volunteer.

"Neither Raj or I are in this for money," Vilelle says. "It's more like a challenge. Can we pull this off? Can we create this impact?"

Opening a Restaurant Takes Sweat, Savvy, Courage, and Cash

By Nancy Leson
Pacific NW Magazine (Seattle Times), November 16, 2012

Why, through boom, bust and 50-50 odds of success, are so many people willing to take a chance on opening a restaurant?

Opening a restaurant is a dreamer's fancy, a risky business. It's brutal work, it ruins relationships, it rarely leads to riches.

So why, through boom, bust and a relentless recession, are so many willing to take a chance?

For some, it's the ambition of becoming the next Tom Douglas, crowned this year with the James Beard Award as America's Outstanding Restaurateur. Others just want to be their own boss after years spent under the tutelage—or thumb—of mentors and meanies.

Then there's the passion.

"Opening a restaurant is such an emotional experience. It's so raw," says chef Maria Hines. "There are so many factors beyond our control that you have to deal with, navigate and survive through."

She's done so twice: first at Tilth, in Wallingford, next at Golden Beetle in Ballard. Both were turnkey operations, restaurant redo's opened on a shoestring. Hines ran high-end kitchens on both coasts before striking out on her own, with help from a few investors.

Ownership has brought her fame—including an opportunity to smoke Morimoto out of his Iron Chef coat. But so far, no fortune.

She lives in a 550-square-foot house, and only recently traded her 15-year-old sedan for a new minivan used to haul food and equipment to caterings that add to her bottom line.

"I'm more in debt today than I was when I opened Tilth" in 2006, admits the 40-year-old chef, whose workweek often extends to 70 hours. That hasn't slowed her plans to open a third, even a fourth Seattle restaurant. "Cooks are all about the suffer-fest," she explains. "We love the challenge. And there's nothing more terrifying than opening a restaurant."

Larkin Young isn't scared. Tilth's former chef de cuisine was at Hines' side when she bested the Iron Chef before an audience of millions. After three years at Tilth, he stood as second-in-command at Golden Beetle's 2010 debut—taking mental notes for the day he'll wield knives at a restaurant he hopes to call Spoon.

Young's business plan includes a menu based on a locavore's love of foraging, and a résumé jump-started when he was a boy, canning, baking and sausage-making with his family on 40 acres of Minnesota woodland.

What he doesn't have is money.

"You don't realize how much it takes," says Young, estimating $250,000 to lease a 50-seat turnkey, do a remodel, secure permits and insurance, and still have "a little cushion" for unexpected items like a faulty hood or failing cooler.

Since arriving in Seattle a dozen years ago, Young has been both grill cook and head cook. Now 38, he's done stints at several high-profile restaurants, most recently as sous-chef at Michael Mina's vaunted downtowner RN74. There, he watched with fascination as the San Francisco–based chef's Euro-luxe newcomer unfolded.

"I want to make something happen," says Young, who since parted ways with the Mina Group. "I don't want to put myself in the position of being someone's sous-chef for another two years."

But he might have to.

"I think it would be close to impossible for me to go into a bank and say, 'Here's my business plan, I need this amount of money.' I rent a house. I barely got accepted for a credit card."

Homeownership and good credit were a godsend for Tony Mann. In 2004, it helped secure $250,000 to lease a prime spot in Edmonds' new 99 Ranch Market complex and build a big, bright 110-seater just north of his original T&T Seafood Restaurant.

It took a $100,000 second mortgage on his home, a $70,000 business loan from his bank, and $80,000 squirreled away during the four years he and his partner, Theresa Lam, worked seven days a week at their first effort—a small cafe in Shoreline.

"Cooking is all I ever wanted to do," says the 52-year-old chef. Born in Saigon to Cantonese parents, he worked his way up the ladder from dishwasher to restaurant owner after emigrating to the U.S. in 1979. It wasn't an easy climb.

Tony met Theresa at Fortune City in Seattle's Chinatown. He cooked; she worked the cash register. They fell in love, soon setting their hearts on opening the restaurant that would bear their initials.

They opened in 2000, when they found and leased a former pho shop, investing $45,000 in savings, knowing the cafe was to be demolished for road improvements. "We were never thinking far enough ahead," recalls Lam.

But they had the foresight to hire an accountant familiar with the restaurant business to keep abreast of daily receipts, taxes, payroll and permitting. He's still working for them.

That's one of the smartest moves a first-time restaurant owner could make, says Anthony Anton, president of the Washington Restaurant Association. "Not understanding the financials is where people get crushed. Fifty percent of restaurants open in Washington today will be out of business—or owned by somebody else—five years from now."

For those that last, "we're still hoping to make a nickel on a dollar, and the average is 4 cents."

Lam was a novice waitress, but learned quickly how to turn a nickel into a buck. When business was slow, she'd drive to a nearby Costco and hand out takeout menus. Meantime, Mann made all his sauces from scratch and soon had a fan club clamoring for his honey walnut prawns and "House Special crab."

Among the fans: the management behind 99 Ranch, which offered him a new venue and attractive lease concessions. Sold!

For nearly a year, the chef recalls, he ran between the two restaurants. One night, his heart racing, he ended up in the emergency room. "You're like an overheated car," the doctor explained. His prescription? "Don't work so hard."

Since then, the couple has married, shuttered the original T&T and expanded their Edmonds restaurant, absorbing the store next door. They've paid off their house and much of the initial bank loan; grown their staff from five to 25, added a wildly popular dim sum kitchen. They've hired a general manager, cut their hours, learned to delegate.

After a recent family trip to Southeast Asia, Lam's son, Wilson, and daughter, Stella, now in college, recalled those early days in Shoreline. After school, they'd come to the café, help bag takeout and fall asleep across some chairs.

Do they see themselves taking over the family business? Wilson laughs, pointing to his sister. "Anything can happen," she says.

Donna Moodie, owner of Marjorie, the jewel-box bistro on Capitol Hill, studied French, art and communications in college, but her real education came after.

Working at Chicago's Drake Hotel—in a small bar perfect for men with their mistresses and celebrities like Oprah—she learned the finer points of fine service. Tips financed a trip to Europe in 1985, and upon her return to Chicago, "I wanted a place where I can invest in the same way the people who own it invest: emotionally."

At Jerome's, she found just that, waiting tables and apprenticing as a baker during her six-year tenure. There the owners sourced organic vegetables and meat from local butchers. "Avant-garde for its day," Jerome's "had a charming patio, comfortable service and an amazing staff," recalls Moodie.

It became the prototype for Marjorie, named for her Jamaican mother, whose "graciously hosted dinner parties" laid the foundation for her daughter's career.

Moodie, who has so far invested in four restaurants, spent $120,000—"our life savings"—to open her first, Marco's Supperclub, with partner Marco Rulff (closed last year after a 17-year-run). Their second, Lush Life, was closed in 2002, renovated and reincarnated as the original Marjorie after the couple split the sheets.

"We had caring people on our staff," Moodie says of that time. "But it was hard for them when we were breaking up," a process that unfolded over several highly emotional years. "It was like they were the children of divorce."

Then, in 2008, five years after opening, Marjorie was forced to close when the Belltown building it inhabited was sold. "When I found out I had to move, I felt really devastated," she said at the time, "but then I looked around and saw it was a great opportunity, too."

That opportunity came after a long search, a year and a half in which she waited tables at Ethan Stowell's tiny Queen Anne restaurant, How to Cook a Wolf.

With the economy in free-fall, "Working at Wolf inspired me to look at a small space and be serious about it," Moodie says. It also found her shelving her original business plan for the new Marjorie—one that called for multiple investors and two more restaurant concepts.

"There's an austerity that makes sense in this economy. One that says, 'If it's doable, I should do it myself.'"

Acting as her restaurant's general contractor, she invested $200,000 to plant Marjorie in the shade of the Chloe apartment complex off 14th Avenue and Union Street—a corner that has since come to house Skillet Diner and the relocated Restaurant Zoë.

"Being adaptable is huge," she says. "I'm not an interior decorator, but I became one. I'm not an HR person, but I do bookkeeping and hiring. I'm not a marketing specialist, but I need to know how to conduct social media. I'm not a sommelier, but I'll purchase wines. I'm not a gardener, but I maintain the patio myself.

"I'm not a trained chef, but I'm going to put my head back there in the kitchen and engage in a conversation."

Emotionally, her investment paid off—something Moodie's acutely aware of while hosting the dinner party disguised as Marjorie's dining room. Financially, not quite yet. "In the early '90s it would have been," she notes. "Everything's increased except for the public perception of the cost of dining out.

"It's hard for people to understand what it takes to run a small business."

Running a large restaurant is no picnic, either, but it's paid off big-time for Nate Opper—who beat the crowds to Ballard when he staked his reputation on a Tex-Mex tequila bar, the Matador, since cloned six times in three states.

Opper was working construction, tending bar part-time at a Pioneer Square pub when he had an epiphany: "Why should I be pounding nails in the rain and getting electrocuted by a Skilsaw?" Why not open a restaurant? Trouble was, "I was living week-to-week."

Ten years and ten restaurants later, he owns a view home in Seattle's Broadview neighborhood.

"I never miss a sunset," Opper boasts after the debut of his company's second restaurant concept: Kickin' Boot Whiskey Kitchen, a Southern comfort-food joint opened in August.

He also never misses a trick, says his partner, Zak Melang.

"You couldn't find two people more yin and yang than Nathan and me," says Melang, a family man whose mellow drawl speaks of his North Carolina roots. A former musician, bartender and restaurant manager, today he wrangles real estate and oversees design for their company while Opper rides herd on operations, food service and nearly 500 employees.

"I'm a really headstrong person," Opper says. "Zak trusts that I'll take care of things, and I do. If he was exactly like me, we'd be arguing."

It took two years to locate and lease the first Matador, since reproduced in West

Seattle, Tacoma, Redmond, twice in Portland and most recently in Boise. "I'm obsessive," says Melang. "I probably lost 25 to 30 locations before I found our first spot."

He's as obsessive about his restaurants' look as their locations.

"When I show people what a Matador looks like, Tacoma is what I like to show them: a historical building, preferably brick. I love corner locations. A small footprint—around 3,500 to 4,000 square feet. High ceilings are always a plus." So is "a cool patio."

Working at Chicago's Drake Hotel—in a small bar perfect for men with their mistresses and celebrities like Oprah—[Moodie] learned the finer points of fine service.

Best of all is a high-density neighborhood, like the one in Northwest Portland where, two months after opening Kickin' Boot, they launched its Southern sibling, Southland Whiskey Kitchen.

Opper, a self-taught cook with a refined palate, depends on a fleet of professionals to oversee his bars and kitchens. He trains them well.

On opening night at Kickin' Boot, Opper kicked butt, showing a prep cook how to better batter fried chicken, expediting at the kitchen window and eyeballing bartenders slow to the task—before taking them to task for that shortcoming.

Says Melang, "He's the kind of guy who excels when thrown into the fire." Only weeks before Kickin' Boot's debut in the handsomely restored Henry Gowan Whyte Building, Opper added fuel to that fire. He gave the go-ahead for demolition on a third concept: Ballard Annex Oyster House, a seafood restaurant aiming to open in December betwixt the Boot and the Ballard Matador.

"It was never our intention to open three restaurants in a two-block radius," says Melang, who finessed a lease that has them owning the building in five years—an important first for the company. "But these locations are magnificent. Someone was going to open a restaurant in them, and we figured we'd rather compete with ourselves."

Eight years ago, the partners set out to control their own destinies and were able to do so thanks to an "angel investor"—a silent partner who'd made his own fortune in the restaurant business. "He lent me $70,000," and financed twice that himself, Opper says. "Not a ton of money, but for me it was—because I didn't have any."

Larkin Young is still waiting for an angel. Last summer he hosted a successful Spoon "pop-up"—borrowing a friend's restaurant for one night. He's showed his business plan to restaurant consultants, small-business mentors and chefs who've taken the plunge and succeeded.

He has friends who've compromised, he says, taking a job at a country club or hotel, exchanging a vision for medical benefits and direct-deposit.

"Instead of thinking about compromising, I'm thinking of ways to support my goal. A food truck or a little sandwich shop, something more feasible. It may take more time to get where I want to go, but at the same time, I'll get there.

"The one person who believes in me is me."

Not so.

Maria Hines says for dreamers like Young, there's nothing like running your own show. "I couldn't think of another thing that Larkin should do."

Check, Please

By John Colapinto
New Yorker, September 10, 2012

One afternoon this spring, Will Guidara, the general manager and co-owner of Eleven Madison Park, a restaurant in Manhattan's Flatiron district, arrived at work limping and gray-faced. He had thrown out his back, a stress-related injury to which he is prone. ("I am an exceptionally anal person," he says.) Often, Guidara, a gregarious man of thirty-two who dresses in dark suits and ties, will enter and stand for a moment in the restaurant's foyer with his eyes closed, listening to the buzz of conversation, the clink of cutlery, and the murmur of his service team moving among the tables; he says that he can tell from the sound of the room how the restaurant is doing. Today, he hobbled into the lounge and eased into an armchair.

He was joined by Daniel Humm, the restaurant's chef and co-owner. Dressed in his usual white chef's jacket and bluejeans, Humm, thirty-five, is six feet four and has an athlete's lean build. Though soft-spoken and outwardly calm, he is as tightly coiled as Guidara.

"So did you go to that acupuncturist, like I told you?" he asked, in his light Swiss accent.

"I did," Guidara said, wincing. "And I went to my chiropractor, too."

Humm and Guidara had been under unusual pressure. In the previous six months, they had bought Eleven Madison Park from their former employer, the restaurant mogul Danny Meyer; published a coffee-table cookbook; and opened their second restaurant, the NoMad—all while striving to maintain the food and service that earned Eleven Madison Park a four-star rating in the *Times* and three stars in the Guide Michelin. They were scheduled to fly to London the next day to attend the San Pellegrino World's 50 Best Restaurants awards, where they would learn their current ranking. Eleven Madison Park first made the list in 2010—but barely, landing at the rank of fifty.

Humm's training is in classical French cuisine, but at Eleven Madison Park he has introduced a witty New York twist: his take on the bagels and lox served at such Manhattan delis as Barney Greengrass uses caviar, cream cheese, quail eggs, a bagel "crumble," and a fillet of sturgeon that arrives at the table under a custom-blown glass dome, swirling with applewood smoke. Guidara's service team eschews the stiff-spined rectitude of European fine dining for a New York casualness that permits an occasional smile and even some light conversation with guests. The restaurant's playful approach caught the attention of the San Pellegrino judges in 2010, but because Humm and Guidara barely made the list, they surmised that

Eleven Madison Park was still too much in the mold of conventional fine dining. Restaurants that rank highest tend to reshape the way people think about cooking: El Bulli, in Spain, held the top slot from 2006 through 2009 with Ferran Adrià's chemistry-set experimentation (frozen "air of Parmesan" with muesli) but was displaced, as fashions changed, by Noma, in Copenhagen, which has a near-Druidical emphasis on foraged ingredients (crispy deer lichen dusted with mushrooms on a bed of moss). Although the San Pellegrino awards do not have the mystique of Michelin stars, their comparative rankings give them marketing power. René Redzepi, the chef and co-owner of Noma, has said that before his restaurant was named the world's best there were days when he had only fourteen customers; after the announcement he had twelve hundred on his waiting list.

For guidance, Humm and Guidara looked to the restaurant's first review after Humm took over, in 2006: the *New York Observer's* critic Moira Hodgson had called Humm "a star," but said that the dining room felt stodgy and needed a "bit of Miles Davis." "We had no idea what that meant," Guidara says, laughing, "but we started to listen to a lot of Miles and read about him." They made lists of words to define Davis's music—"cool," "collaborative," "fresh," "vibrant," "spontaneous"—and hung them, along with a photograph of the musician, in the restaurant's kitchen. They also looked for inspiration in other restaurants—some at the furthest remove from fine dining, like Rao's, a red-sauce joint in Harlem, frequented by mobsters and celebrities, where reservations are impossible to get (tables are "owned" by regulars) and there are no menus. "It's not like going to a restaurant," Guidara says. "I felt like I was at my grandmother's house."

Today, when you step through Eleven Madison Park's revolving door, you see not a maître d' behind a lectern but a greeter, who shakes your hand as if welcoming you into his home. The casualness is illusory. In his left hand he palms a list of reservations, and he has spent the hours before service Googling names and studying Facebook photographs. He says your name in a voice loud enough to be heard by the maître d', who is standing out of sight behind a pilaster. Using a computerized map of the dining room, with the tables color-coded to indicate their stage of readiness, the maître d' decides where to seat you. Meanwhile, he signals to the greeter: a hand across the waist means "The table isn't ready—send them to the bar"; gripping the wrist with the opposite hand means "I need a minute; stall them."

With Rao's in mind, Humm and Guidara thought about abolishing menus, but rejected the idea as impractical. Instead, they replaced the traditional leather-bound board with an eight-inch-square white card, printed with the names of sixteen ingredients that change with the seasons—"trout," "almond," "asparagus," "foie gras"—in a four-by-four grid. (Prices were tucked away demurely at the bottom, without dollar signs: four courses, 74; tasting menu, 195.) Diners are instructed to pick one ingredient from each row, and the courses are built around those choices.

Humm and Guidara also broke down the traditional divide between dining room and kitchen; sous-chefs bring out dishes they have made, and diners are invited into the kitchen, to stand in an alcove overlooking the bustling "pass," where cooks tweeze the final touches onto plates. A server prepares them an applejack cocktail, frozen with a blast of nitrogen, and, at the end of the meal, brings them to the front lounge for free cognac. At departure, they are given a jar of granola and a handwritten check.

Open Table, the online reservation system, conducts a customer poll that rates the food, service, and ambience of restaurants. Two months after Eleven Madison Park introduced these changes, in September, 2010, it was first in the city in every category, and, at the next year's San Pellegrino ceremony, it moved from last place to No. 24. This year, Humm and Guidara learned, on their trip to London, that the restaurant had jumped fourteen slots, to No. 10.

"Every once in a while, in New York, there are restaurants that come along and create an evolution in the dining scene," Joe Bastianich, Mario Batali's business partner in a number of fine-dining ventures, told me. "Babbo was that fourteen years ago, and Gramercy Tavern before that. There are these benchmark restaurants that change the way people eat." For the moment, Eleven Madison Park is that restaurant. It is booked twenty-eight days in advance, with a waiting list of a hundred and fifty people a night—a rare circumstance when many formerly successful places are closing.

But awards, honors, and even full bookings are no guarantee of success. In all restaurants—from fast food to haute cuisine—profit margins are thin and expenses and overhead high; the restaurateurs who survive are those who ruthlessly cut costs and eliminate waste. As Bastianich put it in his recent book, *Restaurant Man*, "You have to appear to be generous, but you have to be inherently a cheap f**k to make it work." He tells how his restaurateur father saved on laundry bills by using chalk to hide sauce stains on tablecloths. Grant Achatz, the chef-owner of Alinea, an avant-garde restaurant in Chicago, eliminated the tablecloths altogether, saving forty-two thousand dollars a year. "It comes down to a day-to-day penny-pinching that you wouldn't necessarily expect from a restaurant that shows a certain level of opulence," Julian Brizzi, the general manager and co-owner of Rucola, a high-end Italian restaurant in Brooklyn, says. "I hold back on changing the menu more than once a week, because that's fifteen dollars in paper, and printer ink is very expensive."

The imperative to be both frugal and generous creates a paradoxical relationship between restaurants and the people who eat in them: the guest has the illusion of control, but the restaurant determines everything that happens—or it should. Indeed, each of the changes that Humm and Guidara introduced to Eleven Madison Park, in order to make the experience of eating there more dynamic, was also designed to limit overhead, maximize turnover, and lift profits. According to one of their financial advisers, these innovations especially impressed potential investors when Humm and Guidara were raising money to buy the restaurant, last fall. "The things they did!" the adviser told me. "Let's not call them tricks—because the experience of eating there only got better. But they're tricks because the profits are only getting better. That's pretty cool, when you can pull off making me feel better as you take more money out of my damn wallet!"

The dining room at Eleven Madison Park looks like a train station in some enlightened European city: thirty-foot ceilings, terrazzo floors, Art Deco lamps, and tall casement windows that look onto the lawns of Madison Square Park. Designed in the nineteen-twenties, the building, near the southern end of Madison Avenue, was originally part of MetLife's corporate headquarters. It was turned into a restaurant in 1998 by Danny Meyer, the C.E.O. of Union Square Hospitality Group, whose restaurants include Gramercy Tavern and the burger chain Shake Shack. Meyer's original concept was a New York take on the unpretentious neighborhood brasserie. But after years of serving French comfort food to middling critical success—the *Times* gave it two stars—he decided to upgrade. "In its DNA, that dining room really wanted to be grander than a brasserie," he says. "That's why I went looking for a young chef who could turn it into something more."

After a five-month search, he found Humm, who was then the executive chef at Campton Place, in San Francisco, where he made unfussy but technically complex dishes: terrine of foie gras formed around a reservoir of aged maple syrup, a deboned suckling pig compressed and crisped in duck fat. "He was cooking with this just incredibly advanced technique and imagination, but not at the sacrifice of flavor or soul," Meyer told me. Humm also had thorough training in the rigors of running a business. Brought up in a small town near Zurich by an architect father and a homemaker mother, he took his first job at the age of eight in a farmers' market where his mother shopped; at fourteen, he left school to apprentice as a chef. For a decade, he worked at three-Michelin-star establishments in Switzerland, including Le Pont de Brent, in Montreux, under the chef-owner Gérard Rabaey, a perfectionist who rooted through the garbage to check for discarded food. At the end of each week, Humm and the other cooks cleaned the kitchen until three in the morning, standing on ladders to swab the corners of the ceilings with Q-tips. Rabaey would reward them with half a glass of cola. "Half a glass," Humm says, laughing. "And not real Coke! Cheap cola. It was insane. But in a way I loved it. It taught me so much about running a kitchen."

After three years, Humm, exhausted, took a job as executive chef at a Swiss mountain inn, Gasthaus zum Gupf, where he became the youngest chef in the country's history to earn a Michelin star. Hired by Campton Place in 2003, he quickly made it a critical success and packed the place every night. Meyer hoped that he would do the same for Eleven Madison Park.

But when Humm started there, in January, 2006, he had a problem with the dining room. The general manager, who hires service staff and sets the aesthetic—décor, plateware, stemware, menu design—was a veteran from Charlie Trotter's, in Chicago, and Humm felt that the room lacked verve and excitement. He complained to Meyer, who asked if there was anyone better in Union Square Hospitality Group. Humm named Guidara, whom he had seen at company conclaves.

Guidara, who was then running Meyer's two cafés at the Museum of Modern Art, was only twenty-six, but he had grown up in the business. Reared in Tarrytown, New York, the son of a successful restaurant executive, he attended the Cornell Hospitality School and a hotel school in Spain. His restaurants at MOMA were elegant but unceremonious, serving panini and ice cream on bare tables, and he was leery when asked to take over at Eleven Madison Park. "Everything about fine dining, as I understood it, was stuffy, it was rigid, and it was not fun at all," Guidara told me. But he agreed to take the job after meeting with Humm, who was then twenty-nine. "I realized he's young like me, he's a fun dude, and, yeah, he's excellence-minded, but we began to talk about how we could build a four-star restaurant that's not rigid or stuffy."

Humm was trained in the high-church tradition of European dining—tableside carving, uniformed waiters, serving from the left—and he was startled when Guidara wanted to abolish some of the more abstruse rituals. They recall fighting until three in the morning over Guidara's insistence on using only one spoon, instead of the traditional two, to drop a bolus of sorbet into a soufflé. Over time, they devised a restaurant that observed the formality that high-end diners expect but that also acknowledged the growing appeal of places like David Chang's Momofuku Ssäm, which serves thoughtful food in the ambience of a burrito joint.

In January 2007, six months after Humm and Guidara started working together, Frank Bruni, then the *Times'* restaurant critic, raised Eleven Madison Park's rating to three stars. Emboldened, they approached Meyer about spending the money necessary to win a fourth star. They wanted to remove some of the leather banquettes and rectangular tables, which impeded the servers, and bring in comfortable chairs for guests who were spending hours eating Humm's twelve-course tasting. They needed new service uniforms, better china and glasses, and various pieces of expensive kitchen equipment, including a Pacojet for frozen purées and a Hold-o-mat slow-cooking oven. They also wanted to reduce the number of seats, to alleviate pressure on the kitchen. Humm explained, "On this level, there is a limit for a chef of how many plates you can let go through your hands and make sure they're perfect."

Meyer was uncertain. The overhaul would cost hundreds of thousands of dollars, and fewer tables meant lost revenue—at least, until the restaurant attracted enough diners to raise prices. "It's a high-risk game," he told me. But after mulling the proposal for two weeks, he said yes. In September 2008, after the renovation was done, Eleven Madison Park hosted a thousand-dollar-a-head benefit for an anti-hunger organization. Late that night, the news broke that Lehman Brothers had collapsed. "The world was changing before our eyes," Meyer says.

In the coming months, restaurants closed across the city, including landmarks like the Rainbow Room and the Michelin-starred restaurants Fiamma and Fleur de Sel. As the recession deepened, Eleven Madison Park was serving as few as twenty customers a night, while still employing thirty servers and Humm's full seventy-five-person brigade de cuisine. "In 2008, I don't think we made a dollar," Humm said. Guidara added, "Then 2009 came, and we were losing money."

They made efficiencies where they could. They instructed cooks to cut paper towels in half, and to trade in their disposable white paper chef toques (which cost twelve thousand dollars a year) for cotton dishwasher caps that could be laundered and reused. They reduced the amount of soap for washing dishes, and enforced strict departure times for chefs to eliminate costly overtime. Although Humm still offered filet mignon, he also introduced, for the twenty-eight-dollar lunch special, less expensive proteins, like chicken and skate. Still, by the summer of 2009 they had emptied their bank account and were within weeks of having to downscale.

But since January, Bruni had been spotted several times in the restaurant, and Humm and Guidara were convinced that a four-star review could bring back the crowds. On days when they ascertained that Bruni was coming, they called up friends to pack the restaurant. "You're not going to get a four-star review if you're struggling," Humm says. Bruni told me that he was unaware of the restaurant's troubles. "Eleven Madison Park just oozed from every one of its pores the fact that it was a place where a number of extraordinarily young and talented people were determined to make their mark," he says. "There was a crackle of excitement to being there that you didn't feel at a Le Bernardin or a Jean Georges—magnificent as those restaurants are." In August 2009, his review, under the headline "A DARING RISE TO THE TOP," awarded the restaurant four stars. "We've been fully reserved every single day since," Guidara says.

Humm and Guidara say that they were inspired by Miles Davis's willingness to reinvent himself—abandoning the minimalism of "Kind of Blue," one of the most popular jazz recordings ever made, for the electric experimentation of "Bitches Brew." A few months after earning the *Times'* highest rating, they decided to recast the restaurant again. Spurred by their last-place ranking on the San Pellegrino list, they wanted to make it livelier—but after the deep losses of the crash and the expense of the previous renovation, it also had to be more cost-efficient. "We couldn't be reckless," Guidara says. "We needed to do it in such a way where we could continue making money." Humm added, "Everything was: How can we streamline?"

The grid menu helped, by overcoming challenges that traditional menus pose for chefs. If, for instance, a restaurant serves snapper, Dover sole, and sea bass, it is obliged to buy those three fish every day, regardless of their quality and their price. Fish that go unordered have to be thrown out—and spoiled food is a significant cost for kitchens. Diners are also unpredictable. "With à la carte it can be all over the place," Humm says. "One person can order three appetizers, or one appetizer and an entrée, or an entrée and a dessert"—which makes it difficult to plan how much food to buy and to project revenues. Humm described the grid menu as "a balance between control and surprise." By paring down to just sixteen items, which can change each day, he eliminated much of the waste; because the kitchen typically offers a single fish, Humm can buy the best one, and just enough of it. "Less ingredients in-house, less waste," he says.

The kitchen tour and lounge visit, deployed late in the meal, also solved a problem that bedevils every restaurateur: how to get people up from the table so that the next customers can be seated, a feat known as "the turn." Fast-food places, which must turn every few minutes, use bright primary colors and loud, fast music to encourage people to eat faster. In fine dining, the turn is enacted differently, but it's no less important. For Eleven Madison Park, which now reduced its seats to eighty-eight, an extra half-turn—forty-four seatings—would bring in thousands of dollars more each night. Daniel, a three-Michelin-star restaurant on the Upper East Side run by Daniel Boulud, monitors patrons with discreet cameras in the dining room.

Before a fork is lowered after a course, cooks watching from the kitchen can insure that the next dish is ready, shaving vital minutes off the meal.

Humm and Guidara rejected the idea of using cameras; it would be too difficult in their cavernous dining room. The kitchen tour and lounge visit was their solution. Indeed, everything about the refurbished restaurant—from the greeter to the lack of dollar signs on the menu, the elimination of supplemental charges for expensive items like foie gras, and the handwritten bill—was meant to elide what Guidara calls the "business-transactional" nature of the visit, to draw customers' attention away from the fact that they were disbursing enough money to buy a week's groceries for a family of five.

The city's high-end restaurants can be outlandishly expensive. At Per Se, Thomas Keller's restaurant in the Time Warner Center, a full tasting menu for two, with wine pairings, costs a thousand dollars. A similar dinner at Eleven Madison Park, at about nine hundred dollars, is not much less. Ryan Sutton, a restaurant critic who monitors restaurant prices on his blog the Price Hike, points out, "Eleven Madison Park has a higher starting price point"—the least expensive prix-fixe option—"than Jean Georges, Corton, The Modern, Del Posto." But in the *Times*, Bruni described it as a cheaper alternative to other fine dining places, and, Sutton points out, this perception has stuck. "That really is the trick of fine dining—or any luxury business," he says. "How can you convince customers to spend eight hundred and seventy-six dollars on a wine-paired tasting menu and make them feel like they got a value?"

Humm and Guidara admit that the refinements they introduced in 2010 contributed significantly to the restaurant's bottom line, but are adamant that their priority was creating the best experience for customers. "We understand that, without making money, we can't stay open," Humm told me. "That's why we are really driven to make money. It's going to end if you don't."

"But if you ever make a decision first and foremost to make money, it will end as well," Guidara added. "Every decision needs to start with it making you better. And then you have to ask yourself, 'Is this also a good financial decision?'"

Humm and Guidara's company, Made Nice, is a private corporation, and they decline to say how much money Eleven Madison Park makes. But some rough calculations are possible. About a hundred and twenty-five people dine there each night, and an average check is about two hundred and twenty-five dollars per person; at lunch, sixty people spend about a hundred and twenty-five dollars apiece. This includes wine and liquor, a significant part of the check. The wine director, Dustin Wilson, says that he routinely sells bottles with a four-figure price, and alcohol is marked up between a hundred and three hundred percent on a four-thousand-dollar bottle, the restaurant makes twenty-four hundred dollars in the time it takes a sommelier to remove a cork.

These figures suggest annual revenues of about eleven million dollars, out of which the restaurant must pay for food and labor, rent, service on debt, and miscellaneous costs—from flower arrangements and publicity to menus, linen service, and those free jars of granola. Bastianich has said that profit margins at fine-dining restaurants in New York are between ten and twenty percent. Assuming a return of ten percent, to account for the bad economy and the spiking costs of food and labor, Eleven Madison Park makes about $1.1 million a year on its main dining room. The upstairs private dining room, however, is booked almost every day, and has far higher profit margins; it charges more, serves a limited menu, and uses only three chefs. With this extra source of income, the restaurant may clear about $1.3 million a year after taxes—at a time when most fine-dining restaurants are struggling.

Jimmy Bradley, who runs the Red Cat and the Harrison, in downtown Manhattan, told me that every successful restaurateur receives offers to expand. "It's paid for," Bradley says. "Why say no? Well, I can give you ten reasons to say no. It's the same thing when your wife says, 'Let's have another child.'" When a restaurateur begins to lose control, Bradley says, "something's going to break."

Since 2009, Humm and Guidara have been invited to open branches of Eleven Madison Park in London, Tokyo, and scores of other cities—sometimes with seven-figure bonuses attached. "That's what happens when you become a brand," Guidara told me. They declined, believing that far-flung outposts would be distracting. But in the summer of 2010 a development firm called GFI Capital Resources approached them about opening a restaurant in a new hotel at Broadway and Twenty-eighth Street—six minutes' walk from Eleven Madison Park. GFI, which was calling the hotel the NoMad (after the real-estate neologism for the neighborhood "north of Madison Square Park"), offered a partnership deal in which Humm and Guidara would share profits but not invest any money. "It was too good to pass up," Guidara says.

They signed in the fall of 2010. Meyer, though he says he admires their entrepreneurial drive, told them that he could not sanction a competing restaurant so close by. According to Humm, Meyer said, "The only way it can work is that either you leave Eleven Madison Park and do the NoMad or you buy Eleven Madison Park." Meyer set a price, which both parties say was "in the millions." With the help of an Eleven Madison Park regular who is a successful banker, Humm and Guidara found an investor: Noam Gottesman, a billionaire former Goldman Sachs banker who created his own hedge fund. Asked why he had invested in a business with famously high risks and relatively low yields, Gottesman said that he was impressed with Humm and Guidara and their staff: "It's just a quest for excellence that I believe—regardless of whether this was a high-margin or low-margin business as a whole—could work out to be a good investment."

The NoMad, housed in a suite of large, dark rooms off the lobby of the hotel, is five distinct dining spaces: a glass-ceilinged

In the coming months, restaurants closed across the city, including landmarks like the Rainbow Room and the Michelin-starred restaurants Fiamma and Fleur de Sel. As the recession deepened, Eleven Madison Park was serving as few as twenty customers a night, while still employing thirty servers and Humm's full seventy-five-person brigade de cuisine.

atrium, a cocktail bar, a book-lined library, and a "parlor" with gilt-trimmed chairs and velvet draperies, as well as a rooftop patio. Food is served from a conventional menu, and the crowd is heavy on Wall Streeters impressing their dates. In décor, the NoMad could not be further from Eleven Madison Park's airy classicism; the dark-leather walls, by the French architect Jacques Garcia, evoke a late night at the Hellfire Club.

By mid-May, six weeks after the NoMad's launch, the strain of running two restaurants had become apparent. One afternoon, I joined Humm as he conducted a pre-dinner-service inspection in Eleven Madison Park's vast white-tiled kitchen. Humm had transferred his former chef de cuisine and top sous-chefs to the No-Mad, and he knew few of the line cooks who had taken over at the flagship. He is ordinarily unflappable, but he became increasingly annoyed as he began to discover problems: a cook at the cold-appetizer station had stored some sweet Maine shrimp improperly, and it had to be thrown out. At the fish station, seconds before service began, another cook was simultaneously boiling a large pot on the stove and cleaning lobsters in a sink, while dirty paper towels littered the counter. "It's a disaster!" Humm cried. To his chef de cuisine, he shouted, "Why is he cooking like a pig here? The line is breaking down!"

In late May, in the NoMad's first major review, New York's critic Adam Platt took Humm and Guidara to task for trying to "monetize" their success. The review said that the prices were too high (hyped as a less expensive version of Eleven Madison Park, the restaurant offered a carrot dish for twenty dollars), and gave the NoMad only two stars out of five. Neither Humm nor Guidara had ever had a negative review. "Our confidence definitely got shaken up a little bit," Humm said.

A few days later, Humm met with his sous-chefs in the NoMad's cramped basement office. Sitting on chairs and on the floor, the six cooks looked glum. "We know we're better," Humm said. "But the best way to fight against it is to just be quiet, put your head down, and work hard." He handed out copies of the NoMad's profit-and-loss statement for the first month of operation, and announced, "What is really exciting is that we are twenty-eight percent over what we had budgeted" for gross revenue. The restaurant, after its well-publicized opening, was packed every night. But there was a problem with costs. Food, Humm pointed out, was about eighty thousand dollars more than projected. "Which is a lot of money, but—"

"A hundred and ten," Abram Bissell, the NoMad's chef de cuisine, interrupted.

"Is it that much?" Humm asked, wrinkling his brow. "So, um, we have a long way to go to become profitable." He looked again at the sheet and saw that losses for the month were in the six figures. According to the rule that every new restaurateur learns, the combined costs of food and labor must not exceed seventy percent of expenses; ideally, food should be thirty. At the NoMad, food was more than thirty-five percent, and labor costs were a whopping fifty, reflecting the overtime necessary to handle the hotel's three crowded dining rooms and two bars.

"You're going to see these numbers every month," Humm told his sous-chefs, "and I'm sure there's going to be a point where we're going to say, 'Stop f**king around.' You lose money every month, eventually there's no restaurant, right? So we've got to figure out that line." He added, "It is so important that we, as chefs, understand how to manage in a way that we are not losing money. Because otherwise there is no point."

Over the next six weeks, Humm and Guidara brought down costs at the NoMad, and in late June the *Times* gave the restaurant three stars, calling it "novel and wonderful." The next month, it eked out a four-figure profit, as President Obama held a forty-thousand-dollar-a-plate fund-raiser there. Guidara, feeling confident, told me, "The NoMad will be real profitable."

Yet, at Eleven Madison Park, the novelty of the changes was starting to wear off. At a meeting of top managers, in May, Guidara learned that a problem had arisen with the end-of-meal kitchen visits: "We're seeing a different crowd of people coming through," the assistant general manager, Daniel Green, said. "They are very much: 'We waited twenty-eight days for this, we're going to sit, we're going to linger, we're going to take our time. You taking me into the kitchen and then asking me to leave is a clear sign that you want me to leave.'"

Guidara, startled, suggested that cutting back on reservations might alleviate the pressure to turn tables. "But," he added, "I firmly believe that going into the lounge at the end of the meal is the superlative way to experience the restaurant. And it makes me concerned that somehow we're not doing it right."

Green insisted that no matter how assiduously he tried to "sell the idea that this is a special, or a new, or different, or unique, or fun experience, people can tell that it's to get them up from their table."

"They feel like they've lost control over their evening," Steven Kelly, the dining-room manager, said.

In August, Humm and Guidara announced a new wave of changes at Eleven Madison Park, which would take effect after Labor Day. They had begun planning to transform the restaurant eight months earlier, hoping to rise still higher on the San Pellegrino list. "Two years ago, when we made the big change, it really put us on the map," Humm told me. "We wanted to make another effort in evolving and moving up a little further." Neither Humm nor Guidara will say that they are aiming to knock Noma from its perch at No. 1, but their former boss, Danny Meyer, told me, "The ranking is very, very important to them. They were justifiably proud to be No. 10, and there's nowhere else to go but No. 1. They are trying to figure out what tactic it might take."

The San Pellegrino list rewards restaurants with a strong sense of place, and of theatre. Accordingly, Humm and Guidara are shaping Eleven Madison Park around a New York theme. They are replacing the waiters' pale-green shirts and mossy vests with uniforms made by a local designer, Bespoken Clothiers: gray two-button suits, white shirts, and dark ties. For the Limoges china, they are substituting plates produced by a Brooklyn-based potter. The wine-list covers, the cocktail menus, and the bar coasters will be produced by Ghurka, a luxury-goods outfit based in New York and Connecticut.

Humm has always paid homage to the city with his dishes—black-and-white cookies, a Long Island-style clambake—but now he will provide more items that are made entirely from indigenous foods, including a course of local cheese and beer, served in a wicker basket meant to evoke picnics in Central Park. Servers will describe the origins of each course, complete with historical dates, names, and facts.

The changes, when announced, provoked a wave of commentary online. Some critics praised Humm and Guidara's boldness in changing a winning formula. Others called the New York theme gimmicky and predicted that it would alienate regulars; Meyer agreed, telling the *Times*, "There does come a point when you just can't see that play another time." But there was surprisingly little outcry over another big change, which Humm and Guidara slipped in behind the talk about the new theme: they are removing the lower-priced prix-fixe options in favor of an obligatory twelve-course tasting menu, for a hundred and ninety-five dollars. Dinners are expected to last as long as four hours, which severely limits the number of customers each night. "Maybe we'll turn, like, two tables," Guidara says. But with the higher minimum price the restaurant can still increase profits slightly. At the same time, Humm and Guidara have kept a close eye on costs: all of Ghurka's leather goods are being supplied free, in exchange for the company's name on the menus and coasters, and similar deals have been struck with other purveyors. Some of the proposed new dishes, too, seemed designed in tribute to outer-borough thrift: a carrot "tartare" ground tableside, and Humm's riff on street ices, flavored with syrups of curry, lemon, and lime.

The most controversial addition is the card trick. "We wanted something that reflects that old, gritty New York, before the place got so cleaned up," Guidara told me. As a teen-ager in the late eighties, he was once relieved of sixty dollars by the three-card-monte players who plied midtown. Theory11, a magic company based in Las Vegas, designed a deck of cards with icons of ingredients: hazelnut, plum, espresso. The trick uses a simple manipulation to make diners select a card that matches the ingredient hidden inside a chocolate dessert. Guidara was enthusiastic—until online commentators began to criticize the card trick as a cheesy gimmick. "It has been pretty brutal," he said.

But he and Humm were determined to keep it. In the weeks before the new opening, Guidara was rehearsing the trick with his service team half an hour a day. One morning in mid-August, before Eleven Madison Park opened for lunch, Guidara sat in the dining room and watched closely as Natasha McIrvin, a service captain who wears her blond hair in a tight bun, ran though the trick. A week earlier, an emissary from Theory11 had come to the restaurant to give the servers a lesson in sleight of hand, and McIrvin had been practicing ever since, walking around with cards in her hands to sharpen her feel for them. She started the trick, hesitated slightly, and then forged on.

"Good," Guidara said, when she was finished. Then he pointed out that she had done part of the trick out of order. "That's when you got flustered."

He asked her to try again. She squared her shoulders and launched into the spiel that servers will deliver. Culled from research by Theory11 and Sandra DiCapua, the restaurant's Harvard-educated special-projects manager, the speech draws on the stories of grifters, scam artists, and profiteers in New York over the past two centuries. "In the summer of 1870," McIrvin said, "the *New York Times* ran a story that had just three words in the headline: 'Three Card Monte.' These card players cheated New Yorkers and tourists out of their money for years. It's illegal now, but we'd like to pay homage to those old scams with our own card trick."

She ran through the trick again, this time smoothly and confidently.

Bibliography

Abate, G. "Local Food Economies: Driving Forces, Challenges, and Future Prospects." *Journal of Hunger & Environmental Nutrition* 3 (2008):384–399. Print.

Allen, Patricia. *Together at the Table: Sustainability and Subsistence in the American Agrifood System*. University Park: Pennsylvania State UP, 2004. Print.

Anderson, J., et al. "5 A Day Fruit and Vegetable Intervention Improves Consumption in a Low Income Population." *Journal of the American Dietetic Association* 101 (2001): 195–202. Print.

Belasco, Warren. *Appetite for Change: How the Counterculture Took on the Food Industry, 1966–1988*. New York: Pantheon, 1989. Print.

Bell, Michael. *Farming for Us All: Practical Agriculture and the Cultivation of Sustainability*. University Park: Pennsylvania State UP, 2004. Print.

Carson, Rachel. *Silent Spring*. Boston: Houghton, 1962. Print.

Cotler, Amy. *The Locavore Way: Discover and Enjoy the Pleasures of Locally Grown Food*. North Adams: Storey, 2009. Print.

Counihan, Carole. *Food Culture: A Reader*. 2nd ed. Routledge, 2007. Print.

Deere, Carolyn, and Daniel Esty (eds.). *Greening the Americas*. Cambridge: MIT P, 2002. Print.

Fromartz, Samuel. *Organic, Inc.: Natural Foods and How They Grew*. New York: Harcourt, 2006. Print.

Guthman, Julie. *Agrarian Dreams: The Paradox of Organic Farming in California*. Berkeley: U of California P, 2004. Print.

Holly, Hughes. *Best Food Writing 2012*. Boston: Da Capo, 2012. Print.

Kimbrell, Andrew, ed. *Fatal Harvest: The Tragedy of Industrial Agriculture*. Washington, DC: Island, 2002. Print.

Lyson, T. A. *Civic Agriculture: Reconnecting Farm, Food and Community*. Medford: Tufts UP, 2004. Print.

Mepham, T. B. *Food Ethics*. New York: Routledge, 1996. Print.

Mitchell, Don. *The Lie of the Land: Migrant Workers and the California Landscape*. Minneapolis: U of Minnesota P, 1996. Print.

Pederson, Donald B., and Keith G. Meyer. *Agricultural Law in a Nutshell*. St. Paul: West, 1995. Print.

Petrini, Carlo. *Slow Food Nation: Why Our Food Should Be Good, Clean, and Fair*. New York: Rizzoli, 2007. Print.

Pollan, Michael. *The Omnivore's Dilemma: A Natural History of Four Meals*. New York: Penguin, 2006. Print.

Robinson, J. M., and J. A. Hartenfeld. *The Farmers' Market Book: Growing Food, Cultivating Community*. Bloomington: Indiana UP, 2007. Print.

Ronald, Pamela C., and Raoul W. Adamchak, *Tomorrow's Table: Organic Farming, Genetics, and the Future of Food*. New York: Oxford UP, 2008. Print.

Rousseau, Signe. *Food and Social Media: You Are What You Tweet.* Plymouth: Rowman, 2012. Print.

Schlosser, Eric. *Fast Food Nation: The Dark Side of the All-American Meal.* Boston: Houghton, 2001. Print.

Sligh, Michael, and Carolyn Christman. *Who Owns Organic? The Global Status, Prospects and Challenges of a Changing Organic Market.* Pittsboro: RAFI, 2003. Print.

Weaver, William. *Vegetable Gardening: A Master Gardener's Guide to Planting, Growing, Seed Saving, and Cultural History.* New York: Holt, 1997. Print.

Welland, Diane A. *The Complete Idiot's Guide to Eating Local.* New York: Penguin, 2011. Print.

Websites

American Community Gardening Association (ACGA)
www.communitygarden.org

The ACGA advocates for gardens in urban neighborhoods, away from the centers of agriculture and farming, as a way to introduce a community-centered appreciation of local foods and foster social interaction. The organization provides information on developing a community garden, as well as resources to support gardens in jeopardy of closure.

American Farmland Trust (AFT)
www.farmland.org

The AFT is dedicated to the protection of farmland by promoting sustainable farmland practices, providing political advocacy for farmers, and educating Americans on the issues in farmland conservation. The organization also funds research and reports on conservation and agriculture on the national, regional, and local levels.

Center for Rural Affairs
www.cfra.org

The Center for Rural Affairs is a Nebraska-based nonprofit promoting a wide range of rural issues related to farming and farm policy at the state and national level. The center is guided by a vision that values rural life. This vision is similar to sustainable farming politics in that the organization advances legislative policy reform and serves as a research leader for sustainable practices.

Demeter International
www.demeter.net

Biodynamic Agriculture is a group of partner businesses under the Demeter brand who sell organic products that adhere and exceed US and international guidelines. The Demeter brand aims to serve as a model of sustainable business practice that promotes the development of biodynamic farming.

Farm to School
www.farmtoschool.org

Working in fifty states, the Farm to School program fosters relationships between schools and local farms in the development of healthy school food programs and in the promotion of food education.

FoodRoutes Network

www.foodroutes.org

The FoodRoutes Network is dedicated to the local food movement and provides resources for consumers and farmers in the promotion of a community-based food system. The organization partners with community organizations in the design, launch, and implementation of "buy local" food campaigns. The FoodRoutes Network also promotes education on the benefits and values of the local food movement.

National Cooperative Grocers Association (NCGA)

www.ncga.coop

Serving food co-ops across the United States, the NCGA is a business services cooperative that represents approximately 136 stores. The organization helps to consolidate best practices for competitive pricing, professional development, and product selection. The NCGA also acts as a central advocacy group on a host of food co-op issues.

Organic Farming Research Foundation (OFRF)

www.ofrf.org

The OFRF works to address policy and education in organic farming through grants that support the development of organic farming. The organization also promotes research in the areas of sustainable farming and organic practices at land grant universities.

Index

❖